Western Christian Thought
in the Middle Ages

Western Christian Thought in the Middle Ages

An Essay in Interpretation

BY

SYDNEY HERBERT MELLONE

M.A. (Lond.), D.Sc. (Edin.)

FORMERLY LECTURER ON THE HISTORY OF CHRISTIAN DOCTRINE
IN THE UNIVERSITY OF MANCHESTER
LATE EXAMINER IN PHILOSOPHY IN THE UNIVERSITIES
OF EDINBURGH AND LONDON

*" Non omnia dicenda sunt quae dicere possumus, ne minus
utiliter dicantur ea quae dicere debemus."*

HUGO OF ST VICTOR.

WILLIAM BLACKWOOD & SONS LTD.
EDINBURGH AND LONDON
1935

BR 252
M52

TO THE MEMORY
OF
PHILIP HENRY WICKSTEED

PREFACE.

THE purpose of this book is one of historical interpretation. The discoveries and studies of the last
fifty years, in the field of mediæval history in all its
branches, have brought to light a wealth of material
previously unknown or neglected. This is true, in
particular, of the thought-world of the period. My
endeavour has been to interpret the really important
movements of thought, gathering the essentials of the
interpretation, as far as possible, round the person-
alities and work of great thinkers who are representative of their times. It is noteworthy that this
becomes more possible, and in the end inevitable, as
we pass from the eleventh to the twelfth and the
thirteenth centuries. I hope that this way of treating
the subject will appeal to readers who are not able to
consult the original sources, and who, at first, may
find the contributions of specialists difficult to follow.
At the same time I have endeavoured to provide
help for such readers as desire to give further study
to particular topics in a field which is full of interest
and instruction for the modern world.

The grotesque fables, which were formerly vended
in the market-place as the truth about the Middle

G.G. Coulton

Ages, seem to be passing out of circulation. But in view of the work of a distinguished British scholar, a very learned writer but a very biassed historian, we must protest against the pathological method of studying history—the method that throws the searchlight mainly on the crimes and blunders, the failures and futilities, of the past, leaving in the shadows its aspirations and achievements.

The bibliography and notes show how extensive are my obligations to other workers in this field ; but reference must be made here to the help received from two friends who have gone. I had the privilege of discussing the plan of this book with the late Thomas Frederick Tout, formerly Director of Advanced Studies in History in the University of Manchester ; and in the writings of the late Philip Henry Wicksteed I have found an unfailing source of insight and illumination. I am indebted to the Hibbert Trustees for assistance in the publication of the book ; but for its contents I alone am responsible.

S. H. MELLONE.

LINCOLN.

CONTENTS.

WESTERN CHRISTIAN THOUGHT
IN THE MIDDLE AGES.

CHAPTER I.

INTRODUCTION.

THE SPIRIT OF THE MIDDLE AGES.

I.

THE traveller under Italian skies who enters for the first time the Duomo in Milan sometimes receives an impression of darkness, which is by no means always due to a contrast between the garish brilliance without and a " dim religious light " within. The impression is due to the sheer vastness of the space into which he enters : too vast to be illuminated even by the serried ranks of great windows, each with its expanse of many-coloured glass. If for a few moments, forgetting where he is, the traveller falls into a dreamy mood, he might imagine that he is beholding a vision, where fragments of massive forms seem to rise out of the dim and the dark ; here the glittering tomb of a famous archbishop ; there and there portions of the fifty-two massive columns which support the roof ; elsewhere white figures seeming to emerge—some of the four

A

thousand statues which the Cathedral is said to contain ; and, far away, as it were the gleam of floating colours—from the eastern windows over the choir. And then, as the visionary mood faded, he would begin to understand the manifold greatness of the reality before him.

It is so, many times, with our apprehension of the past, and, above all, it is so in the case of those ten centuries, from the fifth to the fifteenth, miscalled the " Middle Ages." The unquestioned assumption used to be that these centuries, on the most favourable estimate possible, were a long level stretch of time, with mankind stationary, spellbound under the authority of the Church, absorbed in war or monastic dreams. All these centuries, in the popular imagination, have been thrown together, as deserving but one name—the " Dark Ages." The truth is, that if any age of the past seems to us a dark age, the darkness is as much in ourselves as in the facts. We have carried into it the garish sunlight of the passing day, or the dreamy moonlight of some earlier age, and we are blind to the manifold greatness of the reality before us.

When it became impossible to deny that Monasticism, Feudalism, Scholasticism, the social and industrial groups of the Manor and the Guild, the Crusades, the Pilgrimages, the Friars, the Cathedrals, the great ideals of the Church and of Chivalry, were distinctively mediæval products with a historical importance and human value of their own, then a " mediæval civilisation " was admitted as coming between ancient and modern civilisation. Such crude periodising throws little light on the past and affords no guidance for our understanding of it. There are no watertight compartments in history, no final endings, no absolutely new beginnings. Such appearances are due to the illusions of distance or the exaggerations of romance. Many strenuous students of the subject in recent years have given us organic studies of the past which reveal a more rational picture of the process which produced modern Europe.

The Middle Ages belong partly to " ancient " and partly to " modern " times. On the ancient side these thousand years embrace the fierce life begotten by the young northern nations over the ruins of imperial Rome, and the resurrection, as from the grave, of the spirit of that old world with power to mould in countless ways the mind and feeling of the new. And on the modern side, the attempt to draw a dividing line defeats itself. The line demands breadth and becomes an area, and the area becomes a period of continuous life which unites and does not divide. The fusion of the mediæval and the modern is far longer and far more real than has commonly been supposed. The sources of the so-called Renaissance may be traced within the mediæval period itself. The Humanists which this movement afterwards produced, fascinated by its splendid literary revelations, ignored the achievements of the thirteen centuries intervening between Cicero and Petrarch ; then, by the genius of their work, they fastened their mistaken perspective upon historians and the cultured world at large, and marked it by the term Middle Ages for that which stood between them and their classic ideals. Close upon the indifference of the Humanists came the anti-Catholic polemics of the Reformation and the disgust of men of science at the scholastic philosophy—an attitude well exhibited in Bacon's

'Advancement of Learning.' Thus was erected a threefold barrier against any real knowledge and understanding of mediæval history. There have been romantic reactions, as far from understanding what they admired as classicism had been from understanding what it despised; but it is only through the development of impartial scientific method in the study of history during the last hundred years that a wider and truer outlook has been gained.[1]

II.

The decline and fall of the Roman Empire, as recorded in Gibbon's famous work, covers a period of over twelve hundred years (from A.D. 180 to A.D. 1453). More than three-quarters of the work are occupied with a very full history of the first 460 years of this period (to A.D. 640). We may assume that he regarded the events specifically indicated by his title as falling within these 460 years. We may, however, draw the boundary, so far as there is a boundary, within Gibbon's figure, and regard the essential changes involved in this decline and fall as covering the third, fourth, and fifth centuries. No single date for any uniquely decisive event can be given.

The capture of Rome by Alaric in 410 was a sensationally dramatic and symbolic event; but its intrinsic importance was much less than the profound impression which it made on men's minds, and which moved Augustine to produce what now stands as one of the greatest works of ancient Christian theology. Sixty-five years later, the last Roman Emperor of the West, the helpless boy Romulus Augustulus, fittingly so named, was deposed and banished to Ravenna ; but, again, this event was in itself of no decisive importance. What we find is not an outstanding year, but an outstanding epoch ; for the fifth century did witness the actual dismemberment of the Roman Empire. The new nations in Britain, Gaul, Spain, and parts of Italy and Germany, were forming the rude beginnings of what were to become national States in the centuries following. This had long been preparing in the economic and administrative decline of the Empire, and the steady influx of peoples of northern origin into Roman territory for over two centuries ; but the power of the old civilisation to absorb the new races was exhausted by the fifth century, and the political history of Europe was turned into a different path. The line of political development marked out in the fifth century, that of the national State, still continues.

Nevertheless, for another five centuries comparatively little movement was made in this direction. The northern peoples were slowly acquiring the rudiments of culture, and learning to combine their primitive institutions with the remains of those of Rome. The Empire created by the genius of Charles the Great was politically a union which proved to be premature. It broke up under his successors, when the half-formed civilisation of Christendom was forced to face the migration of Northmen by sea and the onslaught of Saracens on the south and Hungarians and Slavs on the east. Anarchy, as it has been said, " crystallised into Feudalism." Feudalism came into existence during these dark and terrible ninth and tenth centuries, as the only means of defending western Europe against invading hosts who threatened Christendom with extinction. Based upon the armour-clad knight and the fortified castle, it had taken shape, almost spontaneously, in England and on the Continent, as a system of local protection, at a time when the central governments, so far as they existed at all, were too weak to organise any effective resistance to the aggressors. During the eleventh century the struggles with the invaders settled themselves in ways which (we may observe in passing) created some of the hardest problems of the Peace Conferences of 1919 to 1921. But no progress could be made so long as the feudal knights remained the dominant military force in Europe. Their castles were impregnable, their cavalry invincible ; they were constantly at war among themselves, and on the whole the most dangerous obstacle to peaceful industry and civilised government.[2]

In spite of all this, the forces of recovery were already active. The rule of the House of Capet had begun in France. Men of personality, power, and wisdom arose in Germany. The restoration of the Empire in 962, when Otto the Great was crowned in Rome, marks the first milestone on the pathway of progress. Scholarship had found a home in monasteries planted in the heart of German forests. The monks of Cluny were at work. The problem of the feudal knighthood was taken in hand by that greatest civilising force, the Church, and thus she created Chivalry. Chivalry, as an actual way of life and as a spirit and an ideal, arose from the largely successful endeavour of the Church to christianise the knighthood. Historically the results of the endeavour are seen at their best and their worst in the Crusades.

III.

The break-up of the Roman Empire, as a political and economic organisation, set free the idea and ideal of Roman Imperialism, which has influenced the history of Europe through the ages, and largely determined the political history and political thought of mediæval Christendom. What was this ideal ?

The imperial constitution may be said to have been inaugurated in 27 B.C., when the conqueror of Antony at Actium, the great-nephew and heir of the dictator Julius Caesar, was summoned, by the general consent of a world worn out by twenty years of war and anarchy, to the task of establishing a government which, without destroying the traditions of the Republic, should provide the centralisation of author-ity which experience had shown to be necessary for the integrity and stability of the Empire. Octavian was well fitted for the task. Cool-headed, far-sighted, opportunist, tactful, for over forty years he governed, organised, conquered, and left behind him a coherent and well-organised Empire. By request of the Senate he assumed the title of Augustus, and proceeded to gather supreme authority into his own hands. In doing this he roused the self-consciousness of the Roman people, and a great national ideal formed itself in their minds, of which Virgil became the prophetic interpreter. In Virgil's vision it was an ideal at once political, social, and religious. " The supremacy of Rome in his hands assumed the aspect of an ordinance of Providence, to which all previous history had been leading up under Divine guidance ; *his ego nec metas rerum nec tempora pono*. It meant

the establishment of an Empire to which no limits
of time or place were set, and in which the human
race should find ordered peace, settled government,
material prosperity, the reign of Law and the common-
wealth of Freedom." [3] The mission of Rome, seen
almost as a permanent personality, is not only *regere
imperio populos*, not only to establish the authority
of universal law and order among them, but *pacis
imponere morem*, to make peace the habit and custom
of the world. This was the ideal which, thirteen centuries afterwards, gripped the soul of Dante. To him
it became the vision of the whole Christian world
living in concord under its two divinely and legally
appointed Heads.

We are now, however, concerned to understand the
actual course of events as regards the problem of
imperial administration. Even as a practical affair
of business organisation, and apart from the various
characters and capacities of the men who successively
occupied the imperial throne, the problem of administration became one of immense difficulty. In the
case of the eastern provinces the difficulty was destined
to prove insuperable. The countries east of the
Adriatic formed a Greek world, speaking and thinking in Greek ; it consisted of communities which for
generations had been educated by Greeks and accustomed to Greek modes of thought. The countries
west of the Adriatic formed a Roman world, consisting of communities where the traditions of Roman
law and government and military organisation had
entered deeply into the social instincts of the people.
Towards the end of the third century, the Emperor
Diocletian was compelled to make an administrative
division of the Empire for political reasons. It was

found that the central government in Rome could not control the eastern provinces. And when Constantine the Great, after defeating his rivals and making himself master of the whole Empire, removed the seat of his government from the Tiber to the Bosphorus, he intended only to carry on the policy of Diocletian. He did not realise that he had made the separation of East and West inevitable. Much less did he realise that in the West the dominion was to pass to the one power which represented continuity with the ancient splendours of the Roman name, and by its organisation upheld the decaying tradition of national unity.

Nevertheless, to look at the Roman system down to the time of Constantine on the side of its political organisation alone, is to take a partial view. What was the inner moral condition of the peoples of the Empire? Even in the worst days of such men as Nero or Domitian, it is not true that the whole Empire suffered from misgovernment. There were times when Rome was given over to the caprices of an insane or bloodthirsty tyrant, while the provinces were comparatively undisturbed. To the provinces the Emperor usually impersonated peace, well-organised government, and public safety. The Roman system admitted, and in fact encouraged, a considerable degree of local self-government, based on municipalities and differing in different places. It also admitted and encouraged a considerable degree of intellectual and religious liberty so long as the taxes were duly paid, and the supremacy of the State religious ceremonial and the authority of the Emperor were not challenged.

Some modern writers appear to assume that such scandalous stories as those handed down by Suetonius

and Juvenal are typical of the condition of imperial
Rome ; and accordingly they fill page after page with
charges of infamy and brutality such that, if these
were the whole truth, the Empire could not have
existed for a year. Can we not give some definite
and trustworthy account of what was wrong ? [4]
The business of the historian is not to blacken what
was dark and darken what was grey. But when we
allow all that need be allowed in this respect, we still
discover an appalling panorama of a dying civilisation. Outwardly there is wealth and power, splendour
and greatness ; inwardly there is emptiness and
desolation. The externals of the structure of civilisation, political organisation, public finance, criminal
justice, roads and transport, and the like, had been
successfully built up ; but along with all this we find
a deep disillusionment and despondency taking hold
of the mind of the Empire. The earnest propaganda
of Stoicism with its rational philanthropy, the speculative ideals of Platonism, the " secret society "
religions with their appeal to the popular love of
mystery and miracle, all found eager adherents ; for
all thoughtful men were labouring to find a remedy
for what seemed like a mortal sickness. With a true
diagnosis they turned to those problems which arose
out of the two great primary instincts—self-preservation and reproduction. The old civilisation has been
recklessly wasteful in both these matters, attaching
very little value to human life and permitting every
kind of abuse in the indulgence of appetite. The
mental and moral sources of patriotism, economic
wisdom, political capacity, were corrupted and
poisoned.

IV.

Through these tragic centuries the Church was taking the form which would enable her to embody in her own way the old imperialistic ideals.

During the years immediately following the activity of St Paul, we see many small Christian congregations scattered over the Roman Empire, with no bond of organisation more than was necessary to keep order in a union based on supernatural expectations and brotherly love. They were like societies of religious devotees, separated from the world by a rigorous discipline, and working on it only by a direct propaganda. They were scarcely intelligible to one man in a thousand ; and in proportion to their enthusiasm for separation from the world and their eager expectation of its end was their incapacity for saving and educating nations.

The strenuous spirit of the great Apostle to the Gentiles at length passed beyond the veil. Years came and went ; but the expected end did not come. The first enthusiasm could not always live at its former level ; more definition, more teaching, more regulation, were demanded as if by instinct, and most urgently were needed, since Christians were drawn from all ranks and occupations—in the imperial palace, among the officials, in the abodes of labour and the halls of learning, among slaves and freemen. Blindly, instinctively, or consciously, *some change* must needs be made. The second century covered the greatest crisis in the history of religion since the days that followed the crucifixion of Christ. Either must the primitive Church withdraw farther from the world and vanish out of history as other unworldly sects, like the Essenes in Judea or the Montanists among the Christians themselves, were destined soon to vanish, or she must enter into the life of that world to which originally she had stood in such direct antagonism. What *might have been*, in that confused and distant age, is utterly beyond our knowledge ; it is enough that we can discern what actually took place. " She marched through the open door into the Roman State, and settled down there for a long career of activity, to christianise the State along all its thoroughfares by imparting to it the word of the gospel, but at the same time leaving to it everything except its gods. On the other hand, she furnished herself with everything of value that could be taken over from the world without overstraining the elastic structure of the organisation which she now adopted. With the aid of its philosophy she created her new Christian theology ; its polity furnished her with the most exact constitutional forms ; its jurisprudence, its trade and commerce, its art and industry, were all taken into her service ; and she borrowed some hints even from its religious worship. Thus we find the Church in the fourth century endowed with all the resources which the State and its culture had to offer, entering into all the relationships of life, and ready for any compromise which did not affect the confession of her Faith. With this equipment she undertook and carried through a world mission on a vast scale." [5] But it was the Western, and not the Eastern, Church that achieved this work. The Eastern Church had no really effective centre of government or authority, while the Western Churches were growing as it were into a solid body with Rome as centre. Rome became the Mother Church of the West.

It is easy to ridicule the absurd story, devoutly believed in the Middle Ages, of Constantine's " donation " of the West to Bishop Sylvester of Rome, when he himself retired to his new city in the East ; but the legend points to the actual result of the Emperor's action. By his removal of the imperial seat to the Bosphorus, followed as it was by the decay of the imperial power in Italy, Constantine unwittingly placed the Bishops of Rome in the place of the absent Emperors, inheriting their prestige and even some of their titles. It was in that death agony of old Rome, drawn out an awful spectacle to men and angels through the centuries, that the great men among the Popes—and some of them were truly great—proved their spiritual strength and acquired their temporal power.

In truth, the Papacy was a growth. It was not a deep-laid scheme to secure supremacy in the world and among the Churches which the Bishops of Rome handed down from one to another. " Their temporal power," to quote Gibbon, by no means a willing witness in favour of a priesthood, " insensibly arose from the calamities of the times, and the Roman Bishops were compelled to reign as ministers of charity and peace." It is vain labour for Protestant or sceptic to rail at the story of mediæval Christianity, and expose to contempt the vices and superstition and weakness of the Church ; for, after all is said, it is only *human nature* which they convict of every folly and crime which they bring to light ; it is men who by their stupidities and lusts degraded the Church among them to their own level ; and yet, in spite of them, it never failed to witness for truths which the world ignored or was eager to forget, and for virtues of which the world was barely tolerant.

V.

Among the Popes of the fifth century there were some who understood their great opportunity and made the most of it ; and above all is this true of Leo the Great, who reigned as Pope from A.D. 440 to 461. The powers and prerogatives claimed by the future Papacy are all implied in his methods, his policy, and ideals. The historian can see them, as it were, outlined there. We see him, for example, acting as head of the City government ; checking Attila the Hun outside the walls of Rome; enforcing his authority on Prelates in distant provinces ; preaching powerfully on doctrinal questions; and intervening with effect in the Council of Chalcedon, in a lengthy communication which was accepted as settling the problem of the two Natures in the Person of Christ. By word and deed he affirmed that the power of Holy Rome, rising out of the ruins of the pagan Rome, destroyed by the vices of her sons, was absolute and eternal.

Leo did not live to see the actual beginnings of that power in northern and western Europe out of which vast issues were to arise for the See of Rome. Under the leadership of Clovis, a league of Germanic tribes known as " Franks " had extended their conquests from Western Germany into Gaul as far as the Bay of Biscay. The Goths and other tribes of northern origin who had overrun the Empire had been converted by Arian missionaries, and Christ was to them

a hero-god like the deities to which they were accustomed. Clovis was aware that this was not the Roman
doctrine. Rome, of course, stood for the orthodox
or Nicene Christology. Clovis decided formally to
embrace the Catholic faith ; and on Christmas Day,
496, he and a large group of his warriors were solemnly
received into the Church, with the entire authorisation
and approval of the then reigning Pope. This " conversion " has been described as " the crown of a
consistent calculated policy, which displays eminently
statesman-like perception." [6] In any case, even if it
was merely a gesture, its consequences were immeasur-
able. Clovis himself was interested only in the
political exploitation of his change of faith. He knew
he could count on the support of the Catholic Bishops.
Of all the Germanic kingdoms established in Gaul,
Spain, Italy, and Africa, his was the only one which
endured, because he and his successors were of the
same faith as the majority of their subjects.

Before passing on to observe the culmination of
this story, we must call to mind the work of the other
of the two Popes whom men have called " Great."
Gregory I. reigned from 590 to 604. He extended and
deepened what we have called the " outline " of Papal
policy and ideals which had been marked out by
Leo. With his patrician birth and culture he represented the memories of the vanishing age, but he
took command, as he said, of the " battered vessel
of the Church, into which the waves were pouring
on all sides, with decaying timbers moaning in the
tempest." Italy was being invaded by the most
barbarous of the northern tribes, the Lombards, who
soon established themselves in the rich plain watered
by the Po and its affluents, and the country was

devastated by plague, famine, and Lombard raids. Gregory became civil and ecclesiastical ruler of Rome, which he made the religious capital of the Western Church. In the *first* place, he was a very great administrator, capable of effective attention to a vast range of detail. His wise dealings with the Lombards brought some real relief to distracted Italy. He insisted that the primary duty of priests is the care of men's souls ; and on this conviction is based his work on pastoral care (*Cura Pastoralis*) which provided the Bishops with rules for the conduct of their work and that of their priests. And for the first time, with far-reaching vision and great influence upon the succeeding centuries, he took effective control of missionary activity from the religious capital of the Church. In the *second* place, he realised the religious importance and civilising power of the Benedictine monastic rule. He supported the rule in every possible way, and thus provided an effective system capable of organising the ascetic ideals of the West. In the *third* place, he summed up the tradition of the Latin Church, and thus stands, after Jerome, Augustine, and Ambrose of Milan, as the last of the great Latin Fathers. He transmitted the teachings of Augustine, coloured by the ignorance of the age. His book entitled " Dialogues " has been described as " a manual of credulity." He was anxious to express the doctrine of angels, saints, demons, purgatory, heaven, and hell, in a form suited to the understanding of the barbarian peoples, and to make the ritual and ceremony of the Church's worship more impressive. Some writers, who confuse history and propaganda, have dwelt with complacency on Gregory's " denunciations of secular learning." What did these denunciations actually mean in his own mind ? They meant, first, that Nature had no interest whatever for him, either as an object to be known and understood, or as a source of wonder and beauty ; and, further, that in his belief, study of mere rhetoric, or the amours of Horace or Ovid, or the vagaries of the Graeco-Roman deities, was not a good thing in a time of moral chaos like that which surrounded him. We shall meet with that mood of mind about Nature again.

In the meantime, the Kingdom of the Franks, though distracted by the incompetence of most of its rulers after Clovis, did not lose its continuity. But owing to the feebleness of the last kings of the original line, the real supreme authority passed into the hands of the high officials called " Mayors of the Palace." Charles Martel, " the Hammer," a great soldier and a great ruler, completely defeated the Saracens near Poitiers in 732, and claimed that in thus rolling back the Moslem invaders, he had saved Europe for Christianity. The Pope then reigning in Rome, Gregory III., watched these events with the keenest interest, for the Lombards were again pressing south and east and were threatening Rome itself. So Gregory turned to Charles Martel for aid, beseeching him to complete his victories for the faith by delivering the Holy See. Charles died before he could obey the call, but his son Pippin carried out what may have been his father's intentions. The eastern Emperor, nominally the protector of Rome, did and could do nothing. Gregory's successor claimed and exercised the right of deposing the nominal sovereign of the Franks, who, thus freed from their oath, enthusiastically elected Pippin to the vacant throne. The next Pope crossed the Alps for the first time in order to anoint Pippin and his two sons with holy oil, and then conferred on him the title of " Patrician of the Romans."

Although the Lombards were now comparatively civilised and had even embraced the Catholic faith, they were restless for military adventures, and again pushed south and seized the so-called " exarchate," —Ravenna and the surrounding country, the seat of the " exarch," the eastern Emperor's representative, and the symbol of such merely nominal authority as he still possessed in the West. Pippin rescued the exarchate and bestowed the whole territory on the Bishop of Rome—a possession which was to be the nucleus of the Estates of the Church. When on Pippin's death the Lombards once more revolted, his son, Charles the Great—Charlemagne—destroyed the independence of their kingdom, seized it for his own, and renewed to the Pope the gift of his father. This was in 774, and for twenty-six years the government of Rome was carried on in his name as " Patrician." Then he intervened successfully in a serious quarrel between Pope Leo III. and the citizens of Rome, and restored the Pope to his rebellious city ; and in a thanksgiving service in the Church of St Peter on Christmas Day, 800, when Charles was kneeling by the altar, Leo placed upon his head the diadem of the Caesars, and the multitude acclaimed him Carolus Augustus, " crowned of God," Head of the Empire of Holy Rome. What the motives of Leo and Charles actually were, whether indeed Charles expected the event to occur as it actually did, are debated questions which do not concern us here. It is certain that he accepted the position thus conferred upon him, and in that year modern history began.[7]

Charles was a great conqueror, one who may be compared with Caesar, Alexander, or Napoleon ; but above all else he was a creative genius. " The same intense unresting energy," said the late Lord Bryce, " which carried him over Europe in campaign after campaign, sought a field for its workings in theology, science, literature no less than in politics and war. In his legislation and his administrative system, the zeal for education and literature which he showed in the collection of manuscripts, the founding of schools, the gathering of eminent men from all quarters round him, he stands forth as the civiliser of Europe no less than as her conqueror. His work did not perish in the anarchy which followed. He laid the foundations whereon men continued for many generations to build."

VI.

Thus there arose a second power along with that of the Papacy, and there came forth a series of problems which on a careless view might appear to be matters only of theology or theory, while in reality they are of immense difficulty and great practical importance. " Whence did the Emperor derive his authority— from heaven or from men ; and if from heaven, was it at the hands of the Pope ? What was the relation of the Empire to the Papacy ? Was the Emperor the servant of the Pope, or the Pope the servant of the Emperor, or were they equal and co-ordinate, each being supreme in his own sphere ? " The immense difficulty of these problems arose from the fact that the actually existing authorities in Europe were so many. There was the authority of the Pope

and that of the Emperor ; the authority of other
kings ; the authority of the smaller principalities
and of the cities ; the authority of the local bishops
(many of whom were territorial magnates) ; the
authority of established custom. These forces or
" vested interests " were the source of centrifugal
tendencies which threatened with destruction a
dominant mediæval ideal.

The *unity of mankind* was an assured conviction
in the Middle Ages : an organic unity with a spiritual
basis, since all mankind derives its origin from a
single creator. Christendom, which in destiny is
identical with mankind, is set before us as a single
universal community, founded and governed by God
Himself. This was not even a distinctively Christian
idea. It was the offspring of the speculative genius
of Greece and the political genius of Rome, and was
enormously strengthened under the working of the
equalised and equalising Roman Law, when national
distinctions, in the countries round the Mediterranean,
were being merged in the experience of a common
Empire. Here is a statement of it as an ideal based
upon an ethical monotheism : " And there shall no
longer be one law at Athens, another at Rome, one
law to-day, another to-morrow ; but the same law,
everlasting and unchangeable, shall bind all nations
at all times ; and there shall be one common Master
and Ruler of all, even God, the creator and arbitrator
of this law ; and he who will not obey it shall be an
exile from himself, and, despising the nature of man,
shall by that very act suffer the greatest of all penalties, even though he may have escaped from all other
penalties which can be imagined." These are the
words of the Roman statesman Cicero, written in

later life, when he had seen the destruction of all his old republican hopes and the victory of the imperialism which he dreaded.[8]

Such ideals did not die when the Roman Empire broke up. Mediæval thinkers inherited them, either directly or through the writings of the Christian Fathers. And one thing is clear throughout : they would not surrender the ideal of a united Christendom and an earthly Kingdom of God. The leaven of the old conviction, coming from Greece and Rome, was working still. We can trace it down the centuries to the days of Dante.

It meant to them what it had meant to Cicero. The one universal Law of which he spoke was a principle of Justice and Order belonging to the nature of things—a truth always there, waiting to be discovered. They believed it had been revealed to the Romans, as the Gospel had been revealed to the Jews. Hence the Popes of the Middle Ages claimed not only ecclesiastical jurisdiction, but also control of secular concerns. " All kings and governors were baptised Christians, and as such subject to the authority of Rome. Politics, commerce, industry, education, art, literature, philosophy—these, like every other field of human activity, had their religious aspects, and were to be made subservient to the laws of the divine kingship ; and in the multitude of Catholic Christians, of all nations and tongues, organised under bishops, and governed in the last resort by the earthly Vicar of Christ, the Kingdom of God was seen in being and in power."

We have seen how this ideal was outlined in the actual policy of Leo the Great and Gregory the Great. For about two centuries after the death of Gregory, the Chair of Peter was occupied by men of varying capacity. There was no great outstanding figure among them. And, again, we have seen with what statesmanlike perception they grasped the importance of an alliance with the Frankish kings, and the culmination of this policy in the coronation of Charlemagne. In the confusion and anarchy of Europe during the ninth and tenth centuries, the papacy fell into a debased condition which reached its lowest depth from about the last quarter of the ninth century to the middle of the tenth. The details of these events are given in the ecclesiastical Histories ; we refer to them here only in order to introduce the third truly great figure in the line of mediæval Popes : Gregory VII. (Hildebrand), who for several years had been the power behind the papal throne. He found that some of the Cardinals were well aware of the need for reform, and were working for it—and above all for putting an end to " simony " (the buying and selling of ecclesiastical offices) ; for the abolition of the appointment to such offices by secular authority (" lay investiture ") ; for the enforcement of clerical celibacy ; and for the vesting of papal elections in the College of Cardinals. Hildebrand threw his whole energies into the promotion of these aims.

In 1073 the man who thus had endowed the papal policy with his passionate enthusiasm and strengthened it with his imperious will, became leader of the Church. At once he set himself to attain the purposes of the reformers by papal decrees, thus directly challenging the most powerful " vested interests " of the time. His duel with the Emperor Henry IV. over the question of lay investiture has much dramatic interest, but its importance has been greatly exaggerated. The thirteen years of his reign were years of conflict, always strenuous and often embittered ; and in the end he was driven from Rome and died in exile at Salerno. Through all these years of strife, we discern the working power of the same great ideal, the complete supremacy of the Church over the world. As the struggle went on, Gregory looked far beyond his original plan of reforming the morals of the clergy, centralising ecclesiastical government, and raising the papacy from the debased position into which it had fallen and making it independent of the Empire. His idea grew until it embraced Augustine's dream of a Kingdom of God on earth under the rule of the Church.

Never was the supremacy of the Church over the world so nearly realised as it was in the early years of the thirteenth century under Pope Innocent III. His greatness lay not in the assertion of the claim, for others, as we know, had asserted it before him, but in the diplomatic skill and strength of character which enabled him to assert it with such a degree of success. " Nothing in all history," it has been said, " is more astonishing than the spectacle of this man, physically insignificant, by training a theologian and a canon lawyer, regulating the affairs of the entire continent in a time of general disorder." Never, indeed, was the universal regency of the Pope more nearly achieved than under Innocent III. ; and never was it more arrogantly and dogmatically asserted than by Boniface VIII. ninety years later. But after the great conflicts between the Emperor Frederic I. and Popes Hadrian IV. and Alexander III., and between the Emperor Frederic II. and Popes

Gregory IX. and Innocent IV., its tragic failure was
evident to all.

There was more than one reason for the failure.
Because of the great increase in its secular activities,
the Curia, the body of Cardinals organised into
Committees for the transaction of papal business,
was becoming even in the time of Innocent III. a
political and financial institution. The truth is that
the attempt to govern political life was ruined because
the Church adopted the methods of the State for doing it.
The Church as one organised institution set out to
control the State as another organised institution,
and for this it adopted purely secular methods. But
there was another and an even greater reason. Let
us imagine some powerful mind from that time speaking to our modern world in defence of his ideals.

" Men of a distant age ! " we seem to hear him
saying ; " men of an age which we dreamèd would
never be, our voice now comes to you from an age
which you dreamed was dead. Our lives were laid
in centuries of bitter hardship, of constant war, of
devastating pestilence, of paralysing fear, of furious
passion. Against these enemies of our bodies and
souls, we built up no ignoble ideals. We would erect
a presiding power common to all Europe, a power
which should not dethrone the King, but treat him as
an hereditary Viceroy ; a power which should be
charged to prevent strife between kingdoms and to
maintain the order of Europe by being not only the
fountain of international law but the judge in its
causes and the enforcer of its sentences. Such was
our ideal of the Church in relation to the world, to
be embodied in the occupant of the Chair of Peter.

" We believed that the office and the power with

which it endows the holder of it are one thing, and the personal character and aims of the holder a very different thing. Our reverence for the sacred office did not make us blind to the sins of those who held it. There were some in the Chair of Peter whose fearlessness and justice were worthy of their office. There were others who, through their evil example, by their misuse of religion as a means to service, by their cupidity and ambition, have corrupted clergy and laity alike ; who have made their holy office an incitement to war, and placed the spiritual symbol of the keys on their war banners ; who have turned the curia into a place where everything is sold and Christ is daily put up for auction ; whose bishops and priests have taken pattern by themselves and turned to the service of mammon, and made the rites of religion of none effect. All these things, and more, can be charged to the Church of our time ; but not to these do we now look for the ruin of our ideals.[9]

" Forces were growing up in our midst which we did not understand. Nations were growing up in our midst, each with a language, a character, of its own ; nations, growing more and more different from one another in habits and institutions ; nations which would not yield in their strength what they had won in their weakness ; again and again involved in war with one another, or torn within by insurrections and devastating civil wars. We could not destroy nationality nor overcome the antagonisms which it created. We knew not what the issue of these things might be. When we dared to dream of what might be, there rose before us a vision of discordant, mistrustful, suspicious, scheming Sovereign States. We saw the Sovereign State as a predatory force. Its rise was the destruction of our ideals. And we saw it as it might become—eager to be self-sufficing, inflamed with the cupidities of boundless money-getting, and plunging its own prosperity into universal ruin."

If it is impossible to bring an indictment against a whole nation, it is even more impossible to bring an indictment against an age. We cannot against them, nor can they against us. All thoughtful men in the Middle Ages knew as well as we do, or better, that apart from some effective international organisation the nations *taken as separate units* live in a condition of complete anarchy, where self-preservation and justice, for self or for others, can only be secured by the strong hand of the nation which has the will to make these principles effective.[10] But the mediæval mind could not conceive such an organisation except as an international State or Super-state, with a single central source of authority ; and they could not conceive that supreme international State save in closest union with a supreme international Church. Such a Church was in their midst, in all the fulness of its accumulated powers. It is not our intention to make any theological declaration here, unless this be one— that the modern world has decisively rejected the stupendous claim on which the power of that Church was based, and on which whatever real power it possesses to-day is still based. The ideal of a Super-state, with a single central source of power, may be for ever impracticable. In the present condition of the world it certainly is impracticable. Mere negations, however, settle nothing ; and these negations only make the challenge of history more urgent to the people of to-day.

You may reply, What of the Protestant Reformation ? The men who made the Protestant Reformation were not indifferent to the secular welfare of nations ; but they concentrated their conviction into one sublime truth—that only by the soul can nations be great and free ; and they concentrated their appeal on the souls of men. And through their preoccupation with a Book, a thoroughly oriental Book, which they did not know how to read, they lost even a distant vision of that ideal, the greatest legacy of the ancient pagan world, pointing to an eternal principle of Justice and Order, part of the very nature of things, demanding embodiment in human life on earth in the form of an organised community.

VII.

A suggestive metaphor has been employed by Dr C. C. J. Webb to describe the intellectual condition of the men of the earlier Middle Ages : " They did not, perhaps, fully realise—though some of them were not without more than an inkling of it—that they were in the position of shipwrecked children ; but their Christian training had accustomed them to think of books handed down from antiquity as the repository of authoritative truth ; and so it seemed natural to them to seek, as it were, for the necessaries and conveniences of the intellectual life among whatever scanty relics of ancient literature they could find, rather than to catch their own food and invent their own tools." As a matter of fact the first thinkers in our period simply collected together the debris of the knowledge of antiquity wherever they could discover it.

It is usual, even among competent historians, to apply the term " The Dark Ages," certainly not to the whole mediæval period, but to the centuries from the fifth to the eleventh, in contrast to the " Renaissance " which followed. Their use of such a term does not imply that during these centuries all men dwelt contentedly in a state of " darkness." The truth is nearly the opposite. We discern a pathetic haunting sense of being ignorant of much that former ages had known, and an eager endeavour to find what could be known from the past. This was the source of the well-known " encyclopædic " tendency of the time, leading to the formation of collections of all kinds of real or supposed information, and to these the name " philosophy " at first was given. It is the business of the historian to see and understand what the literature of the period *was* rather than what it *was not*. And when he does this, he sees that the period from the fall of the Roman Empire to the great revival of the twelfth century was not one of mere stagnation and darkness, but the workshop in which the transformation from ancient to modern culture was being prepared. He sees that the " confusion of tongues," resulting from the decay of the Latin language in its classical form, and the crudeness of the vernaculars which replaced it, hampered but did not repress the expression of human experience and feeling and thought. During these centuries there were present all the conditions of great literature save one—*an adequate vehicle for its expression*. This remark refers rather to literature as distinguished from philosophy and theology. The appeal of philosophy and theology was so powerful that a universal language, a variety of Latin with distinctive characteristics of its own, was wrought out to serve their needs.

Here we must remember that during the Middle Ages philosophy was never *merely* the " handmaid of theology." If theology is the systematic study of miraculously revealed truths, which are therefore absolute certainties, on which the eternal welfare of men depends, then theology is inevitably the supreme study and the highest type of knowledge ; and philosophy may be useful in explaining the meaning of the revealed truths, and showing their connection with our natural experience, and proving, so far as it can be proved, that they are not contrary to our reason. Moreover, there may be theological truths which are capable of being established by our unaided reason ; and in any case, there is a large field of philosophical inquiry where the problems raised have little or no bearing on theological truth. It is evident, therefore, that the so-called " subordination of reason " will wear a different aspect according to the century and the writer referred to.

On this basis a division of mediæval thought into three periods was suggested by Victor Cousin. The division is chronological in form, but is really more one of principle and inner spirit. At first we find philosophy wholly subordinated to theology ; then a period when they appear as allies ; and finally the beginning of their separation. In other words, we find philosophy gradually extending its claims. What was called " dialectic "—that is, Aristotelian logic (the knowledge of which was largely extended in the twelfth century)—was at first a purely secular art, and only gradually were its terms and distinctions applied to questions in theology. The early results of its application were not favourable to the dogmas concerned. Hence the strength with which a champion of the faith like Anselm insisted on the subordination of reason : *credo ut intelligam*—" I believe, in order that I may understand " ; faith comes first. To St Bernard (Bernard of Clairvaux) and many other conservative Churchmen, any application of dialectic to the things of faith appeared as impious as it was dangerous. At a later period, in the systems of the great thinkers of the thirteenth century, and, above all, in the system of St Thomas Aquinas, the rights of reason are fully established and amply acknowledged. Certain doctrines indeed—an increasing number as time went on—were withdrawn from the sphere of reason ; but with these exceptions, the two move side by side, and accomplish by different means the same ends. These thinkers, at once more profound and more cautious, substituted a harmony for the conflicts which accompanied the first intrusion of philosophy (then only logic) into the theological domain. But the harmony was more apparent than real. The further movement of mediæval thought consisted partly in a withdrawal of doctrine after doctrine from the possibility of rational proof, and their relegation to the sphere of faith. No sooner was the harmony apparently established by Aquinas than Duns Scotus began this negative criticism, which was carried much further by William of Ockham. Hence it is said that mediæval thought failed to rationalise the doctrines of the Church, because the Aristotelian form, as it was then conceived, refused to fit a subject-matter for which it was never intended, and that the matter of Christian theology refused to be forced into an alien form.

This view of the relation of theology and philosophy in the Middle Ages may be called the traditional view. It is not inaccurate, much less is it untrue ; but it does not penetrate to the roots of the question. The comprehensive synthesis worked out by Albert the Great, and by his still greater pupil, Saint Thomas Aquinas, broke down in the hands of William of Ockham and his followers, because William of Ockham held and taught, with far-reaching and powerful influence, a view of the nature and limits of Reason which, if it were true, inevitably shattered the constructive work of his predecessors and left faith with a wholly non-rational basis on which to rest. It by no means follows that the Christianised Aristotelianism of Aquinas is a mere historical curiosity with nothing of value for modern thought.

The constructive work which is characteristic of Christian thought in the West during the thirteenth and early fourteenth centuries—" the Golden Middle Age," as the late Baron von Hügel called it—was, in the first place, the expression of " a side of the Middle Ages to which scant justice has often been done—their immense intellectual enthusiasm " [11] ; in the second place, it was the expression of a conviction that all the ranges of contemporary activity, art and ceremony, law, philosophy and literature, could and must be welded together in a synthesis which while not merely the servant of dogma must be a religious synthesis ; and in the third place, it was the response to a great challenge arising out of the course of events. The situation was in some ways like that in which modern Christian thought found itself in face of the advance of science during the last hundred years. When, alike from the West and the

East, through translations from the Arabic and translations direct from the Greek, the science and philosophy of the Greek and Arabian astronomers and physicians were thrown open to the Christian scholars of Central·Europe, a series of problems emerged which were as urgent as they were new. The merely ecclesiastical theologians at first suspected and resisted the new knowledge ; but the spirit of the age was too strong for them. Christian thought eagerly responded to the challenge. If there was to be peace and not war between faith and knowledge, Christian teachers must develop new aspects of the traditional beliefs, and work out a philosophy, an interpretation of experience as a whole, which would be capable of embracing and amalgamating with all that was sound in the new intellectual life.

This conscious and deliberate endeavour was helped and inspired by another influence, which we may almost describe as " unconscious." This was the influence of Platonism. The Platonism of the Middle Ages was not the philosophy of Plato himself. It was a stream fed by many tributaries ; but part of the spirit of it can be traced directly back to Plato. How can a man attain or forfeit eternal salvation ? Man has a soul which can attain everlasting beatitude, and this beatitude it is the great business of life to attain. The social institutions or the education which fit him to attain it are the right institutions or education ; all others are wrong. It is the soul's vision of that supreme Reality which for Plato is itself Absolute Good, Absolute Beauty, Absolute Truth. It is itself the Source of all goodness, beauty, and truth, which appear " piecemeal," as it were, in this world. It stands to the soul's vision as the light of the Sun stands to that of the body. And the journey of life is a spiritual voyage—the travel of the soul from the temporal to the eternal.[12]

VIII.

In this connection we must point out a striking contrast between the mediæval world and the classical Greek world, in reference to the value of knowledge. Among the Greeks, the capacity for knowledge—not merely knowledge as information but as the rational understanding of the causes and consequences of things—was believed without question to be man's highest endowment, and its development to be at once a duty and a delight. Plato expressed this conviction in his own way when he said, " It is a happy genealogy which makes *Iris* the daughter of *Thaumas* "—*i.e.*, which treats the messenger of the gods, the winged thought which passes to and fro between heaven and earth and brings them into communion, as the child of Wonder, the impulse to know and to understand. Aristotle believed that the highest life is a life of mental self-realisation, of truth-seeking and truth-seeing, ever successful, yet perennially interesting.

Afterwards the enthusiasm which created such ideals died away; and for later Greek thinkers knowledge was valued chiefly as a guide to human good in a dying civilisation. In our modern world there are many who value science only as it ministers to human welfare. Yet it is a fact assured by all the testimony of man's experience of study, that not upon the grounds of economy and the usefulness of

knowledge to man's physical and social wants, but
by some sense of a preciousness inherent in itself, of
a fitness between it and the nature of man, of a privilege in seeking it and a delight in finding it for its own
pure sake—that only so have all the great revelations
of truth come to mankind.

On the other hand, we find early traces of a very
different view, where knowledge is regarded as only
one among other kinds of human excellence or superiority, and the desire to acquire all or any of these
various kinds of excellence is brought under the duty
of *moderation*. To know more than is enough (*quam
sit satis*), said Seneca, is a kind of intemperance.[13]
This doctrine has an interesting history ; but we are
here concerned with its inner meaning. It leads to
a conclusion which is logically inevitable and from
every point of view momentous. It is no question
of the possibility or the difficulty of knowledge.
The conclusion is that *there are things which we can
know but which we ought not to try to know*. And why
not ?

The greater thinkers of the mediæval period gave
cautious answers to this question. Saint Thomas
Aquinas said that it is lawful to pursue any kind of
knowledge which contributes to the purpose for which
man was created—the supreme end of man, to glorify
God and enjoy Him for ever. But this covers a great
deal. It allows for the mind's love for God ; and in the
commandment to love God " with all the mind,"
" mind " was taken to imply a specifically intellectual
power or faculty, different from the "heart" and "soul"
and " strength." Other thinkers had been less cautious. Saint Bernard of Clairvaux, for example, writing
a century earlier than Aquinas, laid great stress on the

motive. To pursue knowledge purely for the sake of knowing, is to yield to an impious and dangerous curiosity. To pursue knowledge for the " edification " of others is charity; for the " edification " of self, prudence. And in all cases Christian moderation must prescribe the conditions under which knowledge is to be sought.[14] Many such utterances might be quoted. They show the drift of mediæval thought and feeling. And the conclusion is that there are things which it is not lawful for men to try to know. It is not God's will that men should know them. This conviction was naturally wrought into the general belief of the time, that mankind is beset by unseen powers, beneficent and malignant. Unlawful knowledge could only be acquired by intercourse with the powers of darkness. So far was this suspicion from being the invention of priests, that a priest was more likely than anyone else to be the object of it ; and some of the greatest churchmen did not escape. A remarkable example is that of Gerbert of Aurillac, a man of extraordinary attainments, considering the meagre material with which he had to work ; insisting on the importance of study of nature, devoting himself to logic, mathematics, astronomy, mechanical invention ; an ecclesiastical statesman of the first rank, dying early in the eleventh century as Pope Sylvester II. How could mortal man, in such an age of widespread ignorance and barbarism, have mastered such a range of knowledge ? Although a Pope, he was believed to have acquired it by unlawful means. After his death, legends grew up round his name. Among his mechanical inventions was a figure of metal, or the head of one, which could *speak*. All through the Middle Ages we find this recurring interest in the manufacture of mechanical men. Gerbert's figure not only spoke, but, what is much more remarkable, always the truth : with the unhappy result that the Pope misunderstood one of its oracles, and died in consequence.

Such quaint and pathetic legends are illustrative. The superstitious form which they assume was natural and inevitable in such an age ; but when we penetrate to their inner meaning, we find their root in an assured conviction that God has given us means of acquiring such knowledge as is necessary for the welfare of daily life. More than that is, so to speak, not authorised. Again we press the question, Why not ? The answer is, Because it is dangerous. There are ways by which men may acquire it, but *they are not to be trusted with it*. If they acquire it, they will use it to the destruction of their bodies and souls. Such was the mediæval assumption. We hear modern voices saying remarkably similar things about modern knowledge ; but at present we are tracing the historic effects of this assumption in the Middle Ages.

Its prejudicial effects on the cultivation of what we understand by the knowledge of Nature, must be obvious. It was re-enforced by another bias even more fundamental and far-reaching. Professor Étienne Gilson has pointed out that before the time of Albert and Thomas, Christian thinkers had no conception of what we call Nature as an independent object of study in its own right. The proper object of all real knowledge was God. God was held to be known before all else in his revelation of himself in Scripture, on which the faith of the Church was founded. Scripture speaks throughout illustratively and in metaphor, and its true sense is not apparent on the surface ; hence Scripture, believed through faith, required the use of reason to be rightly understood. When the truths of revelation were thus established, Christian thinkers turned to the visible world, which must in some sense be a revelation of the same God. But to them the visible world appeared only as it were a shadow of God. So far as they followed Augustine, they went further, and, denying that *sense* is really a source of knowledge at all, they found in sense-perception only the *occasion* for the mind to turn to ideas with which God had already furnished it. This involved an extreme doctrine of "innate ideas." Albert and Thomas rejected every vestige of this view of truth, and allowed to the mind a "natural light," which simply meant that by the exercise of its own rational faculties upon the material given in sense-perception, the mind can learn to understand the created world as an independent object demanding investigation.[15] In one respect Professor Gilson appears to have overstated his case. Although St Thomas Aquinas certainly did recognise Nature in this way, the whole constructive effort of his genius was with questions in philosophical theology, and his influence went to turn Christian thought entirely in that direction and not in the direction of natural science.

In addition to all this there was an inevitable limitation in the mediæval outlook on Nature, arising directly from the scientific tradition which they inherited from the Greeks. In the great period of Greek thought, scientific thinkers, apart from Aristotle, were fascinated by geometry, which seemed to them to provide a means of obtaining real knowledge about Nature by abstract reasoning from first principles or axioms, assumed as self-evident or taken for granted.

The extraordinary development which geometry under-went in their hands diverted their interest from the labour of accurate and extended observation of Nature. This statement is true, with one most important exception, springing from *the desire to cure disease*. It became evident that abstract argument from first principles was useless for this purpose, and extensive observation of the facts was demanded. The work of Aristotle is an impressive demonstration of how this led to the foundation of human anatomy and physiology, and to the beginnings of zoology and botany. Even in astronomy the Greeks seem to have done little in the way of actual observation. Their main interest was in the direction of theory. Interest in astronomical observation as a means of " astro-logical " prediction of the future was an inheritance from the East.

Above all there was a definite doctrine of the " constitution of matter," which, coming down from early Greek philosophy, was widely accepted, though not without criticism, in the Middle Ages. Each of the " Four Elements " of the Greek tradition, " earth," " air," " water," " fire," was believed to have an elementary essence or essential principle. Of these four essential principles all natural objects were composed, and were characterised by four qualities, " hot," " cold," " dry," and " moist." Now many characteristics of natural objects could not possibly be explained on this basis. The phenomena of magnetism made a conspicuous example. Such qualities were called " occult," as distinct from qualities supposed to be derived from the component elements. This view of Nature created the conviction that almost anything was possible—almost anything might happen.

This again created a keen curiosity about the things of this world, and the formation of large " encyclopædias " of all available information about the phenomena of Nature.[16]

If ever the mediæval mind was shaken in its belief that we ought not to know too much, it was in face of the invisible, mysterious, devastating terror of pestilence. There are fragmentary accounts of many outbreaks of epidemic disease during the period, in one district or another ; but there is no indefiniteness in the records of the most terrible of all these visitations—the Black Death, which broke out in the middle of the fourteenth century. The Black Death was bubonic plague in its most virulent and infectious form. It came from Asia through Russia, following the great trade routes, and invaded Italy, France, England and Ireland, Belgium, Holland, and Germany. The mortality was terrific : but the people of that time could not conceive or imagine *how it was propagated from one person to another*. The conventional theological explanations—by reference to divine retribution for human wickedness, or the malignant agency of demons—were not questioned ; but the panic-stricken instincts of the populace were not satisfied thus. The belief spread (as though it were itself an epidemic) that there were individuals and societies who were carrying medicaments in order to propagate the plague. And the cry arose, " Where is the Hidden Hand ? Where are they by whose deliberate design this calamity has come upon us ? Where are they, that we may wreak our vengeance upon them ? " And an immense number of innocent victims— especially Jews—suffered in this way. It was the emergence, in a tragically hysterical form, of a recurring delusion in times of public calamity : that these disasters must have been deliberately planned and brought about of set purpose by individuals.

Amid the horrors of this story—and it is no mere rhetoric to describe it as a most horrible story—it is well to recall these words, written in England at some period in the fourteenth century : " Beloved brother, I hear that thou goest in great fear of the Plague ; but surely a little faith would reassure thee, that thou mightest cast off care and sadness and terrifying thoughts and the like, since they are but accidents of the mind and do but offend and consume the spirit. Strive, therefore, after cheerfulness, for a happy spirit is the very bloom of life, but gloom dryeth up the marrow. And next, after the counsel of wisdom, do thou in all cleanness and sincerity so dispose thy ways that thou mayest live to-day as though thou wert to die to-morrow. Death can have no terrors for him whose life is in the right. And when thy soul is thus washed clean, it may be that thy body will be preserved from the pestilential malady." [17]

CHAPTER II.

THE EARLIER MIDDLE AGES.

OUR purpose in this book is one of interpretation ; and therefore we must fix our attention, not on stories of devastation, destruction, and death, during the tribal migrations of the fifth, sixth, and seventh centuries, but on those constructive forces which prepared the way for the greater constructive work of succeeding centuries.

I.

One penetrating stream of thought and feeling, at once a philosophy and a religion, arose as the ancient world declined. It appropriated almost all the earlier systems, and worked up the results of eastern and western culture. It seemed to disappear only that it might become more powerful as a creative force in the thought of the Middle Ages. This was the movement called " Neoplatonism." The use of this term is too firmly established to be easily abandoned ; but we must not read into it any suggestion of a revival of the philosophy taught in the Dialogues of Plato. The term must be regarded simply as a historic label.

It has been said, with much truth, that never before in Greek or Roman speculation had the consciousness of man's dignity and superiority to Nature found such adequate expression. The ethical mood which Neoplatonism endeavoured to create and maintain is the highest and purest ever reached by antiquity. On the other hand, never was natural science—the investigation of Nature based on experience and systematic observation—so undervalued and despised as it was by the leaders of Neoplatonism. Harnack has said that the inner history of antiquity ended in a despair of this world : " The present world was a thing, which men could neither enjoy nor master nor study : a new world was discovered, for the sake of which everything else was abandoned." This is an exaggeration, even in reference to Neoplatonism ; but it is an exaggeration of the truth. The dominating interest of the movement was a religious interest. Neoplatonism became a philosophy of revelation, claiming to be not only the absolute philosophy, the keystone of all previous systems, but also the absolute religion, re-invigorating and transforming all previous religions. The Stoics taught men to overstep the boundaries of states and nationalities. Through all history the Divine Spirit has moved. But to the Neoplatonists this meant that the older any religious tradition or mode of worship is, the richer it is in divine truth. Hence what they could discover about the ancient religions of the East had a peculiar interest for them ; and even the crudest myths presented no difficulty for they could be understood as allegories.

Although there was no earlier system which did not contribute something to the movement, it intro-

THE EARLIER MIDDLE AGES

duced a new principle into philosophy : the " supra-rational "—that which lies beyond Reason, but which is the fundamental ground of all being and the final goal of all attainment. It is possible to suggest how they were led to this conclusion. They believed that what we call our Reason is a faculty limited by its very nature to a certain kind of work : it is essentially " discursive "—it learns by passing from fact to fact, analysing, classifying, and dividing ; even the quali-ties of the familiar objects of our daily experience are known to us only as we analyse the facts revealed in sense-perception and distinguish them from one another. Neoplatonism perceived that reason (so understood) cannot provide a basis or justification for religious ethics, any more than sense-perception can provide it.

Our purpose here is not to sketch the history of Neoplatonism but to interpret its spirit. The two greatest names in its history are those of Plotinus, who taught in Rome during the middle years of the third century A.D.—the historic founder of the move-ment ; and Proclus, who taught in Athens two centuries later—its " encyclopædist."

Plotinus was profoundly convinced that the capaci-ties of the soul reach forth beyond all that the world of the senses can give, beyond all that the highest knowledge or understanding can comprehend. For him, philosophy falls into two divisions : the theo-retical, setting forth the high origin of the soul and the way in which it has fallen from its first estate ; and the practical, setting forth the way in which the soul may return to union with the Supreme.

The Supreme Source of all Being is beyond all that we can utter or express. It is beyond goodness ;

for to us " good " means being " good *for something* "
and therefore implies limitation. It is even beyond
existence as we understand it : for to us, existence
means being " one among others." We can only say
with absolute truth that it is One. And yet it is the
Source of all Being ; from it, directly or indirectly,
all things proceed, but without any alteration or
diminution of its own Being. This process they described by a vague metaphor for which the English-
Latin equivalent is " emanation "—" flowing forth."
The product has real or complete being only in virtue
of the original Being active within it ; but derived
existence, unlike the original Being itself, is subject
to a law of diminishing completeness : the further the
line of successive " emanations " proceeds, the smaller
is its share in the true existence. Each lower stage
of being is united with the Supreme by all the higher
stages, and receives its share of reality only by transmission through them ; but all derived existence has
an inner " urge " towards the higher, and tends towards it so far as its nature will permit. The world
of our ordinary experience is not evil ; it contains
much that is fair and good ; but it also contains strife
and discord, and the reason for this is that it rests
upon a foundation of " matter," the furthest removed
from the divine Original. In this sense, " matter "
is evil. In this life, our souls are entangled with an
evil principle ; and the divine " urge " within is
blinded and takes the form of personal egoism.

Along the same path by which it descended, the
soul must return. It must first of all turn from the
illusory self of individual egoism and discover its
true self. This is done by the way of Virtue. In the
ethics of Plotinus, all the older schemes of the virtues

are taken over and arranged in a graduated series :
the social virtues, the purifying virtues, and the
divine virtues. The social virtues are only the lowest
rungs of the ladder by which the heavenward ascent
is made. The purifying virtues, by which are meant
ascetic observances, free the soul from sensuality
and make it more spiritual and more enduring, and
open up the higher avenues of approach to the Divine.
The supreme virtues lead the soul to union with God.
The doctrine proceeds in the spirit of the modern
lines :

> He who himself and God would know,
> Into the silence let him go,
> And, lifting off pall after pall,
> Reach to the inmost depth of all.

Thought cannot achieve this ; it is only a prelimi-
nary to communion with the Highest. In order to reach
this supreme attainment, the soul must pass through
a spiritual discipline ending in a condition of mystic
ecstasy in which it loses itself. " The lover approached the dwelling-place of the Beloved, and stood
at the door, and knocked. A Voice said, ' Who is
there ? ' He answered, ' It is I.' The Voice said,
' There is not room here for Me and thee.' After many
days the lover approached the dwelling-place of the
Beloved a second time, and stood at the door, and
knocked. A Voice said, ' Who is there ? ' He answered, ' It is Thou.' And the door was opened."

Notwithstanding these lofty ideals, the story of this
movement is part of the story of the decline of ancient
religion and philosophy. In the hands of some of its
adherents, Neoplatonism became completely subservient to polytheism, and made its chief object

the protection of paganism against the formidable attacks of Christianity. But in the end the victory of the Church had a purifying influence upon it. The leaders gave up all hope of destroying Christianity, and, while maintaining the same religious attitude and the same theory of knowledge, they turned to literary and philosophical studies. Plato remained the divine philosopher ; but the writings of Aristotle were now increasingly read and valued and made the subject of exposition and commentary. Neoplatonic schools flourished in the chief cities of the Empire until the beginning of the fifth century ; during this period, indeed, they were the training-schools of Christian theologians.

The most distinguished among the teachers of Neoplatonism in Athens was Proclus, who died 485 A.D. We have described him as the " encyclo-pædist " of the movement. With a religious ardour as strong as his logical skill, and with a scholarship able to keep in view all the changes which the movement had undergone in the course of two centuries, he set himself to work the whole mass of accumulated lore into a huge system ; and he gave it the form in which it was transmitted to Christianity and Mohammedism in the Middle Ages.

What Neoplatonism meant to Augustine is set forth vividly in the seventh book of the *Confessions*. He had studied the books, in Latin translations, and had deeply assimilated the spirit of the teaching. " I beheld with the eye of my soul, such as it was, the Light Unchangeable, above my mind, above my soul ; not the ordinary light of day, which all flesh may behold, nor even a greater light of the same kind : and not above my soul, as the heavens are above the

earth : but above my soul because It made me :
and I below It, because I was made by It. He that
knows the Truth, knows what that Light is ; and he
that knows It, knows Eternity. O Truth who art
Eternity, and Love who art Truth, and Eternity who
art Love ! . . . I perceived myself to be far away
from Thee, as though I heard Thy voice from on
high : ' I am the Food of grown men : grow, and thou
shalt feed upon Me : nor shalt thou change me, like
the food of thy body, into thyself, but thyself shall
be changed into Me.' . . . Soon was I borne down
again by mine own weight, the habits of my body and
mind ; yet there dwelt with me a remembrance of
Thee, and I doubted not that there was One to whom
I might cleave, but that I was not yet able to cleave
to Thee. . . . Then I considered, whence it was that
I was able to admire the beauty of things in the
heavens and the earth, and whence it was that I
was able to judge soundly on mutable things, and say
' This ought to be thus, and this not ' : considering,
I say, whence it was that I so judged, I found the
unchangeable Eternity of Truth above my changeable
mind. Thus, by degrees I passed from the body to
the soul, which works through the bodily senses ;
and thence to its inner faculty, to which the bodily
senses represent outward things ; and thence to its
reasoning faculty, to which what is received from the
senses is referred to be judged : which, finding itself
also a changeable thing, was made strong to the
understanding of itself, and drew away my thoughts
from the power of habit, that so it might find what
that Light was, whereby itself did see. Then it knew
the Unchangeable, which, unless it had in some way
known, it could not have desired above the change-

able. And thus as with the flash of one trembling glance, it beheld *that which truly Is*. . . . But I could not fix my gaze thereon : I was thrown back again upon my customary habits, carrying with me only a loving memory thereof, and a longing for what I had, as it were, perceived the odour of but was not yet able to feed upon." [18] Augustine believed that three essentials of a lasting religious foundation were wanting in Neoplatonism : it wanted a religious founder, " the Word made flesh " ; it could not provide any means by which the condition of inward blessedness could become an abiding possession ; nor any means of winning those who had no capacity for philosophical discipline.

II.

From the years during which Roman civilisation had been extending into Italy, Spain, Gaul, and South Germany, a racial and social fusion had been going on, which enabled the populations of these countries to act as " mediators " between the northern tribes and the Romans. Christian belief had been drifting in, through hermits and wandering monks, for years, before the extraordinary effects of the mission of Ulfilas (who died in 383) converted the northern barbarians to Arian Christianity and almost raised their speech to the level of a literary language. The peoples from the North were politically the enemies of the Romans, but they were not the enemies of Roman civilisation. In many ways they tried to assimilate it. To say that " there was no breach of culture " may be an exaggeration, but there was no life-and-death struggle between the two peoples, ending only with the downfall of and disappearance of everything which had contributed to the welfare of Rome.

The really decisive loss resulting from the tribal migrations, followed as they were by the breach between East and West, was that for more than five centuries western Christendom was cut off from any effective and direct contact with classical Greek literature, and from any effective and direct knowledge of the spirit and civilisation of ancient Greece. From indirect contact they were not entirely cut off ; and this brings us to the work of man who made possible the " Carolingian Renaissance." We may admit the term, if we remember that " renaissance," in history, means " culmination."

First, however, we must gain a clear view of the ways in which the work of two great figures of the departing age penetrated the thought and feeling of the period on which we are now entering.

The position of Augustine is unique, as personality, thinker, theologian, ecclesiastical statesman, and greatest of the Fathers. He is known best in modern Christendom by the doctrine which counted for least in his actual historical influence—that of Divine Election and Reprobation. Historically, he was the chief channel by which Neoplatonism was transmitted to the Middle Ages, so that when historians of mediæval thought speak of the " Augustinian elements " in the writings, say, of Robert Grosseteste, or of Saint Bonaventura, we might with almost equal truth speak of the " Platonic elements." And he was the source of an authority which largely bound the mind and conscience of Christian thinkers for fifty generations.

Augustine is convinced that the sole worthy and legitimate objects of knowledge are God and the Soul. Men go about to search out the hidden powers of Nature, which are beyond our range (*praeter nos*), and the knowledge of which, even if we obtain it, profits us nothing and may lead us to tamper with magic arts.[19] As to the possibility and reality of *magic* Augustine has no doubt at all; but he attributes its origin to " demons " who are enticed or constrained by methods which it is possible for men to learn. Christian miracles, on the other hand, are wrought through devout confidence and simple faith, not by incantations (*incantationibus et carminibus nefariae curiositatis arte compositis*).[20] His references to *astrology* are not free from ambiguity. On the whole, it appears that he does not deny the influence of the stars on human affairs. This belief was too ancient and deeply rooted to be easily rejected at that time. But he is greatly concerned to discredit all beliefs which made the stars fix as it were mechanically the destinies of individual men.[21] Hence he was often quoted during the Middle Ages as an authority against all belief in the influence of the heavenly bodies which was subversive of human freedom.

Very interesting is his distinction between lawful and unlawful medical art.[22] It is one thing to say, If you drink the juice of this herb, your pain will be relieved; it is another thing to say, If you suspend this herb from your neck, your pain will be relieved; though even this is lawful if done without incantations or superstitious ceremonies, because then, if it acts, it acts *by a natural virtue*. When the reason why a thing is of virtue is not apparent, the intention with which it is used is of great importance. Augustine's recognition of the natural healing powers of natural objects is an example of what we find throughout the Middle Ages. At no time, not even during the period of the barbarian invasions, did medical literature or medical practice cease entirely in the West. Mediæval Christians at no time depended solely and entirely on Divine answers to prayer, or on the healing virtues of the relics of saints, or the miraculous powers ascribed to the Church ; although many times it would have been physically more salutary for them if they had depended only on these, for these, at the least and lowest estimate, are harmless.

There is, then, a legitimate natural knowledge by which bodily ills may be healed. Beyond this, physics, the study of external Nature, is of value only so far as it leads to the knowledge of God, the Supreme Cause. It is worse than useless if it contributes nothing to our salvation. " Wretched is he who knows all this [i.e., has this natural knowledge] and knows not Thee ; blessed is he who knows Thee, even though he knows nought of all this ; he who knows Thee and these things also, is not more blessed through them, but through Thee alone." " More praiseworthy is the mind which knows its own weakness, than the mind which thinks not of this, but searches out the courses of the stars, even though it shall or does already know them, and knows not the way to salvation and abiding strength." " Be not much concerned if thou knowest not the courses of the stars, or the numbers of bodies in the heavens or the earth ; behold the beauty of the world, and praise the wisdom of the Creator ; behold what He made, praise Him who made it, love Him who made it ; for thee also, who lovest Him, He made in His own Image." The holy angels find the knowledge of corporeal things to be as nothing in face of the sanctifying knowledge of the incorporeal and unchangeable God. They understand temporal and transient things far more deeply, because they behold the original causes of all these in the Ideas of the Eternal Wisdom of God through which the world was made.[23]

These convictions of Augustine were of decisive importance throughout the Middle Ages. We shall see their influence in the work of later thinkers, and also the growth of a counter-conviction that the knowledge of Nature has its rightful place in human life, because Nature exists as a distinct object before us with claims on our natural understanding.

III.

What then is Augustine's test or standard of truth ? As Descartes did after him, he found it in our inner experience. In the experience of our own life and thought, we have an immediate certainty which no doubt can assail ; for who *doubts* thinks, exists, lives, and so far knows his own being. For Augustine, as for Descartes, this is a self-evident truth. It is in the accurate sense of the word an *intuition*, something that is seen.[24] Thus, *faith* is the seed of all science, out of which all knowledge grows. Without faith we cannot even assume the existence of the outer world. Strictly speaking, the impressions of our bodily senses are not themselves a source of knowledge at all. They are the *occasions* on which we recollect or are reminded of the ideas already infused into our minds by the Wisdom of God. We see truth by and in God's Light, who is the truth in Himself, the perfect light. He is the direct source of all natural, as of all supernatural, knowledge. Thus the distinction between reason and revelation, faith and knowledge, disappears. The Wisdom of God is, as it were, an active Power embracing within itself the Ideas which, themselves uncreated, are the original causes of all created things.

The soul of man is not a material thing, nor does it occupy space, though it can act with its entire nature at any point of space. In this way, it is present throughout the body but is separable from the body. Its fundamental activities are thought, understanding, and will ; of these, will is the essence of every process of mental life. Even truth implies the active search for it, the attentive effort to know. The soul is immortal, not merely because it is separable from the body, but because it is fitted by Nature to know eternal truths, and cannot be sundered from the Eternal Reason which is the Wisdom of God.

Mental life is therefore a continuous process of attention under the guidance of will, which is the central activity of the soul. Augustine is convinced of this from his own inner experience.

Then arises the momentous question, What can the will of man, thus given the central place in his soul's life, actually accomplish ? Augustine answers the question in the light of the Fall-doctrine which he derived from the Bible and from the early Fathers, and in the light of a vivid memory of his own passionate and tumultuous experiences in early life. He is convinced that fallen man can will nothing needful for his own salvation. In the ordinary affairs of life, human conduct is the necessary fruit of a good or a bad tree ; and for the needs of our eternal welfare, our nature is a bad tree. Only by the continual Grace of God can any human being so live that the will which is central in his own soul shall be wholly inspired and enlightened by the Divine Will, and this and nothing less than this is salvation. As an intellectual dogma, it is the doctrine of an entirely evil human world, a *massa perditionis*, part of which is rescued by God's arbitrary selection.

Augustine, as his writings show, had worked out the essentials of this doctrine by the year 400 ; and about this time there appeared in Rome a British monk, of Irish birth, named Pelagius. Pelagius, by temperament, experience, and conviction, was led to a view of our individual personal responsibility which is at the opposite extreme to that of Augustine. Every individual represents at his birth an entirely fresh start in the moral history of the race, and throughout the whole of his life retains absolute freewill, entirely undetermined by habit or character. So far as there is any transmission of moral evil from one generation to another, it is only through social heredity, bad examples, customs, laws, and the like. In Augustine's eyes this was an unchristian delusion ; unchristian, as destroying the need for a Redeemer, and a delusion, as affirming a kind of freedom which does not and cannot exist. Pelagianism was condemned in the East and in the West, and the writings of Pelagius were as far as possible suppressed. But the eastern Church never accepted any version of the Fall-doctrine akin to that of Augustine ; and even in the West, the history of the Fall-doctrine is the history of the gradual decline of the Augustinian view, until Luther and Calvin revived it. Pelagius had put into private circulation a collection of his own Notes on the Epistles of St Paul, whose authority appeared to be overwhelmingly on the side of Augustine ; and these Notes were circulated and copied for years after the official condemnations.[25] Later it became the ecclesiastical rule, *Augustinus eget Thoma interprete* : Augustine must be read in the light of the teaching of St Thomas.

The capture of Rome by Alaric in 410 profoundly moved the mind and imagination of the age ; and Augustine began his greatest work, " The City of God," which took him many years to complete. His purpose was to find an interpretation of history in which the fall of Rome might be explained. He believes that there are two kinds of men, two " great communities," the one ruled by self-will and self-love, the other by the love of God and man ; the one predestined to suffer eternal punishment with Satan and his angels, the other to reign eternally with God. How do these two " communities " reveal themselves in history ? If we were giving an exposition of Augustine's philosophy of history, his answer, or rather his varying answers, to this question would require detailed investigation. We find that the typical historic representatives of the " earthly city " are Babylon and Rome, while the " heavenly city " is represented by the Christian Church, or more strictly by its elect members. The need of this qualification points to one of the difficulties occurring in the interpretation of Augustine here. For our present purpose it is sufficient to point out that Augustine's successors in the Middle Ages failed to understand his doctrine of the two " cities." Its most distinctive individual features were not assimilated. Augustine's political thinking was influential only so far as he reproduced in his own way the views which the earlier Fathers had inherited from Seneca and other exponents of Roman Stoicism and had restated in their own way.

What were these views? We may call them "theoretical," or "ideal," or otherwise, as we please. As a matter of fact, it was assumed that there had really been a time when all men lived together in peace and harmony, in freedom and equality, having all things in common. Private property and slavery were unknown ; coercive government was not needed, for the advice and guidance of the wiser men was sufficient. This was the age of the pure and absolute "Law of Nature." Then followed long ages of degeneration. Not "each for all" but "each for himself" became the motto of life. The good things of the world were made into exclusive private possessions. The benevolent guidance of the wise gave place to the arbitrary rule and tyranny of kings and princes. Laws became necessary to control rulers and subjects alike. Political organisation, therefore, was made necessary by the actual evils of human nature. It represents a secondary or imperfect "Law of Nature." This theory—which has been of immense importance in the history of political thought—was adapted by the Fathers and wrought into their theological conception of human history. The State, or the organised political government, may be administered by unworthy or evil men ; but in itself, it is a Divine institution, rendered necessary by the imperfections of human nature. Cicero's emphatic declaration, that the State is founded upon Justice, became the first principle of mediæval political thinking. It meant that the State is essentially regulative ; its business is the impartial maintenance of order.[26]

Augustine died in August, 430. His city was in an evil plight. The Vandals, after making their way to the west and crossing the Rhine, had been driven by the western Goths into Spain, and a host of them had crossed over into the fertile province of northern Africa. They were at the gates of Hippo when Augustine died. He was spared the humiliation of seeing the city in the hands of the enemy.

IV.

Nearly a century later (525) under Theodoric the Great, Anicius Severus Boethius, a man of vast learning and lofty character, was put to death in prison at Pavia. He had served his royal master faithfully and well. Theodoric was the greatest of the rulers who arose among the eastern Goths, and had re-created in Italy something of the vanished Roman civilisation. But in his old age he had grown despondent and mistrustful; and his personal friend and ablest adviser fell an untimely victim to false charges and unworthy suspicions.

Boethius stands to the philosophy and science of the Middle Ages almost as Augustine stands to its religion and theology. He had conceived the magnificent ideal of transmitting to the world of western Christendom all the works of Plato and Aristotle, with Essays in discussion of their divergent opinions. This was more than one man could accomplish; but what he actually did accomplish was not unworthy of himself. He may be called the last of the ancient and the first of the mediæval philosophers. Through his work, western thought at this period assimilated

more of the actual doctrine of Aristotle himself than
had entered into the contemporary eastern thought.
His translations and commentaries, and his own
essays on leading topics of logical study, gave his
successors the essentials of Aristotelian Logic and some
of the main principles of Aristotle's general philosophy.[27] And by his method of exposition, through
systematic interpretation and systematic commentary,
he became the pioneer of the literary form which
became most distinctive and characteristic of mediæval thought—that of the explanatory and illustrative
commentary, which none the less left ample room for
independence of judgment and freedom of speculation
among writers who did not fear such things. Together with his logical studies must be named his
writings on arithmetic, geometry (based directly on
Euclid), and music. His purpose in these, in like
manner, is to transmit to his contemporaries and successors some of the work that had been done by
earlier thinkers. These also became highly valued
handbooks of instruction throughout the Middle
Ages.

His theological tracts, on the Trinity and the
Person of Christ, rest on a conviction which dominated mediæval thought in its great period (the
thirteenth century), although Boethius only hints at
it or mentions it incidentally. He accepts these
articles of faith in their orthodox form, and seeks to
show that they are reasonable. He takes as his motto
fidem si poteris rationemque conjungere, to reconcile
faith and reason, to provide by reasoning some support for a belief which stands of itself on the firmest
possible foundation of Faith.[28] And when stating his
intention to make this attempt, he refers significantly

to " the seeds sown in my mind by St Augustine's writings."

All these writings are more or less impersonal. Far otherwise is it with his last book, " The Consolation of Philosophy," written in prison when he was awaiting sentence of death. In this book the prisoner holds a conversation with Philosophy, who shows him the utter insecurity of fortune and of all earthly things save goodness only. The pathos and peril of the author's position, and the power of thought and feeling which inspires all that he writes, have made this book one of the great books of history. It sets forth a complete outlook on life, springing from a pure monotheism more akin in spirit to a platonised Stoicism than to the Theism of the New Testament. As a matter of fact, there is nothing distinctive of Christian doctrine in the book, and the name of Christ is not mentioned. On the other hand, there is nothing in it hostile to Christian Theism.

In the concluding chapters the meaning of Eternity is set forth in words at once profound and simple, in a doctrine which permeated the higher thought of the succeeding centuries. " Eternity is the complete and perfect possession of unlimited life all at once. This becomes clearer by comparison with the things of time. For whatever lives in time proceeds from past to future ; and there is nothing which is established in time, which can embrace the whole space of its life at once : what pertains to to-morrow, it has not yet laid hold of, and what pertains to yesterday, it has already lost. And even in the life of to-day, we live only in the fluctuating and transitory moment. Whatever, therefore, is subject to the conditions of time, although . . . it should never have begun and should never cease to be, and its life should be stretched out into an infinity of time, would not yet deserve for that reason to be called eternal : for it would not comprehend and embrace the whole endless space of its life all at once ; the future it would not yet have, the past it would have no longer. Only that which embraces and possesses the whole fullness of un-limited life at once, from which nothing of the future is absent, from which nothing of the past has flowed away, that alone is rightly deemed eternal ; and of necessity, in possession of itself, . . . it must grasp the infinity of moving time as present." [29]

St Thomas Aquinas suggested a spatial image illustrating this presence to the Eternal of the whole temporal order ; the unmoved Centre of an ever-moving sphere, turning in all directions round that Centre. The time-relationship of the finite to the infinite is constantly changing, not through any essential change in God, but through the constant changing of the finite beings in themselves.

V.

When we move on to the period immediately follow-ing Augustine and Boethius, and take a clear un-clouded view of this " earlier Middle Age," in order to see not what it failed to do but what it actually did during the long drawn out death-agony of Imperial Rome, we can trace the working of a strenuous en-deavour never dying out, working as it were now here, now there—an endeavour to collect and save all that could be found of ancient literature, sacred and secular, amid the ruins of the civilisation in which it had been produced. The mind of the age is represented by those Christian scholars who set themselves to compile out of all the sources that they could reach, encyclopædias of the real or supposed knowledge which had drifted down in literary form. What they reproduced was simple, elementary, and sometimes confused or erroneous ; but they did what they could to meet the needs of the barbarians who were now settling among the political ruins of the Empire.

Two of the ablest and most learned of these " encyclopædists " were Cassiodorus Senator, who died about 570, and Isidore of Seville, who died in 636.

Cassiodorus, a younger contemporary of Boethius, rose to the highest political offices under Theodoric, and notwithstanding the intrigues which surrounded the throne, his abilities enabled him largely to regulate the public affairs of the Ostro-Gothic dominions in Italy. His historical writings and his letters are very valuable authorities for this part of mediæval history, but they do not require special mention here. Shortly before the Ostro-Gothic rule in Italy collapsed in 540, Cassiodorus retired to Scyllacium (Squillace), his native place, in order to give effect as far as possible to the educational plans and ideals which he had cherished for many years ; and he remained there until his death at the advanced age of over ninety. The years which he spent there were of far more importance to the world than the years in which he had held high political authority. He was one of the first and most influential of those who set the monks to literary work—the collection, care, and copying of manuscripts—and thus he did much to preserve the continuity of ancient and mediæval learning. He was the first man in the West to realise the possibilities of the monastery as a centre of liberal culture ; and his ideal was to rouse the clergy from their ignorance and enable them to educate the people.

The scope of his educational programme is set forth in what for our present purpose must be regarded as his two most important works : *Institutiones divinarum litterarum* and *Institutiones secularium litterarum*. The first of these, which appears to have been strangely neglected by his successors, sets forth a scheme of theological training based on a thorough study of the Bible. He gives a careful explanation of the problems which arise out of biblical study, including " textual criticism " (the authority and emendation of manuscripts) and the use of the ancient versions, and he describes shortly the most important commentaries written by the Latin Fathers. The study of Church history is warmly commended, and the best ancient authorities on this subject are named. In the book on secular learning, Cassiodorus advocates the study of the " liberal arts," but not for their own sake alone. They were to be studied for the better understanding of the Bible and the doctrines of the Church. What were these liberal arts ? Cassiodorus gives an account of them in the form of a compilation of extracts from earlier writers. The liberal arts are seven in number : Grammar, Dialectic (Logic), Rhetoric, Arithmetic, Geometry, Music, and Astronomy. These were the studies afterwards divided into the " Trivium," consisting of the first three named above (so called because they were regarded as comparatively ordinary or commonplace), and the " Quadrivium," consisting of the other four. Cassiodorus devotes most of his attention, in this book, to the first three, which he expounds as dealing

mainly with language. His treatment shows little
originality, but it was destined to become one of the
most popular text-books. Many of the Roman schools
in Italy, and some in Gaul, Spain, and south Germany,
had survived; and the text-books of Cassiodorus
came into use especially in the Italian schools. What
seems to us an exaggerated and excessive attention
to language and the *minutiae* of grammar and rhetoric,
was a natural result of the conditions of the time.
The popular vernacular languages, which were already
developing on their own lines, were not yet capable
of use for such purposes as Cassiodorus had in view
when he wrote his two books of *Institutiones* ; and
the educated men of that time felt that it was impossible to take too much care over study of the structure
and laws of the Latin language, and the methods of
using it for systematic exposition and argument. The
Aristotelian Logic, so far as they learnt it from
Boethius, made them eager to carry out this kind of
study, and showed them ways in which to do it.

Half a century after the death of Cassiodorus a
new series of books, presenting in encyclopædic form
the knowledge of the past, was compiled by Isidore
of Seville. Of this city Isidore was Bishop, in succession to his brother, for the last thirty-six years of
his life. Remarkable for genius, learning, and ecclesiastical zeal, by his untiring industry he made himself
master of all the knowledge then accessible to the
Latin-speaking world ; and he acquired an authority
so high that later Popes could think of ranking him
as a fifth Doctor of the Church, with Jerome, Ambrose, Augustine, and Gregory. In a time of dis-
integration and change, when Spain had been for two
centuries under the dominion of the western Goths,

all that he could recover of the learning of classical times was to be condensed and adapted to a lower level of thought. His *Etymologiae*, or *Origines* (to quote its more fitting title), is a monumental achievement in realisation of this purpose. It is a complete encyclopædia, which for centuries remained the most important source from which general information was drawn. Among the subjects treated are the seven " liberal arts " ; medicine ; law ; God and the angels ; the Church and its authority ; anthropology (peoples and languages) ; the animal world and its divisions ; the earth and its parts ; architecture ; agriculture ; navigation. For these and the other subjects treated, he draws on a vast range of classical and ecclesiastical writers.[30]

On another side of his work Isidore set the example of a type of literature which was destined to play a great part in the later history of mediæval thought : the books of " Sentences "—to quote the awkward English rendering usually given for the mediæval Latin *Sententiae*, deliberate or reasoned judgments. Isidore did this in his *Libri tres Sententiarum*, a collection of the opinions of earlier Fathers, chiefly Augustine and Gregory, forming a compendium of doctrinal theology.

Isidore and Cassiodorus are two outstanding figures among the encyclopædists ; and the surviving literature of the time proves that even in this age of turmoil and distress, learning never died out. It might languish at some places and times, but it was never extinguished.[31]

It is easy to ridicule the work of the encyclopædists, and to point to the puerilities which they conscientiously put on record, and their entirely uncritical use of their literary sources. Such a judgment is merely unhistorical. " It was assuredly no small achievement," says a modern student of the subject, " to put together a compendious encyclopædia of the arts and sciences from many sources, at a time when the larger works of earlier authors on different branches of human knowledge were accessible in few places, and when few men, in any case, would have been capable of studying them." This verdict is a just one ; but we must emphasise a strange mental bias common to all these writers. Take the case of Isidore. He gains all his information from old books ; but he makes no attempt to extend or expand it in the light of contemporary experience. He must have seen that much of what he recorded had been based on observation and experience, as well as " hearsay " and tradition ; but for him, the tradition is enough.

VI.

When we speak, as historians usually do, of the "renaissance" under Charlemagne, we must understand that " renaissance " means "culmination." The encyclopædists prepared the way for it ; and so did the Benedictine monks.

Here a backward look is needed. Benedict of Nursia had founded his monastery on Monte Cassino, in Campania, in 529, and his famous Rule became the standard of western monasticism. The Benedictine Rule was a monument of wisdom. Definite and vigorous in the assertion of fundamental principles, and elastic in details, it amply fulfilled its creator's ideal. The mother of the virtues, it declares, is

E

discretio—the wise moderation which is the spirit of the Rule itself. The ideal is to found a *dominici schola servitii*, a training in Divine service, where the monks are not to strive after an absolute perfection, but to train themselves in the way of a purer and more self-controlled life than was possible in the world. The two main principles of the Rule were labour (*otiositas inimica animae*) and obedience. It was the distinction of Benedict that he not only organised the monks into communities, but based their community-life largely on manual labour, in contrast to the merely meditative seclusion which had hitherto prevailed. Probably not even the founder himself foresaw all the advantages of his Rule, which was destined not only to make many a wilderness and solitary place rejoice with fertility, but to expand into a noble intellectual fruitfulness which was the glory of the Benedictine order in its great days. The law of obedience was absolute, but was tempered by the necessity on the part of the Superior of consulting all the monks assembled in council or chapter upon all important business. Food and clothing were of the simplest kind, and all duly regulated ; and the intervals of labour were relieved by a continually recurring round of religious services. The Benedictine Rule spread almost universally in the West—not in rivalry of any other rule, but as the more complete development of the monastic system. The Benedictine monks were able to do a work in northern Europe which the Irish missionaries, with all their contagious enthusiasm and austere Celtic piety, had been unable to accomplish.

They were followed by Anglo-Saxon missionaries, from the middle of the seventh century. Of these the most famous and powerful was Wynfrith of Crediton, "Saint Boniface," who in 719 was authorised by the then reigning Pope to undertake a mission in Germany, for the conversion of the tribes as yet un-Christianised, and for the reform of Church discipline and the correction of irregularities and heathen survivals in worship. For nearly forty years he laboured in the lands east of the Rhine, organising Germanic Christianity and bringing it into closer touch with Rome. The most famous of the monasteries founded by him or his disciples was at Fulda, where the Benedictine Abbey, afterwards a great centre of literature and learning, held the place in the ecclesiastical history of central Germany which Monte Cassino held in Italy, St Gall in southern Germany, Corbie in Saxony, Tours in France, and Iona in Scotland.

All this work not only prepared the way for the revival of literature and learning, but under the commanding influence of the Emperor himself became an efficient cause of it. The story of the great revival carried through by Charlemagne is told in the general histories of the Middle Ages.[32] His own intellectual accomplishments were remarkable for the time. He conversed in Latin, understood Greek, and in the circle of his learned friends laid aside his crown ; but his hand was unaccustomed to the pen, and he began to form written characters late in life, and with great difficulty. He knew how to gather round him scholars and poets from many lands. His " capitularies " or documents of advice and instruction, on matters of educational reform and the reorganisation of monastic and cathedral schools, left a deep and lasting impression on the civilisation of the West. The following is a typical statement, from a capitulary addressed

to the Abbot of Fulda shortly before 800 A.D.,
which appears to have been used as an encyclical
letter : " Since in recent years there have been often
sent to us from divers monasteries letters, . . . we
have observed in very many of these writings just and
good sentiments set forth in uncouth language. For
that which pious devotion faithfully dictated inwardly,
the untutored tongue could not express outwardly
without faultiness, owing to neglect of learning.
Whence we began to fear that as skill in writing was
less, wisdom to understand the Sacred Scriptures
might be far less than ought rightly to be the case.
And we all know that though verbal errors are dangerous, errors in interpretation are far more dangerous.
Wherefore we exhort you not only not to neglect the
study of letters, but with the most humble God-
approved earnestness to be eager in learning, so that
you may prevail more easily and rightly in penetrating the mysteries of sacred literature. For inas-
much as in the sacred pages are found embedded
phrases, figures, tropes, and other like forms of speech,
no one can doubt that any man in reading them
understands the more readily what he reads in a
spiritual sense, the more fully he has been instructed
in the discipline of literature. Let such men be chosen
for this task as have willingness, ability to learn,
and the desire to teach others. . . . We desire to make
you, as is fitting for soldiers of the Church, inwardly
devout and learned, chaste in living a good life,
scholars in speaking well ; so that . . . whoever shall
seek you out to see you, even as his eyes may be edified
by what he sees, so his ears may be instructed by your
wisdom, which he will discern in your reading and
singing." [33]

The school of the Palace at Aachen (Aix la Chapelle) was to be a model for the whole Empire. The man to whom Charles entrusted the greatest responsibility, and who was well fitted to undertake it, was Alcuin of York. The fame of the school and library of York had spread far on to the Continent.[34] In early manhood Alcuin became head of the school and afterwards of the library. He was not a great thinker ; but he was a great book-lover, a great educator, and a great organiser. He had the mind of the encyclopædist, like Cassiodorus and Isidore, but his text-books show the mind of the educator as well. They were written for systematic instruction. He did his utmost also to promote the study of Augustine, and the encyclopædists, and the great grammarians of the Latin language. After fourteen years of strenuous labour Alcuin decided to return to his native land ; but Charles prevailed upon him to accept the abbacy of Tours, where he died in 804 in his seventieth year.

Although this cultural reform was not a natural growth of the popular life, and although it was a culture concerned only with literature of the past, yet even the anarchy of the following century did not destroy its results. It prepared the way for the greater and more enduring " renaissance " of the eleventh and twelfth centuries. The writers whose work is on record show that Christian thought was moving. The work of the encyclopædists was carried on in the same spirit, dominated by the same outlook on the past, and with even greater energy and resolution. The work of Rhabanus Maurus is an important illustration of what we have just said. Rhabanus taught at Tours and afterwards at Fulda, and died in 847 as Archbishop of Maine. He devoted all his energies to raising the standard of education in Germany. His writings reproduce material gathered from Augustine, Gregory, Bede, and Isidore ; and, for better or worse, he handed on volumes of extracts from the Fathers illustrating the allegorical interpretation of Scripture. None the less he deliberately and emphatically proclaimed the value of pagan philosophy—and above all the philosophy of Plato —in whatever sources it could be studied.

We find, again, that the theological and philosophical problems suggested by the traditional dogmas of the Church are beginning to receive special attention. Thus, Paschasius Radbertus, who died as Abbot of Corbie about 860, believing that religion must contain *mysterium* as well as *scientia*, and that these two cannot be identified, published in 831 what was the first formal exposition and defence of the strict doctrine of transubstantiation—that the substance of the bread and wine in the Eucharist becomes converted into the substance of the body and blood of Christ, the same body in which he lived, suffered, died, and rose again. This stupendous miracle takes place under the outwardly visible form (*sub figura*) of bread and wine. There is nothing contrary to Nature in this ; because the essence of Nature consists in entire obedience to the Divine Will (*ut a quo est, semper ejus obtemperet jussis*).

This absolute and uncompromising supernaturalism was contested by Ratramnus, a monk of the same abbey. While fully acknowledging a real supernatural effect in the Eucharist, he endeavoured to rationalise the doctrine as far as possible. The body and blood of Christ are present *in mysterio ;* that is to say, the Scriptural expressions are figurative and are to be

spiritually understood. The elements after conse-
cration produce an effect on the souls of believers
which they cannot produce by their natural qualities,
but this effect presupposes spiritual susceptibility
on the part of the recipients ; and, when the believer
has attained " to the vision of Christ," he will no longer
need such external means of perceiving what the
Divine Love has achieved for him. Here we see the
emergence of the two opposing tendencies which were
destined to play a great part in moulding the form of
future conflicts : on the one hand, that some at least
of the dogmas of the Church are objects of pure Faith
and, in the eyes of Reason, must remain mysteries ; and,
on the other hand, that the content of all dogmas can
and ought to be rationalised and shown to be reasonable.

Ratramnus was a theologian of remarkable capacity,
considering the age in which he lived. This is illustrated in his defence of the doctrine of predestination
in its most extreme form. The repulsive character of
the doctrine need not interfere with our recognition
of the independence and boldness which he showed in
working it out as he did. He maintained that the good
and the evil alike are created and predestined by the
Almighty to their inevitable end. This doctrine was
made a subject of passionate propaganda by his
disciple, the ill-fated monk Gottschalk. It evidently
involved a total denial of human freedom. Hincmar,
the powerful Archbishop, attacked it bitterly on this
side, and at length was moved to urge John the Scot
(John Eriugena, " Erin-born "), already known as a
layman who was winning fame as a teacher, to write
a refutation of it. Here we see the Church employing
the resources of human reason to counteract un-
authorised doctrines.

It is no part of our present purpose to enter into any
discussion of the recorded details in the life of this
extraordinary man. He was born, probably in Ireland,
in the early years of the ninth century. He seems to
have been educated in the best schools of Ireland ;
and his reputation spread so far that Charles (called
" the Bald ") summoned him to the royal school
(*schola palatina*) in Paris. This was about 845. The
reputation of this school or college appears to have
increased greatly under Eriugena's leadership, and
the philosopher himself was treated with the greatest
familiarity and indulgence by the king. A sidelight
on the position which he held at the French court
appears in the story that one day, when he was
seated at table with the king, the latter asked, " *Quid
distat inter sottum et Scottum ?* " and John replied,
" *Mensa tantum.*"

His earliest surviving work was the treatise *De
divina praedestinatione*, of which we have already made
mention. Part of John's purpose was to prove that
Augustine and the other authorities to whom Gottschalk appealed did not support his extreme conclusions. So far, contemporary orthodoxy could have
been satisfied. But he went far beyond an appeal to
the Fathers, and amazed the theologians of his day
by basing his " refutation " on a religious philosophy
which was evidently very different from the historic
meaning of ecclesiastical doctrine. The religious
philosophy in question was that of Neoplatonism,
which John learned in the first instance from an anony-
mous writer who, under the name of " Dionysius the
Areopagite " (Acts xvii. 34), had issued at some period
in the fifth century a short series of works based on
the teaching of Proclus. The writer expounds, with

conviction, the main principles of Neoplatonism, and makes a strenuous attempt to combine them with Christian conceptions. Maximus, called "the Confessor," who died in 662—the last original thinker of the Greek Church—had written a commentary on "Dionysius," and preached the same doctrines with more of churchly fervour. When John published his own excessively literal Latin version of "Dionysius," he added a translation of parts of the work of Maximus, with which he was acquainted. Owing to these labours, "Dionysius" became an object of study and commentary by some of the leading thinkers of the Middle Ages.

In order to find a place for the Trinity and other cardinal doctrines of orthodox Christianity, "Dionysius" insists on the distinction between "negative theology" and "positive theology." He is faithful to the Neoplatonist doctrine of the "supra-rational." The Source of all Being is beyond all predicates imaginable or conceivable by our minds, save that of absolute unity—"the One." This is the "negative theology" which ascends from the creature to the Creator by dropping one after another every definite predicate, because these predicates are derived from our experience and imply the limitations of that experience. None the less, from that Supreme Being proceed in succession the lower orders of existence, by a process which "Dionysius" calls "creation." The "positive theology," on the other hand, admits a symbolic or figurative knowledge of God, and a gradual approximation to his image ; and here the Christian doctrines are given a place, by a free re-statement of their meaning. He believes that both the negative and the positive methods are valid, and that they do

not conflict when each is given its proper place ; but
he could not really reconcile them, any more than
Plotinus and Proclus had been able to reconcile the
" downward " and the " upward " ways.

Eriugena has no thought or feeling of hostility to
the dogmas of the Church. His purpose was to lay a
philosophical foundation for theology. He started his
work against Gottschalk with the bold affirmation
that *true philosophy* and *true religion* are one and the
same. Now this statement is repeated, almost in the
same words, by many of the later mediæval writers ;
but its significance depends on which of the two terms
is regarded as fundamental or primary. By " true
religion " Eriugena did not mean *mere* " authority " ;
but true religion, as an organised force in the world,
involves " authority " ; and to him, reason is primary,
and authority is secondary or derived : *auctoritas
siquidem ex vera ratione processit, ratio vero nequaquam
ex auctoritate : omnis enim auctoritas, quae vera
ratione non approbatur, infirma videtur esse ; vera
autem ratio, quum virtutibus suis rata atque immutabilis
munitur, nullius auctoritatis adstipulatione roborari
indiget.* He does not start with theology as the completed body of truth, requiring only elucidation and
interpretation ; his fundamental thought is that of
the universe, the Whole, the unity which works
itself out into the system of the world. Man and all
that concerns man are parts of this system, and are to
be explained by reference to it ; and the whole of
revealed religion is one factor in this process. Reason
in its own strength and with its own instruments
evolves a system which coincides, according to Eriugena, with the teaching of Scripture. For him, therefore, the speculative reason is the supreme arbiter ;

and in accordance with its results the utterances of Scripture and of the Church have not infrequently to be subjected to an allegorical or mystical interpretation.

Eriugena's great work is entitled *De Divisione Naturae*. His system is based on the idea of the absolute *immanence* of God; but the Divine is exclusively real, and the world of experience in space and time is but a " theophany," a manifestation or *appearance* of God. By *natura* he means, as we have said, the universe or Whole. It embraces four modes of being : (1) that which creates and is not created— God as the Source of all Being; (2) that which is created and which creates—the world of " ideas " or ideal rational principles, active in and from God, after which finite things are fashioned; (3) that which is created and does not create—the world of finite things in space and time; (4) that which neither is created nor creates—God as the goal, end, and aim of all being. The whole realm of created being has no independent reality; it exists, but it exists in God. Creation and revelation are one. The four stages form a process from God to God, which through our finiteness we experience as in time.

Like " Dionysius," Eriugena combines a negative and a positive theology. Real being—in other words, absolute perfection—belongs to God alone; all else has only partial or imperfect being. No predicate applicable to finite being is applicable to God; he is above and beyond all qualities that we experience in finite being. On the other hand, the whole realm of created being is in its measure a " theophany," whereby we may attain to a symbolic knowledge of God, perceiving His being through the being of created things, His wisdom through their order and harmony, His life through their activity and movement. This is the basis for an interpretation of the doctrine of the Trinity : God in His essential being is Father ; God as Wisdom realised in the created world is Son ; God as universal life and activity is Spirit.

The logical structure into which these principles are wrought is that of a vast hierarchy of forms or types of existence, from the natural objects of sense to the absolute being of God. This graded scale of beings, in which each lower form proceeds from the forms above it, is completely parallel to the graded scale of logical conceptions in their successive orders of generality ; and by a " graded scale of logical conceptions " we mean what is illustrated, for example, in the systems of the sciences of classification, as Botany and Zoology, as we know them to-day. If we conceive such a systematic classification extended over the whole universe, we have conceived the outline of Eriugena's main idea. He says, therefore, that the method of knowledge which divides *genera* into *species*, and resolves *species* into *genera*, is no fiction of the human mind, but is founded in the nature of things by the Author of every true method and every true order.

From the ethical point of view, this is equivalent to a hierarchy of degrees of value or perfection ; and increase in perfection means increase in being. Evil, as such, has no real being at all ; it is mere appearance. Nevertheless, Eriugena cannot interpret the doctrine of sin without admitting its reality. The will of the individual imagines to itself something to be good and real when it is neither. This is sin ; but if the imagination is false, the will that imagines is real. Deliverance from sin is the discovery made by the sinner of the illusoriness of what he aims at. To become one with God by becoming like Him is the chief end of man, which humanity as a whole can attain through purification, enlightenment, and completion, with the help of the Wisdom of God, the Word manifest in all things, most of all in the human soul, and most transcendently in Jesus Christ.

The speculative genius and intellectual originality shown in this great work are so impressive that some writers have exaggerated its *historic* importance. John the Scot had a deep and far-reaching influence on mediæval thought ; but it was not through his *De Divisione Naturae*, which was not, and perhaps could not be, understood by the theologians of his time. Three hundred and fifty years later, his authority was invoked in support of a movement of pantheistic teaching which the authorities in Rome believed to be so dangerous that extreme measures were taken to suppress it. The study of John's chief work was forbidden by a Provincial Synod at Paris in 1210 ; and in 1225 a papal Bull was issued ordering all copies of it to be burned, but there is no evidence that the condemnation was based on any real knowledge of the work. To ascribe " pantheism " to John himself is to empty the word of all definite meaning ; as well might " pantheism " be ascribed to Augustine.

It has been said that John the philosopher is like a solitary mountain rising above an undulating plain ; and the result has been that little justice has been done to John the teacher and John the commentator ; but it was as teacher and commentator that his largest influence was felt. Only in recent years has this been realised.[35] If we try to put the result of his work in

one brief statement, it would be this : he taught
Christian thinkers what Neoplatonism can and cannot do for Christianity. The results of the lesson were
to be of the first importance. Aristotelianism was
already approaching, on the way to lend ballast to
mediæval Platonism or to correct it, but never to
destroy all the effects of it.

The remaining years of the ninth century—after
John the Scot disappears from history—show little
that reveals the ways in which Christian thought was
moving. We find many small beginnings of the famous controversy about " universals "—made much
too famous by many historians—of which we shall
speak in the sequel ; and, amid the increasing anarchy
of the time, there is a resolute determination to save
whatever could be saved of the inheritance of Charlemagne. Yet, as the years of the tenth century roll
on, all the effort appears to be in vain. Germany and
France are ravaged by wars. The Northmen—not
yet the " Normans " of history—are invading France
by ascending the rivers and devastating everything
within their reach. Hungarians and Saracens are
attacking eastern Europe. The activity of the
schools seems to be at an end, and Christian thought
to be at best in a condition of suspended life. But the
monks of the reformed Benedictine order of Cluny
are at work, and through them the traditions of the
preceding century are kept alive.

The one outstanding figure of this greatly troubled
time is that of Gerbert of Aurillac, who died in 1003
as Pope Sylvester II. He was a man who could have
held up before the age the mirror of self-knowledge,
if the age had a mind capable of perceiving it. He
was borne along by the stream of the struggle to

restore civil and intellectual and ecclesiastical life ; and he did more than anyone else to advance them. Educated at first under the severe rule of the Cluniac order at Aurillac, he proceeded to Spain, and during three years of study there became acquainted with the science and philosophy of the Arabs. On his return he became famous as ecclesiastical statesman and as teacher. He was a friend of the Ottos in Germany and the Capets in France, and any school which came under his influence became a standard institution. Where he took part in Church Government—as Abbot of Bobbio, as Archbishop first of Rheims and then of Ravenna, and finally as Pope in Rome—he attacked abuses with energy and success. Only his inexhaustible energies explain how he could find time for study. As student and teacher he devoted himself to all the seven " liberal arts," but especially to those of the *quadrivium*—arithmetic, geometry, music, and astronomy. In logic he based his instruction on Aristotle, as in the translations and commentaries of Boethius. He was not a great thinker, but a great personality and a great teacher, whose influence spread far and wide through his disciples. His work stands out as an unconscious prophecy of what was to come.

CHAPTER III.

THE REVIVAL.

WE are now approaching the period when the constructive work of mediæval Christian thought reached its highest level in the West. The twelfth century saw a genuine " renaissance " of thought and learning, partly owing to the contacts set up by the Crusades, and partly to the natural increase of mental activity in a richer and safer Europe. " The zeal for learning," says Trevelyan, " like the contemporary zeal for the Crusades, was compounded of many diverse elements —pure fire of the spirit, professional ambition, greed for benefices, curiosity high and low, love of adventure and of travel. Like the Crusades, the impulse was international, leading men to desert their own country and wander over mountains and seas. Out of this intellectual ferment over the face of Europe, the Universities arose, first in Italy and then in almost all the lands of Christendom. Such was the genius of the Middle Ages for giving corporate life to an idea. Even when each land had set up its own Universities, the more famous seats of learning had ' nations ' of foreign students in their midst, for so long as all educated persons thought and wrote in Latin, learning remained cosmopolitan in spirit. . . .

The mediæval as distinct from the modern University was 'built' of men alone, not of stone and mortar, of colleges, libraries, and laboratories, of endowments from capitalists and from the State. . . . It would have been the freest of all human institutions had it not been for the control of the Church over 'heresy.' . . . And just because the original Universities were not dependent on endowments or buildings, they were able to propagate their species with amazing rapidity, without waiting for the patronage of wealth." [36] Travelling was difficult and often dangerous, but there were no national barriers in the way. The forces which created the "sovereign States" of later ages, and the international anarchy of modern Europe, were only in their faint beginnings. The name by which Europe then knew itself was "Christendom," and its capital was Papal Rome. The same social, religious, and cultural institutions prevailed everywhere in the West. Hence it has been said that the English knight, speaking French, and the English churchman, speaking Latin, could travel through Europe from castle to castle and from abbey to abbey, and find less that was strange to them than Englishmen touring in the same parts in Stuart or Hanoverian times.

England, in all except national feeling and political development, shared actively in the characteristic life of this mediæval Europe. The Norman conquest ensured that it should be so ; but the way had long been prepared. Four centuries before William of Normandy landed at Pevensey, the rivalry between the Celtic and Roman Churches came to a head. In outer appearance the subjects of dispute were technicalities like the date of Easter, and trivialities like

F

the shape of the "tonsure"; but behind these things lay far more important differences of spirit and organisation. King Oswy of Northumbria used his utmost influence in favour of claims of Rome on the religious allegiance of the people of England; and the Synod of Whitby, summoned by his authority in 664, decided accordingly. This decision was of momentous consequence for the history of England down the ages.

On the Continent of Europe political events were moving along the lines which we have described. The struggle between the Empire and the Papacy determined the course of European history during the eleventh and twelfth centuries. In the twelfth century it was chiefly between the great Emperor Frederic I., called by the Italians "Barbarossa" (the Red-beard), and the Popes Hadrian IV. and Alexander III. For seventy-five years the royal power in Germany had been defending itself desperately in the conflict over investiture against the attacks of the Church, seeing at the same time the power of the feudal nobles overshadow its own; and then, in the following twenty-five years, it had fallen into weary resignation. And now (1152) there came to the throne a man who knew how to restore the power and prestige of the Empire. Under Barbarossa, peace at home and prestige abroad were once more enjoyed by Germany. But before all this had been accomplished his adventurous and imaginative mind turned to Italy. He dreamed of that *Imperium Romanum* whose departed splendour fascinated the Middle Ages. Five times he made military expeditions into Italy, until, after thirty years of strife and confusion, the rights of the cities were acknowledged by the Peace of Constance (1183).

One of the most attractive figures among the greater churchmen of this time is that of Otto, Bishop of Freising in Bavaria. Related to the most powerful families in Germany, in touch with the movements of philosophical thought in France and Italy, a keen and impartial observer of contemporary events, absolutely convinced of the uniquely divine authority of the historic Christian Church, inspired by the ideals of Cistercian asceticism, he stands revealed in his surviving writings, a figure as significant as it is attractive. Two works of his have survived. His *Chronicon* or *De duabus Civitatibus* is in part a history of contemporary events as far as 1146, but it is much more than a mere chronicle. It is a " philosophy of history," inspired by Augustine, and vividly reflecting the writer's outlook on life and his intellectual and religious experience. It was written during the time when much of Germany, and all of his own Bavaria, was practically in a condition of civil war. He is convinced that, as it were in the nature of things, the Good form one " city," the Evil another, and that the Church comprises both; but he is not convinced that the forces of secular authority are in themselves evil. Again, he is convinced that the earthly order and disorder in which men were living must be transformed into, or rather replaced by, the divine order of the Heavenly City, but he is not convinced that the nature of that City and the manner of its coming can be understood by a literal interpretation of the biblical writings which, in figure and allegory, appear to describe it. In his eyes " this present world " is transient, and doomed, perhaps very soon, to pass away. Expressed in the jargon of our present historical theology, his outlook is essentially "apocalyptic" or "eschatological"; but in Otto's writings we find strong feeling and equally strong common-sense combining in the treatment of a theme which is usually supposed to be congenial only to unbalanced minds. He is not absorbed in any mere vision of the Heavenly City. He lived long enough to see Barbarossa bringing unity and order to Germany. His hopes for the actual world revived; and in his *Gesta Frederici Imperatoris*, after sketching the history of Germany from the quarrel between Pope Gregory VII. and the Emperor Henry IV., he describes in detail the events of the first five years of Barbarossa's reign. Nevertheless he believes, and feels he must believe, that the preparation for the Heavenly City is seen in the divine power as revealed in the history of the Church; and he finds the strongest and most definite revelation of Good in two great "signs of the times": in the Crusades, and in the life of the new Monastic Orders. In this view of the Crusades he was moved by the passion which prompted them rather than by his experience of the results. He saw the impetuous enthusiasm and fiery eloquence with which Bernard of Clairvaux carried his mission through Northern France and the Rhine country, to arouse Western Europe to another Crusade. In the disastrous expedition which followed, Otto himself took part. The band which he led was almost destroyed, and he returned to Bavaria when the remains of the German armies, disappointed and embittered, sailed for home. We must bear in mind that such convictions as those of Otto of Freising were a vital part of the religious thought of the twelfth century.[37]

I.

We are now approaching the age of what is called "Scholasticism." If the use of this word were abandoned, it would be an advantage to the intelligent study of the subject; but the word is so frequently and variously employed that some discussion of it is necessary. We find the word in use, with no very definite meaning, in later Roman antiquity; but in the Middle Ages it came into use when the teachers of the "seven Liberal Arts," and of systematic theology, in the schools of the Carolingian period, were called *doctores scholastici*. Nevertheless, to characterise the whole of mediæval philosophy and theology by the employment of the word "Scholasticism" is worse than useless. "Scholasticism" stands for different things in the eleventh, in the twelfth, in the thirteenth, in the fourteenth century; it stands for different things in the work of Peter Abailard, of Bonaventura, of Roger Bacon, Thomas Aquinas, Siger of Brabant, William of Ockham—to mention only these; and to cover these centuries of vigorous and many-sided thinking under a single short formula, is simply to empty the formula of any definite meaning.[38]

What we see, in theology and philosophy alike, is that the energies of thinkers are absorbed in dealing with the increasing inheritance of material from the past. They are not occupied with the exploration of new fields of knowledge, in regions hitherto unknown —not with discovery as we understand it to-day. The aggregate of what is coming down to them from other times is at once the object of their criticism and analysis and the foundation on which they build.

The multitudinous character of the mass of material is plainly to be seen in the work of the " encyclopædists," and it increased as time went on. Their greatest endeavour was to make out of it some kind of ordered system ; and this demanded distinction, definition, classification, deduction ; in a word, the methods of deductive Logic seemed to offer a key to unlock all the doors to the treasuries of knowledge. " Deductive Logic " is, of course, the Logic of deductive reasoning. What is " deductive reasoning " ? All reasoning consists in putting together given facts or statements, which when combined yield a conclusion which is new in the sense that it is not inferrable from any of the particulars taken separately. Now it is evident that the combination of facts or statements cannot be made at random, as marbles might be drawn from a bag. We need a guiding thread ; and the distinctive characteristic of deductive reasoning is, that *we start with the guiding thread in our hands*. The " guiding thread " usually takes the form of various " premisses " or propositions whose truth is taken for granted on some kind of authority—whether the authority be that of our natural Reason, or of some other kind. Deductive Logic came into the hands of mediæval thinkers in the form given to it by Aristotle, who laid the foundation of it as a scientific study.

The conditions which we have described produced a common outlook on certain fundamental questions, and a community of method in their investigation and discussion ; and this common outlook and method gained distinctness and thoroughness as time went on. The most important characteristic of the whole period arises out of the relation between theology and philosophy. Philosophy began to be recognised as a separate study with methods and principles of its own. At that time, when men's understanding of Nature was so limited, " philosophy " embraced all the knowledge which the unaided reason of man could acquire of its own operations (in the laws of Logic) and of the natural and spiritual worlds. " Theology " meant the systematic doctrinal statement of the contents of the miraculously revealed Christian religion—the whole system of faith and worship embodied in the Catholic Church. And the questions before the minds of Christian thinkers during these centuries were these : How much of the doctrinal content of the traditional faith can be proved by the unaided Reason of man—even apart from Revelation ? How much of it, while not subject to proof by human Reason, can be explained and interpreted by Reason ? How much of it is altogether beyond the power of Reason to interpret or to explain ? And what fields of knowledge may be studied altogether apart from Revelation ?

The assumption of a definite Revelation is, of course, wholly foreign to ancient philosophy ; none the less, another important common characteristic of mediæval thought is seen in the vitality of its dependence upon ancient philosophy, and especially upon the system of Aristotle. By the end of the twelfth century the contents of all the principal writings of " The Philosopher " were known. They were interpreted in the light of Christian religious ideas and of ideas springing from the ever-active though half-unconscious influence of Platonism ; but the effect of Aristotelianism was to produce a large system of philosophical terms and conceptions which came into general use.

Perhaps the most distinctive feature of Christian

thought at this time was the method of exposition, which came to be applied more and more comprehensively and thoroughly in investigation and in teaching or instruction. It was a method which originated in the discussions of the classroom, and under the influence of the Aristotelian deductive Logic was elaborated in different ways in the Cathedral and Monastic schools and afterwards in the Universities. Its earliest and most natural form was the *lectio*—systematic exposition and commentary, by word of mouth, on some philosophical or theological work prescribed by custom or authority. Often the work thus dealt with was itself a commentary, as in the case of the commentaries of Boethius on the logical treatises of Aristotle or the exegetical writings of the Fathers. The *lectio* naturally led to the *disputatio*. The essential features of the *disputatio*, stated very shortly, were these : the statement of a definite categorical proposition about the question in dispute ; the statement of a counter-proposition ; an analysis of the proposition, with reasons for or against each point ; a similar analysis of the counter-proposition ; followed by a summing-up in favour either of the original proposition or of the counter-proposition. Side by side with the *lectio* and the *disputatio* there grew up the method of investigation by systematic discussion of " sentences," *sententiæ*— that is, of reasoned and deliberate judgments on important questions, selected from the Fathers or other accepted authorities. The field of theological and ecclesiastical learning offered the largest opportunity for this kind of study ; abundant sources could be found in the Scriptures of the Old and New Testaments, in the writings of the Fathers, in the declarations and canons of Church Councils. Then another important consideration arose from the undeniable fact that any systematic arrangement of the judgments of accredited authorities, the Fathers, for instance, showed that the authorities disagreed on important points; and the method of " harmonisation " was developed. Divergent opinions on some leading question were set side by side, and each declaration was analysed in order to discover whether qualifications could not be introduced on each side, so as to show that in application and in effect they did not conflict.

During the whole of the eleventh century all that was known of Aristotelian deductive Logic consisted of the versions which Boethius had made of the two simpler parts of Aristotle's *Organon*, and the logical writings of Boethius himself, which were based on Aristotelian doctrine. Men came forward who made extravagant claims for the value and power of this " dialectic," as they called it. Such self-appointed teachers travelled from place to place, like the Sophists in ancient Greece, extolling " dialectic " as the art of all true knowledge and the standard by which all doctrines, even those of the Church, the Fathers, and Scripture itself, must be judged. From this point of view some of the fundamental doctrines of the Church were attacked—the miraculous birth of Christ, the Resurrection, the Atonement, the Immortality of the Soul. We must not for a moment suppose that all this was serious rationalistic criticism in the modern sense. Much of it was nothing but a display of captious argument. On the other hand, there were some of these " dialecticians " whose criticisms were serious and fundamental. These attempts to apply the distinctions of formal Logic to the mysteries of theology, and the heterodox conclusions which were their first result, naturally produced a reaction, and prompted some theologians to go to the opposite extreme. The more reasonable " dialecticians " appealed to Augustine, who in his work entitled *De Ordine* had not only sanctioned the appeal to our natural Reason, but had urged its necessity. Human Reason is part of that " Image of God " after which we are made ; to ignore or deny the claims of Reason is to dishonour God ; and to appeal to reason is to employ the resources of Logic for the exploration of divine truth. The more reasonable " anti-dialecticians " replied that to employ the resources of Logic for *the exposition and interpretation* of divine truth is one thing, but to claim that formal Logic is *the sole standard and sole source* of divine truth is another and a very different thing ; the one claim is legitimate and necessary ; the other intolerable. This was the attitude of one of the most distinguished teachers of the early eleventh century who in 990 had founded the school of Chartres, for nearly two centuries famous as a centre of humanistic culture. This was Fulbert, who had been a pupil of Gerbert of Aurillac, and whom his own pupils called their " Socrates." In his letters, and we may assume also in his oral teaching, he constantly warned his students not to desert the highway laid down by the holy Fathers. He maintained that the depths of divine truth cannot be comprehended by our unaided Reason ; human disputation can never attain to them ; they are revealed to the eye of faith. In the early years of the school at Chartres, Berengarius, who died in 1088 as Archdeacon of Tours, had been one of Fulbert's ablest students. More than once the

Master was compelled to remonstrate with him for his exclusive devotion to " dialectic." According to the testimony of his opponent and former fellow-student, Lanfrank, he seems even in his student days to have been a rebel against authority. " When we were in the schools together," said Lanfrank, " it was your part always to collect authorities against the Catholic faith." Berengarius insisted that in the investigation of truth, sacred or secular, there is no authority which can possibly be placed above the authority of Reason ; and from this point of view he dealt with the traditional doctrine of Transubstantiation. Examining the logical " category " or conception of " substance " and " accident "—that is, the essential nature of a thing as contrasted with its changing qualities—he concluded that to assume the possibility of an essential change in the substance of a thing while its perceptible qualities remained unchanged, is contrary to the laws of Logic, and therefore inconceivable, and therefore untrue. He was summoned to Rome and recanted his heterodox conclusion ; but there is no evidence that he recanted his conviction of the rights of Reason.

The position of the extreme " anti-dialecticians " of this period is represented by Peter Damiani, Cardinal-bishop of Ostia, who died in 1072. He entered the lists with a work on the Divine Omnipotence, in its relation to the alleged Uniformity of Nature and the logical Law of Non-contradiction. The Law of Non-contradiction was stated by Aristotle in the proposition that a thing cannot both possess and not possess the same quality at the same time and in the same respect (at the same point in time and space). It is evident that to deny the validity of this principle is to deny the possibility of rational thinking or even of rational statement, since precisely contradictory propositions about the same subject might both be true, and the proverbial " 'Tis," " 'Tisn't " would imply no opposition. We refer to Peter Damiani here in order to show the lengths to which the reaction against " dialectic " could go.

As regards the Uniformity of Nature, his statements are less paradoxical, and similar statements have been made by modern writers. He recognises that in our experience there is a limited field where an orderly succession of events can be discerned, where we may know what to expect, and to some extent may anticipate the future ; but there is no necessity about this order, and no rational ground for the expectation ; and over a large part of Nature, he insists, there is no observable order at all. Anything may happen ; and what will happen will be settled not by human disputation but by the unfathomable omnipotence of God. If Damiani had developed this view in relation to the principle of natural causation, he would very probably have been led to anticipate the sceptical conclusions of David Hume. It is only a custom-bred expectation which leads us to believe that anything is really *connected* with anything else : " If we believe that fire warms and water refreshes, 'tis only because it costs us too much pains to think otherwise."

As regards the Law of Non-contradiction, he denies that it has any absolute validity. It is valid in human logic, but only because it states the essential limitations belonging to our capacity of thinking. The Divine Mind knows no such limitations. Did Damiani perceive that his conclusion plunged the human mind into a scepticism which cannot even affirm itself, since the contradictory affirmation might equally be true ? There is no evidence that he saw this. His acceptance of the Law of Non-contradiction as a statement of the limitations of our thinking, leads directly to the doctrine of a twofold nature of truth —a human or natural truth subject to laws which are merely our limitations, and a supernatural truth which violates every principle of our understanding. Yet he does not appear to contemplate this conclusion. What he has at heart is to enforce the entire subserviency of " philosophy " (that is, formal logic) to theology ; and he put into circulation phrases about " philosophy " being " the handmaid (*ancilla*) of theology." These phrases have been found valuable by modern controversialists, who, assuming that " philosophy " meant all exercise of human reason outside the limits prescribed by the Church, have treated them as keynotes of thought in " the Dark Ages."

The controversy between the " dialecticians " of the eleventh century and their opponents died down. Reason could not be simply put under a ban. Orthodoxy itself put on the armour of Reason, and so panoplied, its champions soon proved themselves superior to their antagonists on their own ground. None the less, the question, how the Laws of Thought are related to the omnipotence of God, still remained. A few thinkers were prepared to cut the knot as Damiani had done ; but another view of the matter was opened up by Anselm of Canterbury, who affirmed the universal validity of the Law of Non-contradiction, but found the ground for this in the Divine Will, since God has willed that there shall be truth, and that the truth shall be comprehensible by our minds. Hugo of St Victor denied even this qualification. God cannot do what is logically impossible or self-contradictory. But this, he said, is not a limitation, since to be able to do what is self-contradictory is not a power or capacity but an impotence. A " power " whose activities know no reason, meaning, order, or law is no " power " at all. This solution of the problem may be put in other words. To say that God cannot contradict Himself is not to limit the Divine Power ; and for God to do what is self-contradictory according to the fundamental laws of our thinking would be for God to contradict Himself, since the fundamental laws of our thinking are the expression of the Divine Reason within the range of our humanity. This conclusion, in principle, won acceptance among the leading thinkers of the twelfth and thirteenth centuries.

II.

Credo ut intelligam (I believe in order that I may understand). A new note was sounded in mediæval thought when the greatest thinker of the eleventh century made this principle the foundation on which to build his reconciliation of Faith and Reason. Anselm of Aosta was a member of a noble family of Lombardy, and from his twenty-seventh year (1060) studied in the monastery of Bec in Normandy. Here he succeeded Lanfrank as Prior, and afterwards became Abbot. The school, which was celebrated before his time, became under him the most famous in Christendom. When William II. (" Rufus ") thought to atone for plundering the revenues of

Canterbury by inducing Anselm to accept the arch-bishopric, Anselm accepted with great reluctance and many misgivings. Fifteen years of harassing controversy with William and the first Henry justified his misgivings. He died at Canterbury in 1109, after two years of comparative peace.

His constant endeavour is to render the contents of the principles of the Christian Faith clear to Reason ; but in order that this may be possible, we must first possess the Christian mind. " He who does not believe will not experience, and he who has not experienced will not understand." " Nor do I seek to understand that I may believe, but I believe that I may understand ; for of this I am convinced, that unless I first believe, I shall never understand." For those who have not the capacity thus to understand, belief, submissive *veneratio*, must suffice ; but for the person who is capable of understanding, it would be neglect and indolence not to proceed from belief to understanding and insight (*delectatio*). So much is Anselm concerned about this aim that he sometimes speaks as if he desired to develop the essential doctrines of the Christian Faith from pure reason alone, as if there were no Bible, so that they may be proved even to the unbeliever who admits the validity only of Reason ; and in this connection he lays down the far-reaching principle, that rational grounds which do not conflict with Scripture have implicitly the authority of Scripture on their side. On the whole, however, the qualified statement represents his real view ; the conclusions of rational argument must always be tested by Scripture as interpreted in the light of the tradition handed down from the Fathers. It is only what we should expect, that when the conclusions which Reason is bound to reach are thus determined beforehand hitches will occur in the argument, and some things which we cannot accept as demonstration will be given as such. None the less, Anselm's entire honesty of purpose is as evident as his great ability. His work shows how the higher rational and spiritual possibilities of a dogma may be developed so as to give it a permanent title to respect even when it shall long have ceased to be believed. His direct indebtedness to Augustine and Boethius in no way detracts from his originality and ability as a thinker. For our present purpose we select as illustrative of his method the argument for the existence of God, and the argument for the necessity of the Incarnation.

Anselm accepts without question a fundamental assumption akin to the Platonic doctrine which it is customary to call the " doctrine of Ideas." An example of the ethical import of this doctrine is seen in the saying that " Human ministers of Justice may fail, but Justice, never." In other words, Justice is a real principle, an actual factor, in the nature of things. There are not merely different actions or characters which according to our various standards we may pronounce just or unjust, and which may be classified and named by the " common noun " or " abstract noun," " justice "; there is Justice *as such*. The various actions or characters which are just are so because and only because they partake of or share in the real principle of Justice ; and Justice would still be real even if no just acts were done and no just characters existed, although in such a case Justice would have no embodiment in human life. It is evident that whatever we may think of the validity of this doctrine (and it is not one to be lightly rejected), it is applicable to the meaning of Goodness, of Beauty, of Truth, and indeed to all those " universals," as they are called, which we believe to correspond to the more important similarities in the many different individual things in this world.

Now consider the idea of " good." There are innumerable things which we desire as " good," partly because they are means and utilities (*propter utilitatem*), partly because they have an excellence or worth of their own (*propter honestatem*). All these things are only " more " or " less " good ; their goodness is a matter of degree ; but this very judgment on them implies a standard by which they are compared. This standard cannot be merely *comparatively* good, or it would only fall back into one of the series of degrees, which cannot be endless or go on indefinitely. The standard must be an absolute one ; and if our use of it in judgment is not an illusion, it points to a corresponding reality, a real and Supreme Good. This supreme Good is God. Anselm regards every ideal predicate in the light of the same line of thought. Our human judgments of truth, beauty, good, all point to a Being who not only *has* but *is* all these predicates, not by participation but in Himself, *per se*. God, therefore, is the Being " than whom nothing more perfect can be conceived " (*id quo majus cogitari nequit*). The idea of God is that of the highest conceivable completeness of all perfections realised in one Being.

The conception of God thus gained is then used by Anselm in his famous " ontological " proof of the existence of God. Referring to the opening words of the fourteenth Psalm, he seeks to prove to the unwise man (*insipiens*), who says in his heart that there is no God, that he contradicts himself. Before entering on the argument Anselm assumes only this—that the unwise man knows what he is saying, that he knows what he means by the word " God," that the most important word in his statement is not a mere meaningless sound. He must mean the most perfect Being as defined above ; otherwise we are not concerned to refute his denial. Even the unwise man, therefore, is convinced that something, than which no greater can be conceived, is in his own understanding, because when he uses the word God he understands it. Now a Being, than whom no greater can be conceived, cannot exist in the understanding alone ; for if it were in the understanding only, it could also be conceived to be also in reality, which would be a greater or more perfect thing. Therefore a being certainly exists than whom no greater can be conceived, and exists both in the understanding and in reality. Such is the essence of the argument. The argument was acutely criticised by one of Anselm's contemporaries, Gaunilo, a monk of the monastery of Marmoutier, near Tours. Gaunilo did not question the truth of Christian Theism, but he questioned the validity of this argument in support of it. In a booklet entitled *Liber pro Insipiente*, which we may render " A Few Words on behalf of the Unwise Man," Gaunilo took the case of an imaginary island, replete with every conceivable perfection that an island could contain. It does not follow that such an island exists. The point of this reply is evident. It is never possible to argue from an idea in the human mind to reality. The conception of an absolutely Perfect Being is only an idea of the mind ; and even if it is one which our Reason necessarily formulates, its objective reality does not follow merely from that fact. Anselm's reply to Gaunilo consisted in enlarging on the uniqueness of the idea of God ; but the difficulty remains : we cannot argue directly from the definition to the reality. We may indeed ask : How could a man possibly acquire the idea of a Perfect Being, or even of any being more perfect than himself by comparison with whom he recognises the imperfections of his own nature, if there is nothing in reality corresponding to the idea ? But to take this course is to fall back on Anselm's former argument from degrees of goodness.[39]

To understand the force of Anselm's answer to the question, " Why God became Man " (*Cur Deus Homo*), we must understand that he does not for one moment think of God as needing to be " appeased." Wrath and vengeance alike are conceptions incompatible with the thought of God. It is not the wrath of God from which man needs to be delivered. What is it, then ? To answer this question we must understand what *sin* is. There is an order of the universe, which is spiritual as well as material ; and sin is in one sense a disturbance of the spiritual order, in another sense the substitution of a lower for a higher order. If man voluntarily obeyed God in all things, this would be the working out of the highest order in the measure possible in human life ; but if in anything man disobeys God, he disturbs this higher order, and his sin bears *the penalty inherent in it*. Anselm states this result in the language of traditional theology : man through his disobedience has yielded himself into the power of Satan, although Satan has no kind of right over man or claim upon him. But for Anselm's actual argument the essential fact is that man by his sin has put himself into a fatally wrong relation with God, and in this essential thing the spiritual order has been thwarted. This defect must be made good. Not by mere remission of punishment; that would only make the disorder worse. It remains then that some compensation must be made. Not that God *needs* compensation, for no injury can be done to Him, and nothing can be given to Him that He lacks or that is not His. The " compensation " needed is to redress the balance of the disturbed spiritual order; and this can only be done by man rendering some obedience or honour to which he would not have been bound had he not sinned. But what can man give that he does not already owe to God, apart from any sin? If all our thoughts and deeds and inmost affections had been given to God, we should have given no more than we owe. We owe everything, and we have nothing to give in " compensation " for our sin. And man, who has nothing that is his own to give, owes inestimably more than the whole sum of created things. Unless man can offer it, there remains something unaccomplished, a higher order unrealised, a disturbance in the supreme creative plan for all eternity.

From this point the course of the argument is evidently determined by the conclusion to be reached. God alone can make good the deficiency in the nature of things. But it is man alone who owes it. Therefore God must become man in order that a being who is man may be able to pay man's debt. The God-man is sinless. His offering of Himself is wholly voluntary, and its compensating power is therefore infinite.

Thus Anselm solves the problem of Man's Redemption by carrying it to infinity and making it the result of a contest between the Goodness and Justice of God. The greatness of the book lies not in the solution of the problem but in the statement of it. He teaches that Redemption is the harmonising of man's nature with the Divine Order, and that the only instrument of Redemption is the Divine Love uplifting and purifying the heart and will of man.[40]

III.

In more than one of his writings Anselm refers severely to certain *hæretici dialectici*, teachers of a "logical heresy," which makes a man incapable of understanding any of the most important doctrines of the Christian Faith. He names one of them in particular, his contemporary Roscelinus of Compiègne.

The logical heresy is the doctrine that " universals " are mere words or sounds, *flatus vocis*. We are not here concerned with the doctrine of Roscelinus himself, but with his importance as representing a tendency. For understanding of his position we have to depend upon the statements of his opponents, particularly those of Anselm. It is clear, however, that Roscelinus definitely denied the view of " universals " which we saw to be a vital factor in Anselm's religious thinking, and which is akin to the Platonic " doctrine of Ideas." He is interested in this doctrine only as a theologian ; he does not discuss it on its merits. It is the doctrine which came to be called logical " Realism," and, in opposition to it, the

doctrine of Roscelinus came to be called logical
" Nominalism." What is the meaning of this
opposition ?

The question is about the objective significance of
names—names of classes—*e.g.*, " man," " animal,"
" mineral " ; and names of abstract qualities—*e.g.*,
" whiteness," " goodness,"—the " common nouns "
and " abstract nouns " of our Grammars. The
" common noun " is the name of those qualities,
activities, or uniformities of a thing which it shares
with other things. When we abstract and generalise
these in our thinking, we form the idea of a " class,"
and when we think of a " class " we mean that certain
qualities which characterise the individual thing also
characterise a whole group. Mediæval thinkers, like
some modern logicians, always called the idea of a
" class " a " universal." They also called the abstract
idea of a quality a " universal " ; but we need only
consider their treatment of " universals " in reference to classes. Nominalism is the general theory
that the " universal " has no existence outside our
thinking. Classes of similar things or beings exist,
but the " universal " is merely subjective. Realism
is the general theory that " universals " exist in the
real world, and that a *class* of beings, " mankind "
for example, only exists because its individual members
partake of a single common nature. Naturally each
of these theories, passing through the minds of acute
thinkers, who as we may put it " had nothing else
to do," was analysed and subdivided, until John of
Salisbury, writing about 1160, was able to distinguish
at least eight different views of the nature of " universals " which were current in the schools.[41] For our
present purpose it is sufficient to distinguish an

extreme and a moderate form of Nominalism and an extreme and a moderate form of Realism. *Extreme Nominalism* may be expressed in the words of a modern writer : " The only generality possessing separate existence is the name." [42] Not even in the thought of the knower is there anything general; the universal is merely a *flatus vocis*. This was the view attributed to Roscelinus. It meant that the " universal " is merely something repeated over and over again in individuals ; " genera " and " species " fall apart into so many individuals resembling one another. Carried out to its extreme logical issues, this means the denial of any real community of nature between similar beings ; their similarities become merely unessential accidents. In the case of mankind, for instance, this means that the brotherhood and equality of the human family are mere abstractions, and that the sole reality is *difference*—that is to say, hostility and war, with no right but might, no duty but interest, no remedy but despotism. Roscelinus never drew these conclusions. *Moderate Nominalism* held that the " universal " is not a mere name ; it exists in our thinking ; " mankind," for example, is the verbal expression of an idea, a mental " concept," signifying or standing for many different individuals. *Extreme Realism* held that the common nature of a class of beings exists *ante res*—that is to say, it has a being of its own, independently of the particular things which exemplify the common nature. This was the doctrine of William of Champeaux, who died in 1121. He had studied Logic under Roscelinus in Paris, but he reacted against his master's Nominalism, and carried Realism further than anyone else known to us. As expounded by him, the pantheistic tendencies of the doctrine were plainly apparent. The individual has no independent existence, but is only an " accident " of the real being which is the " universal." From this position he was driven by the criticism of his famous pupil, Peter Abailard. *Moderate realism* held that the " universal " is an objective principle *in rebus*, common to the many different individuals and constituting them into a class. On the whole, this was the view of Anselm. He made no attempt to think out the question on its own merits. But he found that some form of logical Realism appeared to be the only means of rationalising dogma. " Universals," to him, are *in rebus* as objectively real and active principles, and *ante res* as ideal principles in the divine Mind—ideal " plans," as it were, after which things were created.

It is evident that moderate Nominalism and moderate Realism approach one another. They are like converging lines ; and the conclusion to which they point is the one adopted and defended by Abailard, who really brings the strife between Nominalism and Realism to an end, until the early years of the fourteenth century.

Peter Abailard had been the pupil successively of Roscelinus and William of Champeaux, and the contrast between their views doubtless emphasised to him, at an early period, the extravagances of extreme Nominalism and extreme Realism, and prompted him to think out a new *via media* between them. He is convinced that only the individual exists in its own right ; the individual is the only real " substance," and any doctrine which tends to undermine its reality is wrong in principle. An individual thing is the subject of attributes, but cannot itself be regarded as a mere attribute of another thing : *res de re non predicatur*. The " genera " and " species," therefore, which are predicated of the individual subject, cannot be treated as things or substances. This is manifestly true, however real the facts may be which are designated by the generic and specific names. On the other hand, Abailard certainly did not mean to imply that the distinctions of genera and species, which are implied in any kind of classification, are of arbitrary or merely human imposition. They have an objective basis in the similarities of individual things ; and the mind attains to conceptual knowledge by comparing individual things with one another. Such " universals " are involved in all thought, and are the instruments of all knowledge and of all communication between one rational being and another. The " universal," therefore, is more than a mere name. It is a predicate (*sermo*), and for that reason cannot be a thing. Moreover, it is a natural predicate, *quod de pluribus natum est predicari*. The fundamental similarities of things are not accidental, but are due to the fact that the Creator formed them, according to pre-existing types or ideals which in fact constitute the divine plan of the world. This form of moderate Realism, or moderate Nominalism, found sufficient acceptance to put the controversy in the background until the time of Ockham.

Realism appeared satisfactory so long as interest was concentrated on those aspects of things which make them unities or wholes—the world as a whole, the State as a whole, the Church as a whole ; and, in reference to mediæval thought, we must remember that " as a whole " means " as a living whole," an organic unity, like a living body. The subsequent revival of Nominalism is connected with the rise of a new feeling for the importance of individuality. This feeling can be traced in the work of Duns Scotus, who was not a Nominalist, and it was of determining importance in the work of William of Ockham.

IV.

The tragic life-story of Peter Abailard is told, in part, by himself in his *Historia Calamitatum Mearum*, fittingly so entitled.[43] It is not to our purpose here to describe that story or to pass judgment upon his character. It is evident that he was a great personality and a great teacher. Wherever he began to teach, students gathered together. The influence of his work, as a religious thinker, was powerful and penetrating, and was little affected by his condemnation at Soissons in 1121 and again at Sens in 1141. His so-called recantation was only a statement of what, as a sincere Catholic Christian, he had always believed. Some modern historians, who search the Middle Ages for distressed and persecuted champions of Reason, have found one in Abailard; but it is no matter for surprise to find that this rests merely on a partial and biassed view of the facts. To describe him as a " rationalist " is worse than useless, unless that word is already clearly and distinctly defined.

He was keenly, almost passionately, interested in the principles of valid reasoning and the logical structure of language. He believed that these studies had a place of their own and ought to be pursued for their own sake. But his acquaintance with the logical work of Aristotle was limited to what the labours of Boethius had handed down five centuries earlier, and the consequences of this limitation are evident in his treatment of Logic. He believed also that the philosophical speculations of the ancients were not " wanderings of the blind," but had been divinely guided. This was no new or merely revolutionary idea. Even in the second century, Justin the Martyr had worked out his doctrine of the *Logos spermatikos*, the seeds of divine Wisdom scattered, as it were, near and far over the fertile soil of humanity. All mankind, he said, share in this inspiration. Poets and thinkers, according to the measure in which it was imparted to them, were enabled to apprehend divine truth. And those whose lives had been formed by it were Christians, even though, like Socrates and others, they were put to death as atheists.[44] Justin, however, ruined the real meaning of his great conception by yielding to the historically fantastic assumption that Plato and other Greek thinkers borrowed their wisdom from the Books of Moses and the Prophets of Israel. In this assumption the Alexandrian Fathers followed him. Augustine was familiar with the idea, but he deliberately rejected it as historically impossible. Abailard appealed to Augustine, but boldly and even aggressively stated a doctrine closely akin to that of Justin. Since the Son of God is Wisdom, we may hear everywhere in the voice of Wisdom the Son of God. Wisdom in the mind of Plato opened to the latter the understanding of the Christian faith. The superiority of the Jews in possessing the Law and the Prophets is counterbalanced among the heathen by their use of reason. Abailard criticises the crude picture-thinking in which the Hebrews represented spiritual things; he places Socrates on an equality with the martyrs, claims that Plato taught the Trinity and Virgil the Incarnation, and declares that the heathen philosophers, by their possession of truth and the purity of their lives, are assured of salvation. He expressed such opinions with an aggressive vigour which his enemies knew how to turn to his injury; and he had many enemies. A man who was ready to ridicule any whom he had overcome in argument and whose ability he felt to be inferior to his own—and among these was more than one whom in former years he had called Master —could not hope to move with impunity even in the border-land of heresy. The hostility of the greatest churchman of the time, however, had roots far deeper than any merely personal grudge. The two men were temperamentally antagonistic. Bernard of Clairvaux, ecclesiastical statesman, saint and mystic, popular hero, passionate warrior for the convictions on which his faith rested, could not see in Abailard more than the embodiment of a blind confidence in mere Logic and a love of rash and novel interpretations, which made him a mischievous disturber of the peace and order of the Church.

The second and more serious prosecution directed against Abailard, at Soissons in 1141, was instigated by Saint Bernard. It resulted in the official condemnation of a series of propositions purporting to state cardinal points in the defendant's teaching.[45] These statements were substantially authentic; but some of them were based on imprudent or incautious expressions detached from their context. One example, of fundamental importance, must be discussed here. He was charged with teaching that we do not accept a truth because God has said it, but because our reason is convinced; that only the ignorant urge faith before comprehension; and that the so-called "mysteries" of faith no longer exist. But the writer is seriously misrepresented when the full meaning of these statements is pressed, apart from the passages in which they occur.[46] His object is to point out the agreement of dogma with reason by defending dogma against doubts, since heretics are to be refuted not by force but by reason. Hence he seeks to rationalise dogma, so far as this is humanly possible. He objects equally to mere blind faith and mere sceptical doubt. His actual statements concerning the relation of faith and reason are precise. He distinguishes between *intelligere seu credere* and *cognoscere seu comprehendere*. It is difficult to express this distinction in English. The *intelligere seu credere* signifies a partial knowledge—"now I know in part"; this is all that is possible for mortals in this world, but we must insist upon our right to seek for it, and to that end, Logic, which teaches us how to make our ideas clear and distinct and to understand the difference between valid and invalid reasoning, is indispensable. On the other hand, it is an abuse, not a use, of our reason, an abuse, not a use, of Logic, if we force it in this life to claim the *cognoscere seu comprehendere*. This is certainly the fundamental principle with which Abailard works; although, as we have seen, he sometimes applies it with "more zeal than discretion." [47]

On the basal question of God's relation to the world, he was charged with denying the free omnipotence of God and teaching that God could not have done otherwise than he has actually done; that He could not have prevented the evil which he has actually permitted; that this world is the best of all "possible" worlds. In dealing with this subject Abailard throws out novel and important ideas, the precise range of which he does not himself perceive. He lays great emphasis upon the unity of the Divine Nature. In popular speech and thought we may say, for instance, that "God is good"; but in truth we ought to say not that "God is good" but that "God is goodness." He is not the "attribute" but the reality itself. The world, therefore, as a work of divine goodness, is a result or rather a direct expression of the Divine Nature, which is wholly expressed in the world. This statement reminds us of Spinoza; but Abailard makes no attempt to consider its implications. He simply goes on to point out that from this absolute unity of the Divine Nature, the opponents of the Christian faith seek to prove the impossibility of a Trinity of Persons; and then proceeds to discuss, and, as he thinks, to refute, a long series of objections to this doctrine. There is no doubt that his intention was to defend the orthodox interpretation and make it clear to the eye of reason. His opponents charged him with denying the real distinction of "three Persons" and reviving the "Sabellian" doctrine that the Father, the Son, and the Spirit are three expressions, modes, or manifestations of the Divine Nature, corresponding to Power, Wisdom, and Goodness. As a matter of fact, whether he was aware of it or not, this is the position at which Abailard arrives. He insists that the difference between Power, Wisdom, and Goodness, in reference to the Deity, is a difference of definition; and a difference of definition is not necessarily an essential or numerical difference.

The activity of creation belongs to the Father—that is, to the divine Power; the Incarnation, the act of illumination, is the work of the Son, who as Wisdom is called the "Logos," Word or Reason; the forgiveness and redemption of man is the work of the Spirit—that is, of the Goodness of God. Whatever we think of this interpretation, it is not the orthodox one; and, in the view of his opponents, Abailard proceeded to make matters worse by identifying the Spirit with the *anima mundi*, or "soul of the world" —a conception derived from what he knew of the "Timaeus" of Plato; although elsewhere he repudiates the notion that the world is "an immense animal, animated by the divine Spirit." It is no matter for surprise that this "heterodox" interpretation of the Trinity should lead to a "heterodox" interpretation of the Person of Christ. The doctrine of two Natures in one Person is frankly abandoned by Abailard. He insists on the unipersonality of Jesus. Christ as "Word" is a "Person" of the Trinity. The historical Jesus is not a "Person" of the Trinity. What then was the Incarnation? We may not say that "God became man." God, as it were, took possession of humanity in Jesus like a garment with which He is not identical.

Some of these speculations have a curiously modern air; but far more important, as a contribution of permanent value to the doctrine of the "Work of Christ," was Abailard's interpretation of the Atonement. It was a definite and deliberate statement of what afterwards came to be described as the "Moral Theory." The Divine Word was not incarnate to deliver us from the yoke of Satan, but to give us a supreme example of Love. Abailard passionately repudiates the assumption that there was anything expiatory in the sacrifice of Christ, demanded by the "rights of divine Justice." Jesus is not a victim who expiated; He is a model whose Passion has no other purpose than to excite our love.

Abailard's famous compilation, entitled *Sic et Non*, in which he assembled conflicting statements from the Fathers on all the most important topics of theology, has been represented as a "rationalistic" attack upon "authority." Any such supposition is in direct conflict with the letter and the spirit of Abailard's own preface to this work. There is no suggestion that the Fathers are infallible. But they are authorities, and he believed that to assemble and compare conflicting and apparently contradictory statements of these authorities is a method of investigating and discovering truth. Apparent contradictions, says Abailard, suggest questions *quae teneros lectores ad maximum inquirendae veritatis exercitium provocent, et acutiores ex inquisitione reddant.* It is true that such a method is not "milk for babes," and some of the *teneri lectores* to whom Abailard refers must have been dismayed and disconcerted by it. And even the suggestion that our unaided reason may be applied to solve questions which had divided the Fathers must have been resented by the more rigid churchmen as the rash intrusion of an over-confident rationalism. None the less, Abailard is convinced that the study of the problems thus suggested may be made the instrument of understanding and discovery. By doubt, he says, we are led to inquire, and by inquiry we are led to truth. To employ an expression of modern origin, we may say that his ideal is a "faith that inquires." He is not afraid of the rational doubt which goes

deeper than the doubt of scepticism because it doubts
the conclusions of scepticism. Unfortunately he
scarcely attempted to work out the application of
these principles to the material which he had collected; and the conception that apparently contradictory opinions may both contain elements of truth
complementary to one another was apparently beyond
his range.

Abailard did not invent the method of *Sic et non*,
and his use of it is not so large a landmark in the
history of Christian thought as it was formerly
supposed to be. We have already seen that there
had been partial anticipations of it in the work of
previous theological writers; and it was destined
to become the characteristic method of mediæval
theology, philosophy, and jurisprudence. Recent
investigations have shown that in reference to the
systematic method of exposition of which we are
now speaking, the canonists and theologians influenced one another. During the ninth, tenth, and
eleventh centuries students of what is technically
termed "Canon Law"—the successive decrees and
canons of Church Councils and Popes—had been
making systematic collections of these documents;
but there had been no uniformity, and the result
was an accumulation of various and on some points
conflicting material. From the point of view of historical scholarship, and from that of discipline and
order, this state of things was very undesirable.
During the early years of the twelfth century the
study of Canon Law at Bologna was being deepened
and extended largely under the influence of Gratian
(Franciscus Gratianus), a Camaldusian monk, of
whose personal history little is known. Gratian,

H

with what amount of official encouragement is not clear, undertook the labour of constructing a coherent juridical system from the vast body of texts of widely differing periods and origins which he found in the collections. About 1141 he published the results in his famous *Decretum*, known at first by the more significant title *Concordantia discordantium Canonum*. The *Decretum* is not merely a collection of texts ; it is a treatise. He inserts the texts in the course of his dissertation, and where they do not agree, he divides them into opposite groups and endeavours to reconcile them. He drew his materials from the existing collections, from Roman Law, and from the works of the Fathers and ecclesiastical writers. Only ten years after the publication of Gratian's work appeared the *Libri quattuor Sententiarum* of Peter the Lombard, the best known of the pupils of Abailard. The two works had similar histories ; they became the manuals, one for Canon Law, the other for Theology, in use in all the universities, taught, discussed, and commented upon by the most illustrious masters.[48]

Abailard's work was the precursor not only of the famous *Liber Sententiarum*, but of all the *Summae Theologiae* with which the Church was presently to abound. The work of the Lombard was not the ablest of its kind ; but its general character lent itself very conveniently to discussion by a teacher with his class. Opinions for and against a conclusion are presented in the manner adopted by Abailard, and then the solution of the contradiction is discussed, but usually not in a decisive manner nor with any high degree of originality. The conclusion is usually not so strongly supported that the teacher could not modify it or at least the grounds of it. Of the Fathers, Augustine is quoted by far the most frequently and extensively. If, for example, we turn to the first Book, which deals with God as the sole Object of man's fruition—that is, as the sole Object to be desired for Himself alone, or for His own sake alone; and if we consult the first "Chapter" or head, under the third " Distinction " (or Problem), we find the writer treating of " Our knowledge of the Creator through created beings, in whom vestiges of the Trinity appear"; and after a short exposition of the well-known utterance of Saint Paul in Romans i. 19, 20, he proceeds to discuss the " vestiges " or "images" of the Trinity in human and material Nature. Here the references are all to Augustine, and nearly all to Augustine's work *De Trinitate*. The *Liber Sententiarum* is one more indication of the penetrating and profound influence of the great African thinker. Peter does not attempt to discuss any of the questions inevitably raised by Augustine's search for analogies of the divine Trinity-in-Unity among created things, where his comparisons suffer from failure to express the Unity without excluding the Trinity or the Trinity without excluding the Unity.[49] Even more serious are the defects of his treatment of the two Natures in the person of Christ. For this, Augustine is not responsible; but Peter seems in effect to deny the humanity of Jesus altogether. In such ways the *Liber Sententiarum* afforded ample material for critical discussion by its commentators.

V.

During the first half of the twelfth century the most influential and vigorous centre of Christian thought was the school of Chartres, a brilliant example of the old cathedral school, soon to be superseded by the *studium generale*, or University. We have already spoken of its foundation by Fulbert, early in the previous century. Its first famous representative, in the domain of philosophy and theology, was Bernard of Chartres, who died between 1125 and 1130. Our only information about his actual teaching is preserved by John of Salisbury. He devoted himself to cultivate the intelligence and insight of his pupils rather than to overwhelm them under heaps of useless erudition. He insisted on the importance of familiarity with the great writers of classical antiquity. "We are like dwarfs," he said, "seated on the shoulders of giants; we see more and see further than the ancients, not because our own vision is more penetrating or our own point of view more lofty, but because they uplift us and maintain us at their own high level." [50] None the less, the work of Bernard's younger brother, Thierry of Chartres, and especially his "Heptateuchon," so called because it was an account of the sources of the instruction which he gave in the seven Liberal Arts, shows how vast was the intellectual horizon of Western thinkers at this time, and how thoroughly their curiosity had been awakened.

The best known among the pupils of Bernard of Chartres was Gilbert, who afterwards taught in Paris, and died in 1154 as Bishop of Poitiers, hence known as Gilbert de la Porrée. The spirit of his doctrine is akin to that of Abailard. He started from the tradition distinctive of mediæval Platonism which he had learnt from his master, and he applied it essentially as Abailard had done. We have already given a brief illustration of the Platonic " Doctrine of Ideas," and we have seen how Abailard found in it the clue to a *via media* between extreme Nominalism and extreme Realism.* Gilbert proceeds in another way. In the first place, he distinguishes the Ideas in themselves, as they are in the divine Reason, and the Ideas embodied in the objects perceived by our senses, which are inherent in these created things. They are not only embodied but individualised. Their seat is not in the divine Reason, but they are reproductions of the divine Ideas under the limitations imposed by " matter." Although embodied and individualised, they are the ground of the resemblances which we perceive among different individuals within the same species, and they bear a resemblance to their divine originals. In this sense, or regarded from this point of view, they are " universals," but without any independent subsistence of their own. In the next place, Gilbert linked up the doctrine of Ideas with that of " Form " and " Matter." By the " Form " of an object—a stone or a tree, for instance —he meant its inner structure, which makes it what it is and which it has in common with other objects of the same kind. Thus, the embodied and individualised Ideas are " Forms." The individual consists of an assemblage of such Forms ; and it is individual, because nowhere else is such an assemblage to be met with. Gilbert never intended to separate

* See above, pages 96-97 and 104-105.

" Form " and " Matter " ; but his doctrine of individuality was found to be ambiguous in the extreme, suggesting as it does either that real individuality is nothing more than a cluster of abstractions, or, if the reality of the individual is emphasised, that the individual and the universal are dissociated. And when he applied his doctrine of individuality to the explanation of the divine Trinity, he seemed not only to distinguish but to separate the divine Nature, *Deitas* or *Divinitas*, from the distinctive characteristics which make each of the Persons what He is. This bold application of human reasoning to an article of faith excited the wrath of Saint Bernard, at whose instigation Gilbert was arraigned on a charge of heresy, at Rheims, 1148. These heresy-hunts show us Bernard's worst side ; yet they were, in a way, just the obverse of his deep mystical piety. The story of the trial is told by John of Salisbury and by Otto of Freising ; and the latter observes that he (Bernard) " was, from the fervour of his Christian faith, as jealous as, from his habitual meekness, he was credulous ; so that he held in abhorrence those who trusted in the wisdom of this world, and were too much attached to human reasonings." On this occasion Bernard fell short of victory, and Gilbert returned safely to his diocese.[51]

We can trace the influence of the school of Chartres in the work of a number of thinkers who were not members of it. One of the most remarkable of these was Adelard of Bath, *philosophus Anglorum*, who studied in France, and gained a rich store of natural knowledge through his travels in Italy, Greece, Asia Minor, and among the Arabians. His strong desire was to make some of the science of the Greeks and

Arabians accessible in the West. He translated fifteen books of Euclid's Elements from the Arabic into Latin ; and some other translations are attributed to him. Already, in his earlier years, he was acquiring a scientific habit of mind, and was beginning to see the importance of observation and experiment. He compared mere authority to a halter. Reason is given us in order that we may distinguish between the true and the false. Admission of the dependence of all things on the divine Will is not inconsistent with recognition of natural law as the proper object of investigation : " It is the Will of God that plants should spring up from the earth, but God does not act without reason (*sine ratione*)." In other words, there are natural laws of causation which by the use of our reason we may learn to understand.

Adelard is a thorough Platonist, in the mediæval sense. " Since that which we see," he said, " is at once genus and species and individual, Aristotle rightly insisted that universals do not exist except in the things of sense. But since those universals, so far as they are called genera and species, cannot be perceived by anyone in their purity without the admixture of imagination, Plato maintained that they existed and could be beheld beyond the things of sense—that is to say, in the divine Reason." And, as Augustine had done, he developed this doctrine into a theory of innate ideas which is thoroughly Platonic. The impressions of our bodily senses, though they are necessary to knowledge, do not in themselves constitute knowledge. If we rely on them alone, we are led into mere " opinion," and in the end into sheer illusion. They are the indispensable occasions on which we are reminded of, or recollect, the

Ideas already latent in our minds and infused into
them by the Wisdom of God ; and these Ideas correspond to the Forms or inner structures of the manifold
created things around us.[52]

The most typical representative of the culture of
this age—a period more original and more interesting
in many ways than the great age of scholasticism in
the thirteenth century—is found in John of Salisbury.
His works, attractively written in very readable
Latin, reveal a personality as many-sided as the age
in which he lived. The autobiographical account of
his student years (1136-48) contained in his *Metalogicon*
is of the utmost value as a picture of the schools of
the time ; and his *Policraticus* has been described as
an encyclopædia of the cultivated thought of the age.
In him we find an ecclesiastical statesman and man
of affairs—secretary to three successive Archbishops
of Canterbury, of whom Becket was one ; we find a
cultured scholar, who had imbibed to the full the love
of classical learning and the eagerness for extended
knowledge which was traditional at Chartres ; but
we do not find a philosophical or theological thinker.
It is as a historian of opinion that we learn most from
him ; and the first thing which we learn from him is
this : to confound the history of philosophy with the
history of logic, or to oppose philosophy to the life
of religion, is a total misconception of the Middle
Ages. He puts the whole controversy about universals
in its proper place, which is a subordinate place. He
is prepared to defend logic against those who despised
all philosophical training ; but he pours out caustic
criticism on the idle casuistry and aimless verbal
ingenuity of some of his logical contemporaries. Logic,
valuable and necessary as it is, is like " the sword of

Hercules in a pygmy's hand," unless there be added to it the accoutrement of the other sciences.

John has his own philosophical position; in a sense, it is one of scepticism, but it is a scepticism which is carefully defined and limited. He prefers to describe it by the term current in the later Athenian schools—the "Academic" position. Among the adherents of this school a critical attitude was maintained towards the views of others, especially towards the somewhat crude and imperious dogmatism of the Stoics; and for themselves, believing that certainty was impossible, they allowed a large scope to probability as a motive to action. The reservations made by John of Salisbury are much more extensive. He maintains that it is simply absurd to deny the possibility of all knowledge. We have trustworthy knowledge from three different sources: sense, reason, and faith. He who refuses to accept the evidence of his senses is inferior to the lower animals. He who refuses the evidence of reason, and in that sense doubts everything, cannot even know that he doubts. He who refuses the declarations of faith rejects the basis and starting-point of all wisdom. But where not sense, nor reason, nor faith provides inviolable certainty, we must doubt. On the other hand, reasonable doubt does not exclude critical consideration and investigation; it only excludes intolerance and dogmatic assurance. He gives a long list of things which may be doubted, or rather on which suspense of judgment is the only reasonable course (*quae sunt dubitabilia sapienti*); and the list is curious and instructive.

John died as Bishop of Chartres in 1180. He perceived the decline of the intellectual energies which had been vigorous during the earlier part of the century. On the one hand, logical studies were becoming trivial displays of ingenuity; and, on the other hand, Peter Lombard and the "Summists" were devoting themselves to the systematic arrangement of authorities. At first sight, it seems strange that this decline was not affected in any appreciable way by the fact that the remaining logical works of Aristotle, the "Analytics," "Topics," and "Sophistici Elenchi," became known towards the middle of the century, and made their way almost silently into the schools. It is true that the general conception of Logic was fundamentally altered through acquaintance with the contents of these books. It began to be understood that the traditional Aristotelian books, the "Categories" and the "De Interpretatione," were only elementary introductions to the properly logical treatises, which dealt with the nature and method of demonstrative science. John of Salisbury was well aware of the importance of this; and in his *Meta-logicon* he gives a careful account of the contents of the Aristotelian logical treatises, which shows by the way that he was by no means committed to belief in the infallibility of Aristotle. There is no doubt that the fuller knowledge of the ancient logic resulted in an increase of formal acuteness; but it appears to have been of but small benefit to serious studies until there was added to it a knowledge of the other works of Aristotle.[53]

The real source of the trouble was perceived by John himself. It is implied in what he says about "the sword of Hercules in the hands of a pygmy." Elaborate analysis of the forms of logical statement and inference was of little use so long as the material of experience, to which it could be applied, was wanting. The knife was continually being sharpened, but there was nothing to cut with it. Notwithstanding the exceptional cases of a few men like Adelard of Bath, we may say with Professor Étienne Gilson that the point where the men of that age differed most completely from ourselves was in their almost total ignorance of the possibility of natural science (as we understand it) : " the truth is, that Nature did not exist for them (*ils n'ont pas de nature*). In their view, indeed, natural objects possessed a reality of their own so far as they served the daily needs of men ; but as soon as mediæval thought undertook to explain them, they lost this reality. For a thinker of that age to understand and explain a thing consisted always in showing that it was not what it appeared to be, that it was the sign and symbol of something deeper, that it ' manifested ' or ' signified ' something else ; the very substance of things was reduced to their symbolic meaning, and there was merely nothing to understand in the actual material of which they were composed. What was wanting in the twelfth century, in order that Christian thinkers might even imagine a concrete reality behind this world of symbols, was the conception of Nature as having a reality and worth in its own right." [54]

VI.

No picture of the rich and many-sided spiritual life of the twelfth century would be complete if it omitted one of the most characteristic movements of the time—a movement from which vigorous attacks were directed against the so-called "dialectical" and "summist" tendencies whose issues we have described—and which claimed to reach the goal of their endeavours by another and a far better way. This is the movement known as "mysticism." We will not turn aside to criticise this unfortunate term; all its original associations are misleading, and it is still occasionally thrown about as a mere term of abuse; but its use as the distinctive name of a special type of religious experience is too firmly established to be abandoned. The mystical type of religion has well-marked features. It is by no means peculiar to Christianity, although the most instructive examples of it are found in Christianity. It has grown in the most various soils and yet has exhibited the same distinctive features.

The most fundamental factor in mysticism is identical with the nature of all religion of the more vital sort—all religion which involves something more vital than intellectual acceptance of doctrinal propositions or outward conformity to custom and ceremonial. This fundamental factor consists in a certain intellectual conception and a certain practical or experiential attitude of the mind. The conception is the unity of all things in God—a conception which often, in mystical religion, becomes a truth so inviolable that it is not even stated. On the experiential side mysticism holds the possibility, not merely of knowledge *about* God, but of direct intercourse or conscious personal communion with Him. For the mystic, "the chief end of man is to glorify God and enjoy Him for ever"; and this experience is a thing to be achieved, not a mere occurrence in the course of Nature.

We find, in the history of religion, that there are a number of specific features common to all the various forms of mysticism ; and each of these is capable of assuming a degenerate form, destructive of mental and moral and spiritual health. It is not necessary that this should happen ; but in certain cases it has happened. We may enumerate these characteristics of mysticism, and distinguish the normal and morbid forms of each.

(i) The soul has a faculty which is above the ordinary reason of man, and which opens up an avenue of direct intercourse with the spiritual world. It is a faculty of spiritual discernment which can be trained and increased in power until it becomes a full vision of the Infinite. It is above and beyond reason, because the work of reason is assumed to be always of the nature of analysis, separating the things reasoned about. Mysticism would overcome all separation. It desires complete union with the Divine—a union which is beyond reason because it is beyond separation, a union in which self as a separate thing disappears. In its morbid form this ideal lends itself to expression in sensuous metaphors, and may come to be regarded as if it were a union and interpenetration like physical intoxication. The mystical state becomes a pathological physical condition.

(ii) Eternity is no mere future state or endless series in time, but a present reality whose fulness time can neither give nor take away. Eternity is another name for the life of God. It follows that personality, so far as it involves growth in time, would limit rather than express the full truth about the divine. In its extreme form, unbalanced by a living interest in the temporal and the future, this conception makes the eternal world the only real world. The world of experience in time and space becomes unreal. We come to reality and to ourselves by dying to this world.

> Peace, peace! He is not dead, he doth not sleep—
> He hath awakened from the dream of life—
> 'Tis we who, lost in stormy visions, keep
> With phantoms an unprofitable strife.
>
> . . . .
>
> The One remains, the many change and pass;
> Heaven's light for ever shines, earth's shadows fly;
> Life, like a dome of many-coloured glass,
> Stains the white radiance of Eternity,
> Until Death tramples it to fragments.

In its morbid forms this dualism of the divine and the earthly is capable of leading to extreme consequences both in theory and practice. The world and all human experience is not a revelation of God, but a barrier shutting us off from God. We must annihilate that barrier and set ourselves free, not only from outward things, but from every inner desire that points to anything in this world. An ideal is made of the utmost possible detachment from this world. The result is mental vacancy. In certain cases a practical conclusion of a very different kind has been drawn—that all manner of indulgence may be permitted, because it is an affair of the body only, and cannot affect the spiritual nature which is independent of the body.

(iii) A high value is attached to *asceticism* in one or other of its various forms. The Greek word from which this term is derived means " exercise " or " training." So far, this is an essential factor in all life. It is a question of how far it is carried. In the higher forms of mysticism it becomes the training of the spiritual athlete, and manifests itself in moral efficiency. In the morbid forms, it becomes mere physical self-mortification, a torturing to death of the impulses of the body.

(iv) The true mystic tends to sit loosely to institutional and legal religion in general. Some mystics have regarded institutional religion as harmless, and have been merely indifferent to it ; others have passed to open revolt and rebellion and become "heretics." Both attitudes have at times been carried to extremes. Some yielded the most absolute submission to the Church ; others have gone to the extreme of revolt and died as martyrs.

In western Christendom, from the time of Eriugena there was a constant stream of what must be called mysticism, originating for the most part from neoplatonic influence transmitted through the mind of Augustine, or more directly through "Dionysius" and other sources ; but with the partial exception of Eriugena, who occupies a unique position, the mystical element in all those writers who are in any real way representative of the period was in definite subordination to the doctrines of the Church. These doctrines might be interpreted symbolically—that is, treated as standing for truths which went beyond the logical meaning of the words in which the doctrines were stated ; but their authority was still regarded as inviolable.

Saint Bernard of Clairvaux, great man of action and gifted leader of men, who represented and, we may even say, embodied in himself the religious genius of an entire age, is one of the founders of mediæval mysticism and least dependent on Augustinian or other sources for his presentation of it. He has no thought of denying the utility of secular learning and study in its own place, nor does he engage in mere general denunciation of philosophers and logicians. But he is convinced that the value of secular knowledge is utterly insignificant compared with that of sacred knowledge : *haec mea sublimior philosophia, scire Jesum et hunc Crucifixum.* His ideal is not the objective demonstration of truth by systematic logical thinking, but the subjective experience and apprehension of truth in direct contemplation. The pursuit of knowledge " for its own sake " is to him disgraceful inquisitiveness ; the pursuit of knowledge is justified only so far as it leads to edification. Hence he had and could have no understanding of the ideals of sincere and strenuous thinkers like Abailard and Gilbert. He can speak of the *ventosa loquacitas philosophorum;* and of Abailard he can say " it were better that the mouth which uttered such things be smitten with a bludgeon." Yet, when he had forgotten all this, and had returned to his own way, we find in his sermons and hymns—those rhymed Latin hymns which in the Middle Ages became one of the purest forms of religious art—a spirit so simple and sincere that under a superficial appearance of sentimental credulity it penetrates deep into reality.

Jesu dulcis memoria
Dans vera cordi gaudia :
Sed super mel et omnia
Ejus dulcis praesentia.

Nil canitur suavius
Nil auditur jucundius
Nil cogitatur dulcius
Quam Jesus Dei filius.

Jesu spes poenitentibus
Quam pius es petentibus,
Quam bonus es quaerentibus.
Sed quid invenientibus ?

On the other hand, his religious experience begins with a profound and invincible pessimism about the secular natural world. Man's natural condition is one of misery. From this the only possible way of deliverance, the beginning of the way to divine truth, is the way of "humility," understood not as a vague sentiment but as a deliberate conscious effort. When we become effectively aware of our own wretchedness, then we understand the misery of others; this is "compassion." Arising from this experience we attain to "contemplation," again understood as an active effort, when through the endeavour after righteousness and purity of heart we aspire to the enjoyment of heavenly things. This enjoyment is based on vision. More exalted still, however, is the *ecstatic* vision, such as was granted, for example, to Saint Paul. This is the reward of those who, as it were, are "dead" to the body and to the world: *te enim quodammodo perdere tanquam qui non sis, et omnino non sentire te ipsum, et a te ipso exinaniri et pene annullari, coelestis est conversationis.* Love grows with the knowledge of its objects, and at the highest stage self-love is so merged in love to God that we love ourselves only for God's sake or because God has first loved us. "As the little water-drop poured into a large measure of wine seems to lose its own nature entirely and to take on both the taste and the colour of the wine, or as iron heated red-hot loses its own appearance and glows like fire, or as air filled with sunlight is transformed into the same brightness so that it does not so much appear to be illuminated as to be itself light, so must all human feeling towards the Holiest be self-dissolved in unspeakable wise, and wholly transfused into the will of God. For how

I

shall God be all in all if anything of man remains in man ? The substance will indeed remain, but in another form, another glory, another power." [55] Bernard uses the suggestive metaphor, a favourite one with later mystics, of the " spark " (*scintilla*, or *scintillula*) in the soul, the " spark " whose faint and seemingly transient glow may be intensified into a pure absorbing flame. Such are the characteristic similes of mysticism wherever it is found.

The exponents of mediæval mysticism are fond of marking out stages or degrees of progress on the mystic way to the Highest. Some writers among them carry this to an extent which makes an unpleasant impression of sheer artificiality—an artificiality not exceeded by the verbal ingenuities of some of the " dialecticians." It is difficult to acquit Saint Bernard of this charge when we examine his exposition of the twelve degrees of " humility." But there can be no reasonable doubt that the doctrine of degrees is in principle sound, and essential to any adequate interpretation of religious experience. Such passages as the following illustrate the sound and helpful use which he made of the doctrine. " I confess that the Word has come to me (I speak as an ignorant man), and that many times. And though He has often entered into me, I have not perceived when He came in. I have felt Him to be there, I remember His presence, sometimes I have had foreknowledge of His advent, but His entrance I could never feel, nor even His departure." And again, when expounding his doctrine of contemplation, he finds that the vision of the Highest is realised or attained through what in terms of modern psychology we should call constructive imagination. This means nothing else than the weaving of certain spiritual images (*similitudines*, likenesses) in order that the meanings of the Divine Wisdom may be brought into the sight of the mind which is contemplating, so that it may perceive, as in a mirror and imperfectly (" darkly ") what it cannot as yet look upon face to face : " What I speak of are things divine, and wholly unknown save to those who have experienced them—how in the mind, in this mortal body, while yet the state of faith lasts but the reality of the Perfect Light is not made manifest, the contemplation of pure truth can yet anticipate its action in us, at least in part ; so that some even among us, to whom this has been granted from above, can employ the Apostle's words (1 Corinthians xiii. 9, 10). For when something from God has momentarily, and as it were with the speed of a flash of light, shed its brightness upon the mind, then, whether for the tempering of this too great radiance or for the sake of imparting it to others, certain spiritual images arise in the mind—images of inferior things but suited to the meanings which have been infused from above. By these images the pure brightness is in a manner shaded, and becomes more bearable to the soul and more capable of being communicated to others who may desire to hear." [56]

Saint Bernard died in 1153 at the age of sixty-two ; and in the meantime mysticism had been more systematically developed by his contemporary, Hugo of St Victor, who died in 1141. It is usually said that the Augustinian Monastery of St Victor near Paris became the headquarters of mysticism during the twelfth century. This is true, especially in reference to the work of Hugo and his pupil Richard of

St Victor; but it is misleading to describe the theologians of St Victor simply as "mystics." In their comprehensive studies they desired to provide a place for each of the distinctive spiritual activities of man; alike for the philosophical thinker, the theologian, the mystic. The close and harmonious union of mysticism and reason is a remarkable characteristic of the great "Victorines." [57]

VII.

We now come to a topic which, though it lies almost outside the range of our subject, has living links of connection with it; that is, the "heretical" movements which come into prominence during the twelfth and thirteenth centuries.[58]

We have interpreted the work of some leading thinkers who claimed the right to rationalise the dogmas of the Church to an extent which the exponents of traditional orthodoxy regarded as dangerous. We have shown that these thinkers had no intention of denying the dogmas of the Church. Eriugena and Abailard are conspicuous examples, although in very different periods and in very different ways. If we are to ascribe to such men an ideal of "free thought" we must be clear about what we mean. There is no evidence that they desired any general emancipation, but only their own relief from certain restraints. If this is "free thought," it means the claim for liberty made by a select and enlightened class. To the end of the chapter this "free thought" never desired to quarrel with the established order, or to challenge a system on which social peace and welfare appeared to depend. It never meant any demand for the relaxation of the bonds of civil law or Church discipline. During the period on which we are now entering, the critics or challengers of Authority came from an instructed class who wanted no public revolution, but only personal liberty to write and think.

Quite apart from the influence of such men, of exceptional talent, there were genuinely popular movements of enthusiastic dissent, some of which created a greater panic among ecclesiastical and civil rulers than the menace of Islam itself. Few subjects are more interesting, or more obscure, than the real origin and significance of the popular " heretical " movements of the twelfth and thirteenth centuries. There can be no reasonable doubt that part of their impulse came from outbursts against a worldly hierarchy. It is certain that this was by no means the whole explanation ; but it was a contributory cause of the success of these movements, more particularly in Southern France. Pope Innocent III., who ruled from 1198-1216, not only admitted this, but insisted on the essential need for reform. Men looked with scandalised eyes on the lives of some of the priests and monks. To this was added political and social discontent. The distinction between rich and poor was becoming more and more apparent as the distribution of wealth became more unequal in the life of the towns. More might be said of these things ; but under such conditions it is not difficult to understand how the ground was prepared for new beliefs, new in the West but very old in the East, held and taught with passionate conviction by self-appointed missionaries. In truth, the oriental world was penetrating Europe. The great trade routes to and from Asia were channels not only of commerce but of ideas and beliefs. They came along the roads, over the mountain passes, along the rivers ; across the Balkans through Dalmatia into Italy ; over the Alps into South-eastern France ; up the Rhone and through the valley of the Rhine into the Low Countries. What were these beliefs ? They rested upon a number of general principles. This world is created by, or is entirely under the dominion of, an evil power, and everything arising out of embodied life is evil ; there is no hell, because nothing could be more evil than this world ; this world itself is purgatory, where the faithful may learn to fit themselves for another world in every respect the opposite of this one ; all ceremonial or institutional religion is worse than worthless, and the only Church consists of those who under the inspiration of the Divine Spirit are preparing themselves for another and a different world. We need not observe that these ideas, stated in this general way, are not a description of the actual teaching of any of the sects of the time. We have stated them as common characteristics of these movements, actually held in more, or less, extreme forms, and assuming different aspects in the different communities in which they took root. Fundamentally, the East was responsible for them.

The mediæval chroniclers, when professing to describe the various forms of " heresy," are far from exact in their nomenclature, and employ a large variety of designations ; but two dominant " heresies " stand out historically. The more revolutionary of these had established itself during the twelfth century in the south-east of France, and its adherents were called " Albigenses " from the small town of Albi, although the larger city of Toulouse was the real centre of the movement. The other was due largely to the work of a remarkable teacher, Peter Waldo, and its adherents were called " Waldenses."

Among the Albigenses, the principles which we summarily stated above became matters of absolute conviction ; but their practical application was limited by the division of the movement into two groups, the " Perfect " and the " Believers." The " Perfect " led a life of extreme austerity and asceticism ; for them, even the begetting of children was an evil, since it prolonged the inherently evil life of this present world. The " Believer " was not required to order his life on these extreme principles. He might eat meat ; he might marry. The result was a strange amalgamation of asceticism and laxity, of lofty ideals with aberrations which were perverse and unhealthy ; and, it has been truly said, we cannot wonder that the Catholic, ever ready to suspect the heretic of immoral practices, should do so with conviction in the case of a sect whose fanatical attitude towards material existence was plainly inconsistent with the elementary facts of life.

Social conditions in South-eastern France favoured the increase of the Albigensian movement. The States and Communes of the district had become virtually independent. It was a cosmopolitan land, to which from the dawn of history adventurous folk had found their way and created a strange mixture of races. The heretics were supported by the nobles, the Communes, and even by some of the local bishops, who resented the authority conferred upon the papal Legates sent to direct operations against the " enemies

of God." The "Holy War" of extermination proclaimed by Innocent III. against the Albigenses, the
atrocities to which it led—which the Legates made no
attempt to prevent—and its transformation into a
secular struggle between North and South, are
described in the general histories of the period. More
than a century passed before the religious movement
was extirpated. Little attempt appears to be made
among Roman Catholic historians to justify the
methods adopted. But there is more to be said.
Whatever the subversive or revolutionary or even
antinomian tendencies of the sectaries may have
been, they were working to a certain extent for
religious freedom, and they attacked only an authoritative Church establishment supported by coercive
methods and the civil power. This, judged by some
modern standards, was, of course, a movement in
the right direction. We must, however, press the
question, *to what extent* were they working for
religious freedom ? It is a mere delusion to suppose
that the new temper shown by the sectaries would
have been more tolerant and propitious than the
Church to the cause of enlightenment and progress.
Their movement was more fundamentally and thoroughly obscurantist than the Roman system had
ever been.

When we pass to the Waldenses we find ourselves
in a different atmosphere. About the year 1170,
Peter Waldo, a rich merchant of Lyons, who had been
studying the New Testament and comparing the
record of Galilean Christianity with the character of
the contemporary Church, decided to distribute his
wealth among the poor, and to go forth to preach
what he believed to be the Gospel in its primitive

purity and simplicity. His movement only gradually became " heretical " in the ecclesiastical sense. Its adherents claimed that every good man is competent to expound the Bible and to preach. Then they proceeded to denounce the low moral standard of many of the clergy, and to appoint their own " leaders," as we may call them ; that is, men devoted to extreme strictness of life who gave their whole time to the teaching of religion. The ideal of the movement was voluntary poverty and the greatest possible simplicity and purity of living. In spite of pitiless persecution they were never entirely suppressed. The leaven of their ideas worked itself into the Reformation. Nevertheless we may say of them what Harnack said of the early Christian " Montanists." The primitive Christianity to which they looked back consisted of small congregations scattered over the Roman Empire and provided only with the most indispensable forms of organisation, such as were required by a religious bond resting on supernatural expectations and brotherly love. Their enthusiasm was for a life of holiness and separation from the world, and an eager outlook for its end. The Waldenses could never have been more than a society of religious devotees, separated from the world by a rigorous discipline and working on it by a direct propaganda—an insignificant sect, barely intelligible to one man in a thousand, and utterly incapable of saving and educating nations.

While Peter Waldo was labouring to preach his Gospel on the highways and byways of the country round Lyons, another remarkable man, of kindred spirit but widely different teaching, was founding a special order of Cistercians in the monastery of Flora or Floris, now San Giovanni in Fiore, among the mountains of Calabria. This was Abbot Joachim, known as Joachim of Floris. He was of noble birth, had travelled in the East and West, and had friends in high places ; but he had won fame as an exponent of the allegorising art, which extracted moral or spiritual significance from every statement in the Bible and every event recorded there. Pope Clement III., writing to him in 1188, had urged him to devote himself entirely to this work ; and now, in the year 1200, he reverently submitted his principal writings to the consideration of Innocent III., to receive his sanction, correction, or condemnation. Whether the Pope ever looked at them we do not know. At any rate, no official opinion was expressed upon them till long afterwards, and then on the occasion of quite another appeal. But the modern reader who glances at their contents will be sufficiently amazed at the boldness of their speculations and at the naïvety of the Abbot's good faith in submitting them to Papal revision. For while in the main they conform to the general character of the allegorising mysticism of the time they contain certain revolutionary speculations, the acceptance of which would be fatal to the whole theory of an organised and authoritative Church.

Joachim divided the history of the world into three great and decisive periods. The first dispensation was the Kingdom of God the Almighty, a time of trial, in which obedience was the highest duty of men ; this passed away with the coming of Christ. The second dispensation was the Kingdom of the Son, a time of wisdom and action, in which men were freemen ; this was even now nearing its end. The third dispensation, soon to begin, was the Kingdom of the Holy Spirit. The first dispensation was embodied in the letter of the Old Testament Law; the second, in the letter of the Gospel of Christ. The third is embodied in no " letter " at all, " for the letter killeth, but the Spirit giveth light." It proceeds from the Gospel of Christ, but transcends it, even as the Gospel of Christ transcended the Law of Moses; " for that which was committed to us by Christ and the Apostles, concerning the faith of the Sacraments, is but for a time and passes away—that is, as regards the Sacraments themselves; but as regards that which is signified by them, it is eternal." This is the Everlasting Gospel proclaimed by the Apocalyptic angel: " and I saw another angel fly in the midst of heaven having the Everlasting Gospel to preach unto them that dwell upon the earth, and to every nation, and kindred, and tongue, and people." This is the Gospel that shall reveal the hidden meaning of all that has gone before it. It shall put an end to all schisms and divisions, and shall endure to the end of the world. It underlies the conflicting creeds of Eastern and Western Christendom; and when it shall be preached to the whole world, its spiritual understanding " shall pierce even unto the Jews, and like a thunderbolt shall shatter the hardness of their hearts." In this connection Joachim quotes the prophet Malachi : " And behold, He shall turn the heart of the fathers to the children, and the heart of the children to their fathers."

The subsequent history of this doctrine of the Everlasting Gospel is instructive. Joachim having fixed the period at which the Everlasting Gospel was to fructify at about 1260, himself died in 1202 ; and about fifty years afterwards a certain Brother Gerard, a

Franciscan, wrote an "Introduction to the Ever-lasting Gospel," which we only know from the sentence passed on it by a Papal commission, held at Anagni, soon after its first appearance. From this we learn that Gerard held the writings of Joachim not to proclaim only, but actually to constitute the Ever-lasting Gospel, Joachim himself being the Apocalyptic angel to whom it was committed. Francis of Assisi was another angel of the Apocalypse—that one who " bore the seal of the living God," and the Franciscans themselves were at any rate the provisional custodians of the Everlasting Gospel. The life had gone out of the Old and New Testaments about the year 1200, and in 1260 (according to the prediction of Joachim himself) the Gospel of Christ was to come to an end.

This lapse into the literal conception of the Gospel as a book, and reconfining of the channel through which it flowed to a single personality, is a striking exemplification of the irony of history. And yet Joachim himself had prepared the way for the sterilis-ing of his own conception, for, as we have seen, he had assigned a definite date (1260, forty-two genera-tions after the birth of Christ) for the fructification of the Everlasting Gospel, and, while declaring that the sacraments and the priesthood would be done away, and quoting the great saying that no man should teach his brother, saying, " Know the Lord," because all should know him, from the greatest to the least, he had nevertheless announced the name of the order of monks who would be the guardians and repositories of the Everlasting Gospel. On the other hand, it is impossible not to trace in Joachim's speculations the kernel truth that the final test of revelation consists in its harmony with an inward experience, which can never perfectly express itself in any outward utterance, can never formulate itself in any creed, can never embody itself in any sacrament. Hence the profundity of the conception that the divisions, whether between the Eastern and Western Churches, or betwen Christian, Jew and Gentile, are due to the channels through which the Spirit has flowed, and not to the breathings of the Spirit itself. Codes, creeds, and sacraments are for a time. Could the Everlasting Gospel, which underlies them all, and is one in them all, be liberated from its bondage in them, it would be recognised as the universal and the everlasting Gospel, that unites and divides not.[59]

CHAPTER IV.

THE CULMINATION.

THE twelfth century is in many ways the most interesting period in mediæval history. It was an age
of remarkably free and varied intellectual activity ;
but as we approach the end of the century, we find
that the logical and speculative impulses which had
given life to the work of Western thinkers were
exhausted for lack of material. Historical and
scientific knowledge scarcely existed ; the logical
interest, and the kindred interest in scientific
methodology, had to feed on themselves, or at
the best had to be turned back on the dogmas of
the Church and analyse them into details of ever-
increasing complexity, or, again, had to be devoted
to the systematic collection and arrangement of pat-
ristic authorities. In the meantime, however, an
epoch-making change was maturing.

I.

We have seen that during the first half of the
twelfth century the remaining logical works of Aristotle gradually found their way into the schools.

This by itself would not have brought about a great change ; but at the end of the century the medical, scientific, and philosophical works of several Arabian thinkers were introduced into France from Spain, where for more than fifty years these writings had been studied and translated. The chief initiative in the labour of translation was due to the enterprise of Archbishop Raymond of Toledo, who organised a company of translators in that city, and the work was carried on there with vast industry under the superintendence of Gerard of Cremona. The material conveyed to France included translations of the principal works of Aristotle — physical, psychological, ethical, and metaphysical — and of the Arabian commentaries on them. Among these were two other works, which in the Arabic manuscripts bore the name of Aristotle, and at first were simply accepted in the West as coming from him. These were the " Treatise on Causation " (*Liber de Causis*), which was really an Arabian compilation of theses from Plotinus ; and the " Theology of Aristotle " (*Theologia Aristotelis*), which was a compilation from Proclus. Both these books were destined to have a powerful influence on Western thought, especially in the period immediately following. Such was " the rich but dangerous gift made by the Mussulman schools to the Christian." To this must be added the Neo-platonically inspired *Fons Vitæ* of the Jewish philosopher and poet, Ibn Gebirol, whom the Westerns cited as " Avicebron," and believed to be an Arabian.[60]

It is, however, a mere delusion to suppose that Western thinkers were ever dependent entirely, for their knowledge of Aristotle, on translations from the Arabic. When the Crusaders took Constantinople in the year 1204, they made the original country of Greek philosophy more accessible than it had been to Western scholars, and manuscripts were eagerly sought for and carried to the West for translation. The result was that by the middle of the thirteenth century the Westerns were in possession of all the works of Aristotle, with the exception of a few fragments which have since been discovered ; and they were prepared to use them, for their minds had been trained in Aristotelian Logic as they had learnt it from the books of Boethius. These translations enabled them to distinguish the genuine Aristotle from the extraneous accompaniments with which he had made his first appearance in Western Europe. Arabian Aristotelianism was conceived in a Neo-platonic sense ; and in its most distinctive forms it implied a doctrine of God which excluded the possibility of creation as an individual act at a particular period of time and the possibility of personal immortality. In truth, both the Jewish and the Arabian philosophies of the period are entirely under the influence of Aristotle and Neo-platonism. Nothing distinctively national appears in them. They are, moreover, largely moulded by the fact that their founders and exponents were not priests but students of medicine and physical science. And when we think of the civilisation in the midst of which these thinkers taught and worked, with its centres at Bagdad and Cordova, we are thinking of something far removed from the life of the Arabians of the desert. " Islam," says Professor E. M. Hume, " was the heir of older civilisations. Within its frontiers the lingering civilisation of Hellenism blossomed better than anywhere else. In Egypt were remains of the civilisation of the Ptolemies. Then there was the rich civilisation of Persia ; and Persia had inherited and acquired much from the distant East. It was especially the Persian influence that affected Islam at this time. . . . It was the Persians who tempered the materialism of Islam with oriental mysticism ; and this influenced literature, art, and life. . . . And now that Arab influence was no longer predominant, conquests were abandoned, and attention was turned to political consolidation and social improvement. Thus was created the civilisation which we call ' Saracenic.' From the Arabs it received its unity of tongue and religion, and its irresistible tendency to expand ; but at bottom it retained all the characteristics of the oriental civilisations from which it was derived." [61] The interest of the Saracens was absorbed in the Logic and Philosophy of Aristotle, who, they believed, had summed up in his writings the substance and meaning of Greek thought ; although in coming to this conclusion they had, as we have seen, intermingled many characteristically Neo-platonic ideas with the Aristotelian doctrine. The " Arabian " philosophy was " Arabian " only in respect of the language in which it was written. It was the continuation of a stream of thought derived from Aristotle, modified by Neo-platonic ideas on one side and by the ideas and mental proclivities of Islam on the other. The Jews played an important part as carriers of learning from place to place ; but the character of their philosophy was not really different from that of the " Arabs."

By far the most influential and dangerous of these thinkers, in the Western view, was Averroes (Ibn Roshd), a native of Cordova, who died in 1198 at the

K

age of seventy-three. The general aim of his thinking was to adjust the relations between philosophy and religion. Freedom of philosophic thought and speculation must be preserved; but there are those, the majority in fact, who are naturally incapable of understanding any rational discussion of philosophical questions. Averroes finds three types of mind among men. These are, in the first place, those who desire demonstrative proof, and endeavour to attain the truth by passing from one necessary truth to another; in the second place, those who are satisfied with reasonings leading to conclusions which are probable; in the third place, those who are fitted only for rhetorical reasonings which appeal to the imagination and the emotions. The Koran is the depository of truth, but it cannot be read in the same way by these three types of mind. There must be these three degrees of interpretation of one and the same truth, corresponding respectively to philosophy, theology, and simple faith. This was the doctrine which, misunderstood and distorted, was destined to give rise to the theory of a " double truth."

The voluminous commentaries which Averroes composed on the works of Aristotle were the culmination of the labours of his predecessors during two centuries; but the Westerns were only vaguely aware of this, and they spoke of him as " The Commentator" *par excellence*—a description which lasted to Dante's time: *Averrois che il gran commento feo*. We are here concerned only with those doctrines of Averroes, based on Aristotle, which came to be of decisive influence on Western thought. We may distinguish these as four in number :—

(i) The world is produced by God, the Absolute

and Infinite Being who is perfect Unity, through an eternal process, realised in a series of emanations. By an eternal process is here meant a process which has no beginning or end in time, because it is beyond the limitations which time implies. The successive emanations form a series of Intelligences, until we come to the world of human secular experience. (ii) This world and the substance of which it is composed are in like manner eternal. The world is composed of Matter and Form. These highly technical terms are derived directly from Aristotle, and we shall meet with them again. Here the distinction may be conveniently illustrated, not from the forms of inanimate objects, but from the forms of life. The constituent tissues of an oak-tree, or a horse, or the chemical elements out of which these tissues are built up, are of the same kind as those of an ash-tree or an ox ; but the oak differs from the ash, or the horse from the ox, in characteristic structure. In any individual thing we can distinguish the " stuff " of which it consists (and which may be identical in kind with the " stuff " of which things of a very different kind consist) and the structural law of formation or arrangement which is peculiar to the special kind of thing under consideration. In our examples the " structural law " is a law of growth, through which the acorn becomes not an ash but an oak. If, then, we think of Matter in abstraction from the Form from which in reality it is inseparable, we have to think of it as something which is entirely potential, involving latent capacities which may be even infinite in their extent or range. This is essentially the Aristotelian doctrine. " Matter," therefore, in this technical meaning of the word, must not be confused

with corporeal existence. The "bodies" which we
perceive in the world are examples of realised Matter
and Form. Moreover, both Matter and Form may
be incorporeal. This is essentially the Aristotelian
doctrine. Now Averroes believed that the function
of the highest Intelligence, under the Absolute Deity,
is eternally to evolve from Matter the Forms which
are involved in it. This continual and eternal emergence of the wealth of latent capacity in Matter is
the immediate cause of the world which we perceive.
(iii) Averroes believed that our merely human intelligence is the lowest of the Intelligences proceeding
from the Absolute Deity. Founding on a difficult
doctrine of Aristotle, he concluded that there is but
one sole unique Intelligence active throughout the
human race, and it is through the activity of this
Intelligence in us that we think, so far as we think
logically and rationally. (iv) From this last conclusion it follows that immortality belongs only to the
Active Intelligence which is common to all mankind.
Personal immortality is impossible. Everything in the
mind of the individual thinker, which is capable of
being eternal, is absorbed into the one Active Intelligence ; everything distinctive of the individual personality is dissipated at death.[62]

We have emphasised these ideas thus, because
throughout the Middle Ages they were considered to
be characteristically "Averroist." Discussed, as they
usually were, in detachment from their place in the
author's own scheme, they were liable to be exaggerated and even distorted. Hence we must distinguish
mediæval "Averroism" from the teaching of Averroes.
Sometimes "Averroism" proved to be thinly disguised materialism.

The wealth of new material, made available for Western thinkers almost within a single generation, would not have produced such a far-reaching and profound upheaval if it had not coincided with the organisation of the Universities and the growth of the "mendicant" Orders, the Dominicans and Franciscans. " In 1100," says Professor Haskins, " the school followed the teacher [as in the days of Abailard] ; by 1200 the teacher followed the school. At the same time these intervening years created a more advanced type of school by the very fact of the revival of learning. At the close of the eleventh century, learning was almost entirely confined to the ' seven liberal arts ' of the traditional curriculum ; the twelfth century filled out the *trivium* and *quadrivium* with the new Logic, the new mathematics, the new astronomy, while it brought into existence the professional ' faculties ' of law, medicine, and theology. Universities had not existed hitherto because there was not enough learning in Western Europe to justify their existence ; they came into being naturally with the expansion of knowledge in this period. The intellectual revolution and the institutional revolution went hand in hand." And as for the Dominicans and Franciscans, it is impossible to understand the history of mediæval thought without paying attention to the new incentives and rivalries caused by the existence of these two militant organisations. The Dominican Order received papal approval in 1216, and was from the first intended to be devoted to study, learning, and teaching. Its members were selected not only for their knowledge of theology, but for their powers of persuasion. Their fields were to be the pulpit and the University lecture-room ; and so in time they came to be known as the Friars Preachers. Very different in their original purpose were the Franciscans. The story of Francis of Assisi, his early experiences of the world and its gaiety, his illness, his ideals and the founding of his Order, his ways of work and life, have a lasting interest and even fascination. But the early enthusiasm began to decline. Worldly interests entered in; and the habit of " mendicancy " led to great abuses. Most significant of all was the change in mental outlook. Among the friars were now some who had studied in the Universities, who entered with ardour into the theological and philosophical discussions of the day, and who did not wish to spend their time tending lepers and begging their bread from door to door. John of Fidanza, who had received from Francis himself the name of " Bonaventura," by which he came to be known, gloried in the learning of the Order. " It is this," he said, " which has made me most of all to love the life of Saint Francis, that it is like the beginning and consummation of the Church, which first began from simple fishermen and then advanced to famous and learned doctors." [63]

II.

The first effects of the immense acquisition of new material are seen in a stream of confused and erratic speculation, the leading tendencies of which are revealed in the materialistic pantheism of Amalric of Bena, who died in 1207, and the kindred doctrine of David of Dinant, who died in about 1215. Amalric (Amauri de Bène) enjoyed great popularity as a teacher of philosophy and theology in the University of Paris. He taught an extreme form of what is now called "immanence." God is immanent in everything; and in this changing world, everything, including man, becomes God. David's pantheism was more definitely materialistic. The professed followers of Amalric became a heretical sect, animated by an antinomian fanaticism which exposed its adherents to fierce persecution after the Lateran Council of 1215.

The result of all this was that along with Averroism the study of all the Aristotelian writings except the purely logical treatises was proscribed by the Church. It is the merit of the Dominicans and Franciscans alike that they used all their influence to capture Aristotle for the Church; and in capturing him "for the Church" they were doing more than they knew. This result was achieved after a long struggle, which may be said to have ended in 1253, with the establishment under papal authority of two Chairs in the University of Paris for study of the Aristotelian philosophy.[64] This was the most conspicuous success of the Friars at this time. The University of Paris was the leading centre of Christian theology in the West; and any doctrine taught from one of these Parisian Chairs was bound to be widely broadcast and to have international echoes if it gave the slightest opportunity for them. Thus the issue of the struggle was that Aristotle, after being suspected and condemned, was placed on the same level with Augustine, and came to be regarded as the forerunner of Christ in matters of Nature, as John the Baptist had been in matters of Grace. From the point of view of orthodox theology, therefore, the problem became quite definite : to combine adherence to Aristotelianism with fundamental criticism of Averroism, and with effective defence of the doctrine of a transcendent creative God and the doctrine of the immortality of the soul.*

The thinkers of the Franciscan Order never set themselves in mere opposition to Aristotelianism ; but while making full use of the tools of analysis provided by the Aristotelian Logic, they advocated an Augustinian or Christianised Platonism as the true philosophical setting for the dogmas of the Church, in preference to the philosophical principles derived from the Metaphysics of Aristotle. Among these Franciscans there was one standing out above all the rest. This was St Bonaventura (John of Fidanza), contemporary and friendly critic of Thomas Aquinas, who organised and defended the principles implied in mysticism, especially as mysticism had been expounded by the "Victorines." And yet to regard Bonaventura as only a "mystic" would be to take an utterly inadequate view of him. The defect of some modern accounts of him is that they imply an attempt to separate his "philosophy" from his "theology" or his "religion." In his experience and teaching these three are entirely inseparable ; we might even say that they are one. In principle he stands over against Aquinas ; they represent two different and contrasted theories of the relation between faith and reason, between Christian theology and philosophy. His whole conception of knowledge differs essentially from the theory of Aristotle and the theory of St Thomas Aquinas. He begins with a doctrine of "illumination" which applies to all knowledge the

* See above, pages 31-32.

literal meaning of the Psalmist's saying, " In Thy
Light shall we see light," and which historically goes
back through Augustine to the famous passage in
Plato's Republic about the parallel between the
" Good " and the " Sun." [65] Just as the perception
of colour requires something more than the presence
of a coloured surface to be seen and an eye to see it,
so the simplest act of knowledge requires something
more than a knowable object and a knowing mind.
There must also be something which answers to the
light of day, an " illumination " of the mind by its
spiritual Sun, the divine Reason or uncreated Word.
Thus knowledge of any kind depends on divine
illumination. What then is the difference between
our human reason and faith, between " natural " and
" supernatural " knowledge ? It should follow logically that this difference must be only one of degree,
not one of kind ; that there is a *continuity* between
them, and that the " supernatural " illumination is
more intense, and therefore covers a wider range,
than the " natural." But such a "difference of
degree " actually becomes a " difference of kind " ;
and Bonaventura employs the language of contrast
in the usual way. Nevertheless his central thought
is this doctrine of a " hierarchy of illuminations " ;
and from this point of view all aspects of his philosophy
must be regarded.[66]

There are a number of details of a more or less
technical character in his doctrines, which follow
from the principles of degrees of illumination, and
with these we are not now concerned ; but there is
much interest in observing the position which in
consequence is given to the " proofs of the existence
of God." For Bonaventura, the argument from

creatures as effects to God as their Cause, is itself
only possible and only valid in virtue of the actual
presence of God to the human mind as the light of
its understanding ; and this of itself involves in all
minds an implicit or *latent* knowledge of God's existence. In like manner Anselm's " ontological argument " is, for Bonaventura, really not an argument
at all, but an interpretation of God's immediate presence in the supreme experiences of the human soul.
Thus the " proofs " represent the apprehension of a
soul in the successive stages of its pilgrimage towards
God, and therefore at different levels of illumination.
Conceptions of this kind, stated in scholastic language
and with special reference to the questions which
loomed largest in the thirteenth century, may seem
remote from the religious outlook of our own time ;
but we see that they are the essential questions when
we ask, What is the real nature of religious experience
and religious knowledge ? For Bonaventura the
experience and the knowledge are inseparable ; religious knowledge is not a mere inference but the
interpretation of an experience. In this way the idea
of God is implicit or latent. His great contemporary,
Thomas Aquinas, cannot admit this. For him the
soul comes into this world endowed, not with any
implicit or latent ideas, but with the all-important
potentiality or capacity of deriving " universals "
from the particulars of sense-experience. On a superficial view we might be tempted to conclude that the
doctrine of " illumination " is a mere metaphor. It
is far from being a mere metaphor. It is part of a
genuine " philosophy of light," deliberately adopted
with full understanding of its meaning. It has a
point of contact with Scripture in the statement that

Light was created before the creation of the sun, moon, and stars, or any luminous body. And in some points it strangely resembles the nineteenth century doctrine of an all-pervading " ether," and the modern doctrine of radiation as a fundamental property of matter. Bonaventura maintains that light has the capacity of spontaneous increase from itself alone. It is not in itself a body, but is something inherent in bodies. All bodies partake in the nature of light, and according to the measure of this participation hold a higher or lower place in the scale of being. Light is the " Form " of a luminous body—that is, the constitutive principle or law on which the luminosity of the body depends. Moreover it is the universal Form (*forma communis*) of all bodies, determining the common structure of matter, as we should say, throughout the universe. We shall meet with this doctrine again in Robert Grosseteste. It was held by more than one of the great Franciscan thinkers.

Every object in the universe speaks to us of God, represents Him after its own manner, and invites us to turn to Him. The whole meaning of life is to be a journey to God (*Iterarium mentis in Deum*), and the world of our senses is the pathway which leads us to Him. The things with which the path is filled are all " signs " or " symbols " which at first appear utterly mysterious to us. But when we study them attentively with our reason illuminated by the light of faith, we read through the multitudinous variety of characters the one Word—God. To do this demands a constant effort of our will and confidence in divine Grace—a constant trust in God and our better selves. We thus are able, through created things, to rise to

God. We must observe that this is not a doctrine of the " divine immanence " in any modern meaning of that vague word. It is not a doctrine that created things reproduce or imitate God. Bonaventura is convinced that God has nothing in common with created things, and that the finite cannot reproduce or imitate the Infinite. The resemblance or " analogy " which exists between God and His creatures is one of *expression*. They are related to God as signs are to the meaning which they express. They are a kind of language ; and the whole universe is only a book in which the Divine Nature may everywhere be read (*creatura mundi est quasi liber in quo legitur Trinitas fabricatrix*). We may express another side of the truth by the use of another metaphor. Even when we perceive in the world its orderly movements, its harmonious structure, its beauty and sublimity, even when we discern the unity of its structure, the truth which it expresses, the good which it subserves, we are, as it were, turning our back to the Divine Light and finding in created things only its reflection—or its " shadow " (*umbra*) as he sometimes calls it. But when we seek God within, we are turning towards Him. We find within no mere " vestige," no " shadow," no " reflection," but the very image of God. This is explained, so far as explanation is conceivable, by the doctrine of degrees of illumination. Beyond the experience of the outer world, beyond the apprehension of the inner " image of God," there is the supreme intuition of the soul in its union with God ; and here Bonaventura falls back on an abundance of rich metaphors, recalling those of Bernard and the Victorines. He develops the suggestive simile of the *scintilla*, the small spark of pure divine light within the soul, which in the supreme intuition becomes a flame. The imagery of the *scintilla* attracted mystical thinkers throughout the Middle Ages. It is the natural will towards Good, implanted in us all, though weakened by sin. It cannot be extinguished. It was created with the soul, moving the will away from sin and towards virtue, and always seeking the Source from Whom it came. It is a power or potentiality in the soul in which God works directly and unceasingly.

Bonaventura has no hesitation in claiming the right to employ a fourfold interpretation of Scripture, which avoided many of the difficulties resulting from the assumption that the historic sense, of parts of the Old Testament for instance, is the only sense. In this he follows Augustine. The historic sense is not the only one. All Scripture has its " allegoric " sense, disclosing the hidden contents of Faith ; its " tropic " sense, disclosing rules and warnings for the guidance of life, implied in its narratives or directly stated ; and, above all, its " mystic " sense, disclosing, as it were here and there, or little by little, the way to the supreme intuition of God. In his belief, the Bible is above all else God's Book of Redemption ; and therefore everything which concerns the constitution of the world must be read out of God's Book of Creation—that is, from Nature.

His feeling for the Person of Christ is different— evidently different, yet with a difference which is not easy to define—from the feeling natural to a modern evangelical Christian. Bonaventura finds that the supreme experience is attainable only through the grace which has appeared in Christ ; but from this he concludes that he must take Christ up entirely into himself and become completely one with Him, and nothing facilitates this so much as absorption in the history of Jesus, especially in the account of His sufferings. In some passages he enters into this so minutely as to give the modern reader an impression of tragic trifling. His little book, entitled ' Meditations on the Life of Christ ' (*Meditationes vitæ Christi*), written for a Sister of the Order, is on another level. Here the blanks which the Bible leaves in the life of Christ are filled with products of poetic fancy. He begins with portraying the conflict between the Justice and the Mercy of God before the Incarnation, as Saint Bernard had dramatised it ; and he ends with lessons on the active and the contemplative life, derived from the picture of Martha and Mary. It is impossible, however, to overlook the fact that the love of Bonaventura for Mary the Virgin is uttered in all his works with scarcely less warmth than his love for Christ, and that, next to Mary, the founder of his Order receives from him the highest honour. Both of them are always quoted as examples of the closest union with God.

III.

We have seen that it is possible to state the fundamental and essential principles of Bonaventura's philosophy of religion without bringing forward any distinctive principles of Aristotelianism. In the detailed exposition and defence of his positions he does employ Aristotelian principles ; but these are in a subordinate place, and do not affect the spirit of the whole. This is true of all the leading Fran-

ciscan thinkers. In the case of the two great Dominicans, whose work we are now approaching, it is different. Here we have a Christianised Aristotelianism.
The influence of Platonism can be discerned ; indeed
it is vital in their doctrine of God's relation to the
world. None the less, " Christianised Aristotelianism "
is a true description of these systems.

We must emphasise the fact that the whole controversy about " Nominalism " and " Realism " had
now " died a natural death." There was substantial
unanimity upon this question in the " moderate
Realism " which was implied in the position of
Abailard, and was independently defended by John
of Salisbury ; * and the same conclusion was supported by the Arabians. The " universal " arises
through comparison in thought ; it is the product
of our thought. But there are actual resemblances
among the objects of our experience, and among these
we may distinguish the likenesses which are " accidental " and those which are " essential " ; and it is
on the latter that the true " universal " is founded.
These true " universals " were in the mind of God
before creation ; in this sense they were " before
things " (ante res).

The acquisition and study of the works of Aristotle
turned the minds of the thirteenth century thinkers
and their successors in new directions. It compelled
them to define very precisely the relation between
theological and scientific knowledge, and between
those theological truths which are known only by
divine revelation and those which can be discovered
by the natural light of human reason. It also provided them with certain fundamental principles, of

* See above, page 105.

a philosophical character, which acted as an intellectual stimulus, setting their thought free to study and interpret human and physical nature. All this is illustrated pre-eminently in the work of the two great Dominicans of whom we have now to speak.

Albertus Magnus was born in Swabia in 1193, and lived to the great age of eighty-seven, dying at Cologne in 1280. The limits of his life thus include that of his still greater pupil, Thomas Aquinas, who was born in 1227 and died while still comparatively young in 1274. Albert had a warm personal affection for his distinguished scholar, whose genius he discovered at an early period of their intercourse. When he went to Paris in 1245 to lecture and take his doctor's degree, his pupil accompanied him ; and, on their return to Cologne, Aquinas taught along with his master at the great Dominican school there. At a later date, when Aquinas proceeded to Paris to lecture independently, we find him in occupation of the Dominican chair at the same time that Bonaventura held the Franciscan professorship ; and they received the degree of doctor in the same year, 1257. Though they were, in a manner, rivals, and though they differed fundamentally over the philosophical theory of knowledge, they were always united in personal friendship and charity.

Albert and Thomas are at one in labouring earnestly to show that reason and revelation are neither identical nor mutually opposed, but harmonious, in the sense that certain truths, while not contrary to reason, are yet beyond reason. Our unaided reason can discover and establish by argument a great body of truth, including natural religion and ethics, because the methods by which these truths are established depend on principles which the mind carries within itself. But the truths distinctive of faith are revealed to, not discovered by, the human mind. It is possible for our natural reason to refute arguments brought forward against them, and even to produce some considerations in favour of their acceptance ; but we cannot discover them of ourselves. They are divinely revealed, and they have the authority of divine revelation behind them. We shall see, very shortly, the precise way in which this doctrine is worked out by St Thomas.

We observed that there were certain fundamental principles of the Aristotelian philosophy which acted as a powerful intellectual stimulus at this period. The most important of these principles was the distinction of " Matter " and " Form," to which we have referred when speaking of Averroes.* Aristotle extends this distinction to everything in which we can distinguish a comparatively indefinite " raw material," and a law or type of order and arrangement, giving it definiteness and organisation. Thus, consider the " formed " character of a man in adult life. We may look upon this character as produced out of the " raw material " of instincts and other innate and acquired dispositions which have received a specific development along definite lines, according to the kind of environment and experience to which the mind has been subjected during the " formative " period of its growth. In the Aristotelian sense, the innate and acquired dispositions are the " Matter " of which character is made ; and—Aristotle would have said—the practical problem of education is to devise a system of training which shall impress upon this

* See above, page 147.

L

" Matter " the " Form " required if the grown man is to be a good citizen of a good State. And as regards the general question, we must add that Aristotle regarded " pure Matter," that is, " Matter " entirely devoid of any definite structure, as an abstraction or mere creation of our thought. In his view, " Matter " entirely devoid of " Form " does not exist.

Now when we concentrate attention on the process of natural change, or growth, or manufacture, as the case may be, by which the " raw material " becomes arranged and organised, then the contrast of " Matter " and " Form " becomes the contrast of " Potentiality " and " Actuality." The following has been given as an illustration, and it is an effective one. " Consider the embryos of two animals, or the seeds of two plants. Even a botanist or a physiologist may be unable to pronounce with certainty on the species to which the germ submitted to him belongs. Even at a later stage, the embryo of one animal may be indistinguishable from that of another. Yet it is certain that one of the two originally indistinguishable germs will grow (for example) into an oak and the other into an elm, or one of the two originally indistinguishable embryos into a chimpanzee and the other into a man. However indistinguishable, they may therefore be said to have different latent tendencies or possibilities of development within them. Hence we may say of a given seed, ' though this is not yet actually an oak, it is potentially an oak,' meaning *not merely that, if uninterfered with, it will in time be an oak, but also that by no interference can it be made to grow into an elm or a beech.* So we may look upon all processes of production or development as processes by which what at first possessed only the tendency to grow along certain lines or has become actually endowed with the characters to which it possessed the tendency." Hence the distinction of " Matter " and " Form " may also be expressed by saying that the " Form " is the " Actuality " of which the undeveloped " Matter " is the " Potentiality." Aristotle usually employed the term *energeia* (ἐνέργεια) for the actual manifestation of the " Form." It is evident that the English word " energy " is no adequate rendering of this term. The mediæval thinkers rendered it by *actus purus* or simply *actus*. We must always remember that Aristotle was a scientifically trained physician and a biologist ; and many of his philosophical conceptions were suggested by thinking about the biological processes of reproduction and growth. The process, proceeding in the " Matter " and culminating in the appearance of the " Form," Aristotle always called by a term (*kinesis*, κίνησις) of which the traditional and established English rendering is " motion," and for which the corresponding Latin word was current in the Middle Ages. The word " motion " is thus used in mediæval thought in a much wider sense than that of change of place or motion from point to point in space. It covers all the processes by which things came to be what they are or cease to be what they have been. Motion in space is only one important variety of it.

All this suggests something like an approach to the modern doctrine of an age-long natural evolution of living forms, if not also of inorganic matter. But nothing of the kind was recognised by Aristotle. In every case, development from the unformed " Potentiality " to the formed " Actuality " has a last stage. The oak does not grow into something else. It can only reproduce its kind. The world of life is the perpetual reproduction of unchanging species. There is no natural evolution of creatures of one species from those of a different kind. And in like manner many different kinds of inorganic matter proceed on their round of change through combination and dissolution of unchanging elements. In this sense, "motion" is eternal. Professor A. E. Taylor, of Edinburgh, has made a striking comment on the mediæval use of this Aristotelian doctrine : " Even the great Christian theologians who built upon Aristotle could not absolutely break with him on this point. St Thomas, though obliged to admit that the world was actually created a few thousand years before his own time, maintains that this can only be known to be true from Revelation ; philosophically it is equally tenable that the world should have been ' created from all eternity.' And it is the general doctrine of scholasticism that the expression ' creation ' only denotes the absolute dependence of the world on God for its being. When we say ' God created the world out of nothing,' we mean that he did not make it out of pre-existing matter, and that it depends for its being on Him only ; the expression is purely negative in its import." [67]

What, then, is the source of the process by which the " Forms " latent in matter are brought into manifestation ? What is wanted is the presence of an adequate " efficient cause " or source of motion. One source is sufficient ; to assume several is a gratuitous, groundless, and confusing assumption. We must assume One Source ever present throughout the never-ending process of the world. This is the Aristotelian God. Aristotle finds no evidence that

God actually enters into the world-process; if He did, He would be both "Matter" and "Form," in other words, a product of development,—a "growing God." God is ever present to it, but, as it were, He is outside it. How then does God initiate and maintain the world-process? Aristotle can answer this question only by a metaphor,—the metaphor of "desire." He is severe on the poetic metaphors used by Plato; but his own theism culminates in the doctrine that God moves the world by being the object of the world's desire. The Divine Life is that of an Unmoved Mover, a life of eternal self-contemplation but not one of mere inaction or stagnancy. It is an "activity which is not one of motion" (ἐνεργεία ἀκινησίας). By this is meant that it excludes, not all change, but just that kind of change which involves gain or loss, excess or defect, increase or decrease of being. Only in one direction does Aristotle recognise a real communion with God, and in this direction he joins hands with the mystics. When we give ourselves up to the pure activity of scientific thought or contemplation, we enter for a while into the Divine Life and share the happiness of God. From this doctrine the mediæval thinkers worked out their theory of the contrast between the "contemplative" and the "active" life, though their view of the former, intimately bound up with the ideals of monasticism, was foreign to the spirit of Aristotle.

We have said that Aristotle was a scientifically trained physician. He was also a great naturalist, and his influence not only brought about a final break with the Augustinian tradition that our bodily senses are not real sources of knowledge; it also helped the thinkers of the thirteenth century to re-discover Nature as an independent object of study on her own account. Nature was, so to speak, turned over to man as a field for free and independent study.

It is in the sphere of natural history that Aristotle proves his capacity for minute and accurate observation. But in the departments of science which we now call Physics and Astronomy, his work suffered greatly from two causes. He had only a slight knowledge of Mathematics, and he had an invincible prejudice against mechanical explanations of natural events. Moreover, his scientific doctrines are not typical of Greek science in general, for he deliberately rejected views of his contemporaries and predecessors some of which look like " faint anticipations " of modern knowledge. He denied the mobility of the earth, which was a serious hypothesis in current Greek science ; he treated the "four elements," "Earth, Air, Fire, Water," as incapable of further analysis, so that the whole material universe was to be regarded as composed of solid, gaseous, and liquid matter, and heat ; and, in opposition to previous physicians and naturalists and in defiance of what might have been a matter of plain observation, he insisted that the heart, not the brain, is the centre of the nervous system.

His ascendency in astronomy is one of the misfortunes of the human race. The conviction that the earth is at rest in the centre of the universe was of course not peculiar to Aristotle. Although questioned by some Greek mathematicians, it appeared to be warranted by sense-perception ; and, three centuries afterwards, the Alexandrian mathematicians regarded any other supposition as absurd. The

alternation of day and night was accounted for by
assuming a revolution of the whole universe round
an axis passing through the centre of the earth. The
universe was thus conceived as bounded by a spherical
surface, on the concave side of which were the fixed
stars. The stars, therefore, are all at the same
distance from us. This sphere, under the immediate
influence of God, revolves uniformly on its axis once
every twenty-four hours. All that was known of the
solar system was that it consisted of seven " planets "
all revolving at a uniform rate round the earth. These
were, the Moon, Mercury, Venus, the Sun, Mars,
Jupiter, Saturn. But their movements were observed to be irregular; and the Greek mathematicians worked out a theory that the apparent irregularities in the movement of each " planet " were the
result of several combined circular motions. It was
customary to speak of these motions as due to the
rotation of celestial " spheres "; but the scientific
meaning of the theory was essentially mathematical.
Now Aristotle, in what has been called " one of the
most retrograde steps ever taken in the history of
science," " converted the mathematical hypothesis
into a physical fact." In other words, he took up
the theory in such a way as to make the material
character of the spheres the essential feature of it,
so that the spheres became real bodies. The outermost one, containing the fixed stars, and moving
under the direct influence of God, communicated
motion to the " Matter " of each of the lesser spheres
through its " Form." This conception was inherited
by the mediæval thinkers directly from Aristotle,
and also through the famous Alexandrian astronomer
Ptolemy, who had before him more accurate know-

ledge of the apparently irregular movements of the
" planets," and had worked out an extremely complicated mathematical theory to account for them.
But the mediæval thinkers, under the fatal influence
of the Aristotelian astronomy, concentrated their
interest on the physical aspects of the theory; and,
fascinated as they were by the possibilities of the
doctrine of " Matter " and " Form," they came to
the conclusion that the " Forms," which were the
means of communicating motion from one celestial
sphere to another, were not mathematical laws but
angelic intelligences, and the spheres a succession of
" heavens." So it was natural for Dante, in his Ode
to the angels controlling the movement of Venus—
the third in order from the earth—to say: *Voi ch'
intendendo il terzo ciel movete.* Indeed, it is a theory
which gave itself more readily to poetry than to
theology; and, linked with belief in the " music of
the spheres "—music too vast and deep and high for
embodied souls to hear—it has served that purpose
well.

> Look how the floor of heaven
> Is thick inlaid with patines of bright gold:
> There's not the smallest orb which thou behold'st
> But in his motion like an angel sings,
> Still quiring to the young-eyed cherubim.
> Such harmony is in immortal souls ;
> But whilst this muddy vesture of decay
> Doth grossly close it in, we cannot hear it.

When we spoke of Aristotle " joining hands with
the mystics," in his doctrine of the highest life as one
of perennial truth-seeking and truth-seeing, we
touched upon his famous and debated doctrine of the
" active Reason." In the Aristotelian psychology,

the successive grades of mental life are carefully distinguished, up to and including that of "passive Reason," so called because it has no innate structure of its own, not because it "does nothing." Its function is no more and no less than to discern, in the objects of our bodily senses, the "Forms" which are the real natures of those objects. But over and above all this, there is the "active Reason" which is not dependent upon the vital functions of the body. It is creative and "immortal." Here Aristotle bequeathed a difficult problem to his successors. We have seen what Averroes made of the doctrine. The Christian thinkers fell back on the conclusion that the "active Reason" is not God, nor is it the same in all men ; it is the highest and most rational activity of the individual soul.

The full influence of the scientific works of Aristotle —the methods and ideals animating them as well as the detailed results—was felt by Albert the Great. It has been customary to speak of Luther and Calvin as liberators of human thought, and to look upon Albert as the chief of mediæval obscurantists. This would be almost amusing if it were not a serious symptom of a radical misapprehension which has vitiated the traditional estimate of the Middle Ages. The very fact that Albert made so clear a distinction between theology on the one hand, and philosophy and science on the other, simply means that he was setting thought free upon Nature and the natural aspects of human experience at large. He was a good naturalist and a good observer, but not a good theorist. In matters of theory he was afraid to go beyond Aristotle. His encyclopædic mind worked over every branch of philosophy and science, and of theology ;

in the field of theology he claimed for reason all its rights in reference to those religious truths which the human mind can discover of itself, and in reference to those dogmas which are held on the authority of revelation, he made it his business to show that they were not contrary to reason.[68]

His importance in the history of Christian thought arises from the fact that he was the first of the mediæval thinkers to reproduce the whole philosophy of Aristotle in systematic order, with constant reference to the Arabian and Jewish commentators, and with many independent discussions of his own. On this account he was called *Doctor Universalis*. His works, in the edition published under the auspices of Pope Leo XIII., occupy thirty-eight quarto volumes. But it is evident that the material was still too new and too vast to be mastered even by a mind like that of Albert. The fabric is not well joined together in all its parts ; the theologian and the philosopher speak sometimes with different voices. In the work of St Thomas this is no longer so. His system is that of his master, rounded to a greater completeness and elaborated in parts by an intellect not more comprehensive and laborious, but finer and more penetrating.

There is, however, an important difference between the two men. St Thomas, like his master, was convinced that natural science has a rightful place and utility of its own ; but, unlike his master, he was not really interested in such inquiries. Historically, the importance of this can scarcely be exaggerated. The genius of St Thomas diverted the interests of mediæval thinkers from natural science to philosophical theology. Roger Bacon, despite the perversities of his embittered imagination, struggled hard and long to recover for science the ground which was being lost. None the less, so far as philosophy and theology are concerned, the systems of Albert and Thomas need not be separated.

IV.

In the Church of Santa Catharina at Pisa there is a picture, painted in 1345, which illustrates well the position occupied by St Thomas in the minds of mediæval churchmen. He is sitting with four books on his knees, representing the four parts of the *Summa contra Gentiles*. In his hands he holds the open Bible, displaying, in the Vulgate version, the words " For my mouth shall speak truth, and wickedness is an abomination to my lips " (Proverbs viii. 7). Above sits the enthroned Christ, from whom rays of light descend directly on the saint's head. From Christ rays proceed also to each of the six Biblical teachers, on the left, Moses, St John, and St Mark, and on the right, St Paul, St Matthew, and St Luke, and from each of these a ray proceeds directly to the head of St Thomas. To the right stands Plato holding open a book probably representing the *Timæus ;* and to the right, Aristotle, holding open his *Ethics.* From these also rays of light pass to the saint's head. From the books of St Thomas rays pass to illuminate the faithful, habited as Dominicans, who are placed right and left below. Between the groups of the faithful lies the prostrate Averroes, and by his side is flung the great *Commentary*, transfixed by a ray, not of illumination but of refutation, from the Thomistic works.[69]

From the Aristotelian presuppositions of St Thomas there follows a clear distinction between philosophy and theology. This distinction is illustrated in the scope and method of his greatest works, the *Summa de veritate catholicæ fidei contra Gentiles*, which was probably finished in 1265, and the *Summa Theologica*, which was begun in that year and left unfinished at his death. The *Summa contra Gentiles* is essentially and fundamentally an appeal to Reason. It may be accurately described as a treatise which in scope and method is philosophical and not theological. Certain doctrines of theology are discussed in it,—doctrines which are common to Christian, Jew, and Moslem, and which claim to have been demonstrated by ancient philosophers without any special divine Revelation. These are accordingly discussed as demonstrable propositions in philosophy ; and when Scripture is quoted, it is merely to show that the truths demonstrable by philosophy are part of what the Church teaches on the authority of Revelation. In the fourth and final division of the book, we are introduced to theological propositions incapable of philosophical demonstration and known only on the authority of a special divine Revelation ; but the aim of the philosophical arguments employed is merely the negative one of showing that these propositions do not contradict any principles of rational philosophy, and that the " rationalistic " objections brought against them by the unbeliever are therefore invalid. Such are, the doctrine of the Trinity ; the doctrine of the Creation of the world " out of Nothing " at the beginning of time ; the doctrine of the Incarnation ; and the immediate inferences which follow from these. There is no attempt to provide the unbeliever with *reasons* for accepting these dogmas; if he accepts them, it must be by an act of *faith* in the revealing Authority. The method throughout is demonstration from first principles and axioms claiming to be self-evident.

The better known, though not more important, *Summa Theologica* is a book for the theologian and not for the philosopher. It makes frequent appeal to philosophical arguments and authorities; but its subject is God as revealed to us authoritatively in the Scriptures of which the Church is the custodian and interpreter. Its method is the appeal to authority; the authority, in the first place, of Scripture which contains the text of Revelation, in the second place, of the Church as authorised interpreter, and in the third, where the Church has not spoken officially, of interpretations given by the Fathers and Doctors of the faith. This view of the matter not only enabled St Thomas to draw the line between reason and what it can demonstrate and faith and what it accepts simply on authority, but it also enabled him to mark out the field of what was afterwards called " Natural Theology." The doctrines which make up Natural Theology are those which claim to be demonstrable by philosophical argument. These same doctrines fall within the purview of the theologian; but, so far as he confines himself to the theological point of view, he treats them simply as acceptable by faith. The importance of Natural Theology, in the history of Roman Catholic doctrine, is indicated in the following statement, which appears among the doctrinal decrees of the Vatican Council of 1870 : *Sancta Mater Ecclesia tenet et docet Deum . . . naturali humanæ rationis lumine e rebus creatis certo cognosci*

---

posse: the existence and attributes of God may be known with certainty, by the unaided reason of man, from the works which He has created. This is essentially the position taken by St Thomas. And as it is held that there is a body of demonstrable theological truth constituting Natural Theology; in like manner it is held that there is a body of demonstrable moral truth constituting Natural Ethics.

This view of Natural Theology and Natural Ethics was certainly connected, in the mind of St Thomas, with his conviction (which the mediæval thinkers in general firmly held) of the reality of Nature as independent of the mind which apprehends it. To him, and to the mediæval thinkers generally, this was an axiomatic truth. The world around me is " the object of my knowledge "; I think about it and know many things about it, and in this way my mind is directly related to it; but the world is independent of my thinking in the sense of being—

" Actual ere its own beginning, operative through its course,
Unaffected by its end."

They were strong " realists," if we use this term not in special reference to the question of universals but as it is used in recent philosophy; in other words, they assume as a primary datum of our rational nature that there is an immediate apprehension of the world as beyond and independent of the mind which knows it. The distinction between understanding (or intellect) and sense, as two different kinds of knowing, is always insisted upon; but in each case the mind is directly related to the objectively independent world. St Thomas and others sometimes speak as if they held a doctrine of what in recent times has been called "representative perception." This doctrine, in principle, means that the mind does not know or apprehend the real world directly but only by means of some mental process which *represents* it. St Thomas speaks as if the interaction of the mind and the real object produced in the mind a kind of copy of the object, which is universalised by the intellect and becomes a permanent mental possession.[70] We find, however, that he is prepared to reconcile this view with the immediate objectivity of perception and conception. "In the process of understanding," he says, "the intellectual impression received in the . . . intellect is that *whereby* (*quo*) we understand ; just as the impression of colour received through the eye is not that *which* (*quod*) is seen but that *whereby* (*quo*) we see. On the other hand, that *which* (*quod*) is understood is the nature of things existing outside the mind ; as also it is things existing outside the mind that are the objects of visual perception." [71] In brief : our perceptions and our ideas are not the objects of our knowledge but the instruments or means by which we know ; or rather, they are themselves the knowledge.

To infer from all this that St Thomas was hostile or indifferent to religious "mysticism" would be a serious error of interpretation. There is no evidence in his writings that he was interested in "mystical phenomena," if by this term we mean states of trance or ecstasy with abnormal experiences of sight or hearing. He has no interest in mental conditions which are, to say the least of it, very unusual, and which modern science would probably call "pathological." The standard Roman Catholic books have given descriptions of these supposed supernatural favours, with instructions how to distinguish them from diabolical imitations. But the mysticism in which St Thomas is supremely interested is the endeavour of the human mind to enjoy the blessedness of actual communion with the Highest.[72] The principle of his supernaturalism may be expressed in the sublime saying which found its way into the "Shorter Catechism" of the Presbyterian Church: "The chief end of man is to glorify God *and enjoy Him for ever.*" But though God is the chief End of man, He is a transcendent End (*finis superexcedens*). Man is fitted by his original nature to attain to God (*ordinatur ad deum*) as the End of his being, but an End which is beyond the comprehension of his purely rational nature, and which therefore must be made known (*praecognitum*) to men, in order that their thought and action may be directed to that End. The poetic expression of this ideal is given once for all in the *Paradiso* of Dante. In the closing lines he tells us, with entire simplicity, how it was granted to him, at the supreme point of his journey, to realise "what eye hath not seen, nor ear heard, what hath not entered into the heart of man." He realised all things and all their relations to one another, not in fragmentary incompleteness but as one perfect whole. And in thus realising, as one, the whole essential being of the universe, there was only the simple limpid flame of the divine all-embracing Love, "the Love that moves the sun and all the stars."[73] The constancy of the heavens in their courses was to him the sign and symbol of the everlasting Order which is one with the everlasting Love.

V.

The reasoning by which St Thomas endeavours to provide a rational proof of the existence of God starts from the reality of Nature,—the existence of the world, with known and knowable qualities, as a fact to be explained. It is an inference from effect to cause. It is based upon Aristotle; and it is an attempt to combine the Theism of Aristotle with the Theism of early Christianity. St Thomas had no access to Plato's last work; otherwise he would have found in the tenth Book of *The Laws* an exposition of Natural Theology in which the central thought, employed by Aristotle and developed in a Christian setting by Thomas himself, was used in a way more akin to the presuppositions of Christianity. This central thought is thus stated by Plato. " When we have one thing making a change in a second, the second in turn in a third, and so on,—will there ever, in such a series, be a first source of change ? Why, how can what is set moving by something other than itself ever be the first of the causes of change ? . . . But when *something which has set itself moving* alters a second thing, this second thing a third, and the motion is thus passed on in order to thousands and tens of thousands of things, will there be any starting-point for the whole movement of all, other than a change in the movement which initiated itself ? . . . Let us put the point over again in this way, once more answering our own questions. Suppose all things were to come together and stand still, . . . which of the movements we have specified must be the first to arise in things ? Why, of course, that which can

M

move itself; there can be no possible previous origination of change by anything else, since, by hypothesis, change was not previously existent in the system. Consequently, as the source of all motions whatsoever, the first to occur among bodies at rest and the first in rank among moving bodies, the motion which initiates itself we shall pronounce to be necessarily the earliest and mightiest of all changes, while that which is altered by something else and sets something else moving is secondary." [74]

Plato finds that all motion is either imparted or communicated motion, or self-originated motion; and by appeal to experience, he finds that Soul is the only kind of being capable of self-originated motion. The "motions of Soul" are memories, desires and purposes, emotions, acts of will. Its life is—to use a modern metaphor—a *growth from within*. Looking out again on the world, Plato finds that the all-pervading changes in the universe are orderly and regular; partial disorder is everywhere over-ruled. He therefore concludes that the supreme Soul, the Source of all cosmic changes, is "the best Soul." The contrast with Aristotle has been effectively stated in this way. "Aristotle insists on getting behind such a Source of motion to a still more ulti-mate *unmoving* Mover. The activity of Aristotle's God is strictly immanent within himself; it is an activity of unbroken self-contemplation; *outgoing* activity is essential to the God of Plato. He is then, as Aristotle's God is not, a *Providence*," capable of Purpose and Design. Nevertheless, St Thomas starts from the Aristotelian conception, not the Platonic. [75]

St Thomas follows Aristotle,—and, through Aris-

totle, follows Plato,—in using the word " motion "
in the widest sense, so as to include under it *change* of
every kind. The meaning of the word is by no means
limited to change *of place* or motion *in space*. It
includes every kind of " becoming," every kind of
origination and passing away, every kind of development, every kind of transition from one state to another ; and it includes every kind of change in mental
life,—the passage from premisses to conclusion in an
act of reasoning and the passage from motive to deed
in an act of will. The argument rests upon what
logicians afterwards called " the Principle of Sufficient
Reason " ("Whatever exists must have a sufficient
reason why it should be as it is and not otherwise "),
and it may be concisely stated as follows : " We find,
throughout all our experience, that wherever motion
or change takes place, we can distinguish between
what is moved or changed and that which moves it
or changes it ; that which is moved or changed is one
thing, and that which brings about the movement or
change is another thing. Now it is impossible that
this chain of things moved and things which move
them can go on to infinity. Everything which is
moved or suffers change is in a sense an instrument of
some originating source of motion [if St Thomas had
known of the possibility of the steam-engine, he would
probably have taken as an illustration a series of
interlocking wheels, in such an engine, all moved by
the source of power,—the steam]. And if there is no
originating source of motion, then every one of the
series of movements is nothing but an instrument or
means to further movements. Now if the series,
every term of which is at once moved and moving,
goes on to infinity, there is no absolute Source of

motion, and every term of the endless series of the moving and the moved is nothing but an instrument or means. Yet even an unlearned person can understand the absurdity of the assumption that every changing thing is nothing but an instrument or means without any originating cause to change it ; as well might he ascribe the construction of a chest or a bed to the saw and the axe without any craftsman's hand to use them. There must then be one absolute and supreme originating Source of motion and change ; and this we call God." [76]

The metaphysical attributes of God—immutability, eternity, omnipresence, omnipotence—are expounded by St Thomas with much acute reasoning ; but for our present purpose it is more important to understand his exposition of the moral attributes. He dwells on the purposes which not only inanimate objects but also living creatures fulfil, although the ends thus attained are utterly beyond their knowledge ; and he agrees that the attainment of such ends is evidence of the action of a supreme rational Will. This is the "argument from Design," which requires to be re-stated but not rejected in the light of the modern doctrine of Evolution. He then passes to place great emphasis on the "hierarchy" of degrees of Perfection which we find in our experience. There are degrees of goodness, of truth, of beauty, and other such perfections. Now these degrees, of "more" or "less," imply a standard of comparison ; and the standard of comparison, being superior to the ever-varying degrees of perfection which are tested by it, is an absolute standard, and implies the existence of an absolutely perfect Being in whom it is realised : "All of the many kinds of perfection, wherever in the world they are found, must be in absolute fulness in the nature of God as their Source. For whatever moves another being to some kind of perfection, must have in itself the quality which it moves the other to attain ; just as the teacher must first have in himself as a mental possession the doctrine which he imparts to others. And since God is the Source of every kind of movement, and since He imparts to every being the kind of perfection corresponding to its nature, all these perfections must pre-exist in absolute fulness in the nature of God." [77] This implies that the manifold evils in the world are failures of perfection, not independent realities existing on their own account ; " when we speak of ' a good ' or ' an evil ' we have in view something which has failed in some degree of perfection which it ought to have attained ; a *man* who cannot see is in that respect in an evil condition, but not a *tree*, since vision is not one of its possible qualities."

The culmination of this doctrine of God is reached in the proposition that the supreme End of all things is the divine Goodness (*quod ultimus finis omnium est divina bonitas*). This follows from the assumption that the Goodness of God is nothing else than His essential Nature, and His essential Nature is nothing else than His Goodness. And God is the Source of all change. His rational creative Will has brought forth a world in which the nature of everything is to come to pass or come to be, as we see most clearly in the case of living beings ; and this realisation or fulfilment of the nature of the thing is its " chief end." We see also that " like produces like " ; that which is produced is like in nature to that which produces it ; man begets man. The resemblance need not be complete ; indeed in the order of Nature it is very often far from complete ; but the principle holds. This principle St Thomas takes as a clue to understanding the purpose of creation as a whole. Its purpose is to express the Nature of that which has produced it,—the originating Source of its existence. In other words, the supreme End of all things is the Nature of God, which is His Goodness ; but in the case of every finite thing within the world, its " end " is the attainment of its nature *through a process of real change*.[78]

It is impossible for our minds to penetrate into the Nature of God if that means seeing His Life as it is for Himself ; we are finite and He is infinite. But there is necessarily a real relation, and therefore a certain resemblance, between cause and effect. We may, or rather we must, think of the character of God after the analogies which hold between God and the things which He has created. The Cause is infinite and the effects are finite. It is impossible for the effects to be or to exist in the Cause as they are, or as they come to be, in finite things ; but there is a real though partial or imperfect analogy between the two extremes. We are justified in attributing to God in an infinite form all the perfections which we can trace in created things, and which, passing thus to infinity, constitute one perfect Whole.

VI.

The idea of *Analogy* is vital in the Thomist system. An " analogy " is usually defined in Logic as a resemblance between two things, such as to justify us in inferring of the one what we know of the other. Thus, if it were known that the conditions which are necessary to make life possible on the earth exist also on the planet Mars, then we should be justified in inferring that some forms of life exist on that planet. But the resemblances must be " important " or essential to the question at issue ; otherwise, the inference is worthless. The planet Mars does resemble the earth in several ways ; but we have no knowledge that it resembles the earth in the conditions necessary for the possibility of life. By " life " we mean the existence of organisms which depend upon the possession of a nitrogenous compound, protoplasm, for the chemical changes by which the phenomena of living are exhibited, and upon the presence in the atmosphere of the element oxygen, with which their nitrogenous constituents combine. This requires also a temperature free from extremes of heat and cold much greater than those occurring on the earth. It is evident that an " argument from analogy " requires great care in its application even to objects of our natural experience ; how much more, then, in its application to the contrast of the finite and the Infinite ?

Let us take an illustrative passage from a once famous exponent of nineteenth-century agnosticism. " It seems strange," he says, " that men should suppose the highest worship to lie in assimilating the object of their worship to themselves. Not in asserting a transcendent difference, but in asserting a transcendent likeness, consists the element of their creed which they think essential. It is true that a bodily form and substance, similar to that of man, has long ceased among cultivated races to be a literally conceived attribute of the Ultimate Cause ; the grosser human desires have also been rejected as unfit elements of the conception ; and there is some hesitation in ascribing even the higher human feelings, save in greatly idealised forms : yet it is still thought not only proper, but imperative, to ascribe the most abstract qualities of our nature. To think of the Creative Power as in all respects anthropomorphous is now considered impious by men who yet hold themselves to think of the Creative Power as in some respects anthropomorphous ; and who do not see that the one proceeding is but an evanescent form of the other. It is, then, our highest wisdom and our highest duty to regard that through which all things exist as The Unknowable." If it had been possible for St Thomas to have a passage like this before him, he would at once have recognised the doctrine. In principle it is the ancient doctrine of the *via negativa* in theology,—the doctrine which seeks to reach the idea of the Infinite by dropping one by one all the attributes of the finite, until there is nothing left,— but with its negative implications emphasised instead of its positive implications. He would have detected in it an important truth and a serious error.

St Thomas repeatedly points out that no conceivable affirmation can be made *in exactly the same sense* of God and of the creatures ; but this does not mean that God has *nothing in common with* man, nor man with God. " The names which we ascribe both to God and to created things [such as ' existence,' ' life,' ' wisdom,' and so on] are used both of God and of the creatures not entirely in the same meaning and not entirely in different meanings. The definition of a quality [such as ' life '] is not the same when we ascribe it to the creatures as it is when we ascribe it to God. On the other hand, the names which we ascribe both to God and to the creatures are not used in entirely different meanings. When names are used in meanings altogether different [as, for example, ' vice ' as the name of a mechanical instrument and of an immoral quality], we have the same name used of two things between which there is no real relation, and *we cannot draw any inference from the one to the other*. A name which we ascribe alike to God and to the creatures is ascribed to God on the basis of a real relation in which He stands to the creatures whose qualities, grasped by our thought, are connoted by the name ; and from this reason we can pass in our thought from created things to God (*ratiocinari de Deo possumus*)." All creatures are related to God as their Origin and Source ; therefore there is a real analogy between the perfections of created things and God.[79] However *inferior* the effect may be to the cause, so far as there is real causation at all there must be a real resemblance between the nature of the cause and the nature of the effect, however slight the resemblance (on the side of the effect) may be. The sun, for example, is the cause of heat in an inferior body, say a stone ; in this case " inferior " means " immeasurably smaller in size and in mass." But the warmth of the stone, engendered by the sun, has a real resemblance to the radiant energy of the sun, which warms all bodies exposed to its rays ; and we are justified in saying that the sun is " hot," although, along with the real resemblance, there is a vast difference between the warmth of the stone and the radiant energy of the sun. In like manner we say that created things, proceeding from God and dependent upon Him for all that they are and are capable of becoming, have a certain limited resemblance to the Creator. The immensity of the difference does not annihilate the resemblance.

VII.

We have observed that the old controversy regarding "universals" had died a natural death, because there was general agreement in favour of what we have called "moderate Realism." St Thomas states and defends this view of the matter with his usual lucidity and definiteness; for example : " the universal is a common quality of the many individual things, but it does not exist above them or apart from them, except in our thinking " (*non praeter multa, nisi sola ratione*). Again : " the ' universal ' is a natural predicate of the many individual things " (*aptum natum de pluribus praedicari*). In other words : the " universal," as a factor in our knowledge, is the means by which we come to know the " universal " as a natural predicate of objects. " Our intellect, in its active nature, produces the universal by abstracting from the material of experience " (*intellectus agens causat universale abstrahendo a materia*). In this sense, " the knowledge of the details of experience is, for our thinking, prior to the knowledge of universals " (*cognitio singularium est prior quoad nos quam cognitio universalium*). [80]

We refer to this subject again because of the range and import given by St Thomas to the doctrine that the true universals, which represent the essential similarities of things, exist, and existed before creation, in the intellect of God. In the light of this doctrine

we must understand the use which he makes of the
time-honoured expression that God creates " out of
nothing " (*ex nihilo*). In the first place he uses it to
exclude from our idea of the divine creative act
everything which implies or suggests the work of an
artificer using material already existing. But the
expression has not merely a negative meaning. To
speak as if " nothing," or non-existence, could be a
kind of source from which things are created, would
be absurd. " Being " can only proceed from " being."
Created things exist only because the essential nature
of everything is derived from the divine nature (*omnis
essentia derivatur ab essentia divina*) in the sense that
it has in God its " exemplar " or ideal " pattern."
A kindred thought, derived probably from Alexandrian Platonism, was in the mind of the author
of the Epistle to the Hebrews when he spoke of the
religious ceremonies of the visible Temple as a " copy
and shadow of the heavenly things," " even as Moses
is warned of God when he is about to complete the
Tabernacle : for, See, saith he, that thou make all
things according to the pattern that was showed thee
in the Mount " ; [81] but St Thomas would have re-
pudiated any suggestion that created things, though
they are in every way limited and imperfect, are
without a substantial reality of their own. Hence,
when he speaks of a created thing as " participating "
in the divine Nature, he never means that it is God or
a part of God ; he means that there is a real analogy
between it and the divine ideal of it which belongs to
the nature of God.

The infinite and eternal intellect of God brings
forth " ideas," as we may call them, of all things
possible. The divine idea of a thing is at once its

essential nature and its perfection, so that instead of its " divine idea " we may speak of its " divine ideal." Why, then, out of the infinite extent of the divinely conceived perfections, has God brought into being this world, in which His ideal of everything is expressed only in processes of constant change, under the conditions of embodied existence in space and time ? St Thomas answers by appealing to the very nature of Goodness. It is the nature of Goodness to extend beyond itself. Its characteristic is to communicate itself to other beings according to the measure in which they are capable of receiving it. And if this is true of every being so far as that being is *good*, it is above all true of that Supreme Goodness which is God. The natural expansion beyond self, and communication of its quality to others, when we apply it to the Goodness of God, means the unbounded wealth of an Infinite Being whose Perfection expands and distributes itself through a hierarchy of beings who share in it. The universe is a hierarchy or graded organisation of beings, or rather, of kinds of being, extending from the infinite fulness of the life of God down to the lowest materialised forms of existence whether known by our senses or not. To each kind of being in the hierarchy corresponds a kind of activity which is distinctive and characteristic of it ; while all alike proceed from and are dependent upon the Supreme Being.

VIII.

There is a real connection between the old controversy of " Nominalism " and " Realism," on the one hand, and the famous doctrine of " Matter " and " Form " on the other. This doctrine, as we have seen, had its origin in the work of Aristotle ; but the mediæval thinkers of the thirteenth century understood it in different ways and applied it in different ways to the contents of the natural world.

In order to illustrate the importance of the question at issue let us take a simple case of natural action and state it in terms more familiar to modern thought. Experience shows that one stone falls to the earth when allowed to drop ; another stone does the same. Is there any *real connection* between the two cases ? If there is none, then it was a chance coincidence. If a million stones fell to the ground under the given conditions, it would be a series of chance coincidences, and would afford no *reason* whatever for believing that the next stone would do the same. The events would be independent in their real nature, and Science would be impossible. Consistent " Nominalism " cannot avoid this conclusion. If, on the other hand, the events are not independent, if there is a real connection, then we have a real " universal " *which proves on examination to be a Law of Nature.* Behind the question of the reality of " universals " stands the question of the reality of Laws of Nature and the meaning of natural Causation. From this point of view, " Nominalism " means that any Law of Nature is merely a convenient mental formula summing up the fact that the events have happened in a similar way ; and " Realism " means that a Law of Nature is a real factor in the nature of things, such that under the same conditions the same result will always follow.

It was not possible, however, for mediæval thinkers to state the doctrine in this way. The Aristotelian doctrine of " Matter " and " Form " would indeed have admitted of such a statement, because the true universal, in which our thought grasps the essential nature of an object, is equivalent to its " Form," and, as we have seen, is another name for the constitutive or structural law governing the growth or the possible changes of the special kind of object under considera-tion. And much of the mediæval discussion of " Matter " and " Form " is intelligible only when regarded from the point of view which we have just stated. On the other hand we find—most definitely in St Thomas—a tendency to regard the " Form " not merely as a structural law but a *kind of being* capable, at least in the superhuman world, of existing and acting independently of " Matter." The Thomist doctrine of Angels as " pure Forms " is of interest and importance ; but any discussion of it here would lead us far afield.

It is in relation to the natural world, revealed to us through our bodily senses, that the mediæval doctrine of " Matter " and " Form " becomes most interesting. The Thomist doctrine is best explained by comparing it with that of St Bonaventura. We must always remember that behind the whole discussion stands the question of the reality of natural Law and the meaning of natural Causation.

Bonaventura argues from an assumption, the absol-ute validity of which is taken for granted. God alone works or creates "from nothing," that is, without needing anything pre-existing to work with. Nature never acts "from nothing," but always from something already existing, at least potentially : *Deus enim operatur ex nihilo ; natura autem non facit ex nihilo, sed ex ente in potentia.* Neither animals nor men, neither angels nor demons, are able to create,— that is, to confer reality on something thought of, directly from the thought of it. We can act upon Nature only by submitting to her, and learning her ways, and making use of the knowledge. Our position in relation to Nature may be compared to that of a man cultivating a garden. He certainly produces the fruits of the earth ; but in order to produce them he must collect the proper kinds of seed, and sow them in suitable soil, entrusting them to the earth to act as " efficient cause " on the vitality latent in the seed.

If it had been possible for St Bonaventura to become acquainted with facts brought to light through the modern developments of agricultural chemistry, he would have found in these facts further illustrations of his conception. Chemists and physiologists have analysed plants to find what they are made of, and have discovered the chief factors controlling their growth. They have shown that plants can be made to grow better, and with far greater certainty, by merely adding to the soil certain easily procured substances essential for their growth, the lack of which had in the past caused low yields and even failure, with much subsequent human suffering. These " artificial fertilisers " are manufactured by industrial chemists and for many years have been supplied in enormous quantities to farmers. It has also been found that plants do not grow simply by themselves. Associated with their growth are minute organisms living in the soil, some preparing the plant food, others consuming it, others again causing injury or disease. These organisms are exceedingly small and amazingly numerous; and some of the most useful of them are now cultivated in factories and sold to farmers. We have mentioned these facts simply because they afford excellent illustrations of what Bonaventura meant when he said that in every case of natural causation we find an " efficient cause " acting directly upon something which already exists but exists only potentially or in germ. The repro-duction of animal life is an example of the same thing at a higher level of existence. The animal begets offspring after its kind only in virtue of the life latent in the act of conception. In the case of material motion, we have an example at a lower level of existence, if we interpret spatial motion by the familiar doctrine of nineteenth-century science, which distinguishes " potential " energy or energy of *position* from " kinetic " energy or energy of *motion*.

Bonaventura finds in such facts a clue to the understanding of every kind of natural causation. All natural objects, as created by God, involve at their various levels of existence " seminal Forms " or " natures " (*rationes seminales*) ; and only by means of these can the natural relation of cause and effect occur. This principle differentiates Divine from human or natural causation. For natural causation, something must be given, but it is given in a potential or germinal form.[82]

For reasons which are not easy to explain clearly, St Thomas was not satisfied with this interpretation of Nature. The two thinkers were at one in the fundamental doctrine that God alone is creative, in the full meaning of this word, and that in producing natural objects He has produced " Matter " and " Form " *together*. They are at one in the recognition of natural laws,—that causes and effects occur in a regular order in our experience ; heat produces heat ; an animal procreates after its kind. The nature of the effect produced is essentially related to that of the productive cause. And we must always bear in mind the inviolable certainty ascribed by both thinkers to our " common-sense " belief in the independent reality of the natural world, affecting our bodily senses and known through our mental acts of perception and understanding ; but St Thomas cannot admit that God created " Forms " which are imperfect in the sense of being undeveloped or latent.

IX.

When we turn from St Bonaventura to St Thomas, we find that the doctrine of " Matter " and " Form " has to be stated differently. Consider any kind of natural object ; gold, for example. We find that it has a constitutive principle,—in other words, a distinctive " essence " or " nature," in virtue of which it is what it is and does what it does ; and without this essence or nature it could not be distinguished or defined. So far as its nature is completely expressed in it, we say it is *perfect after its kind ;* and, technically, we say that this condition is its " actuality," and the essence or nature on which its actuality depends we call its " Form." But the natural objects occurring

N

in our experience are constantly undergoing all kinds of *changes;* and if the " Form " explains what the nature of the object is,—if its " Form " is, so to speak, just that which is positive in it,—this does not account for the fact that it may change, or become something else, or even cease to exist. Its existence involves a certain " indeterminateness," a range of the *possible* as well as of the *actual;* and, technically, we say that this range of possibility is its " potentiality," and this indeterminate or changeful aspect of natural objects we call their " Matter."

What, then, really takes place in any case of natural causation ? The answer given by St Thomas to this question defines one of the principal characteristic features of his system. When a natural cause produces an effect, the cause acts creatively, in that it reproduces in the effect a " Form " like to its own ; but it does not act creatively in the sense of conferring *being or existence* on the effect, since the latter may remain after the cause has ceased to act. In other words, the effect depends on the cause for what it *becomes,* but it does not depend upon the cause for its very *existence* as the whole created world depends upon God. The animal, for example, procreates after its kind ; but the offspring may remain after the parent is dead : whereas without God the world would cease to be. St Thomas appears to have been led to this conclusion through his realistic view of Nature. Natural causes must be real productive agents, but not productive in the sense in which God is so. Hence he regards natural causation as the reproduction of a given " Form," and not merely as the impulse to the development of a " Form " existing germinally, as St Bonaventura had regarded it.

If it had been possible for St Thomas to become acquainted with the methods and results of " plant breeding " at the present time, he would have been extremely interested in them. The inborn properties of a plant are a kind of mosaic, each fragment of which comes unaltered from one of the parents, which in turn derived it from its parent, and so back to the beginning. The mosaic contains only such fragments or " characters " as come from the parents,—though, of course, the fragments may be differently arranged. The " characters " are transmitted in " chromosomes," minute bodies some twenty-five thousand of which placed end to end would barely cover an inch ; but the actual " character," called the " gene," is much smaller,—so small, indeed, that it has never been seen ; its existence is a matter of inference. One gene carries a colour, another the character of producing hairs, another the character of growing tall, another that of ripening early : each gene faithfully preserves its " character " intact and hands it on to the next generation. The plant breeder, knowing the " characters " of the parents, can predict with considerable certainty the properties of the offspring. We have said that St Thomas would have been extremely interested in such results ; but he would not have regarded them as illustrative of his own view regarding the place of " Forms " in Nature. With his intense belief in *unification* as part of the divine method of creation, he had convinced himself that the life of each individual is the expression of a single controlling " Form," not a plurality of " Forms." He would have said that the metaphor of a " mosaic of fragments " is only a metaphor, and misleading if pressed too far ; and that the most obvious characteristics of a living organism are its *individuality* and its *unity*.

The difficult questions raised by the Thomist doctrine of " Matter " and " Form " are fully revealed when the doctrine is applied to human nature. Man is both an embodied soul and, if we may so express it, an ensouled body. The word " Soul," as used here, and as it was used by St Thomas, includes not only our rational and spiritual nature, but all that we mean by " Mind," conscious and unconscious. His fundamental doctrine may be thus expressed : the Soul is the " Form " of which the body is the " Matter." What exactly did he mean by this ?

In the first place, there are certain conceptions of the relation between mind and body which the Thomist doctrine excludes as its contradictories. The mind is not related to the body as a modern materialist conceives it to be,—wholly dependent for its activity on the life of the body, and perishing when the body ceases to " live." The mind is not related to the body after the manner of a mixture, as when two substances,—two kinds of metal, for instance,— are chemically mixed. The mind is not related to the body after the manner of a charioteer controlling his horses, or an oarsman guiding his boat. The body is not evil in itself ; neither is it the " prison " of the soul, and embodied life does not represent any kind of punishment of the Soul. The union of Soul and body is a beneficent union, necessary in order that the Soul may express its proper life, individually and socially, in the created world. But St Thomas appears to have supposed that the metaphor of the " charioteer controlling his horses " or the " oarsman guiding his boat" represented the doctrine of Plato ; and he substituted for it what he believed to be the doctrine of Aristotle,—that the Soul (as St Thomas understood the word) is the " Form " of the body, and the body the " Matter " of the Soul.

We have seen that the Thomist conception of " Matter " in general is just the abstract idea of " changefulness " with its implication of real possibilities,—" real," because based on conditions actually given in the nature of things. Now when we pass from the abstract to the concrete and consider any natural object in our experience,—for instance, a living organic body, it is evident that something more than " possibility " is involved. The " something more " is the " Form," giving actuality to the possibilities. If the abstract idea of " Matter " may be defined as that of real possibilities, the " Matter " of the objects which we perceive in our experience is *actualised* by " Form." The two factors are inseparable in the natural world. This is assumed to be the principle according to which the natural world is constructed ; but the assumption at once gave rise to a difficult question. In fact, the difficulties which embarrassed a former age in trying to conceive the mode in which the " universal " exists in the " individual " reappear in the systems of Albert and St Thomas as the problem of " individuation." What is the origin or explanation of individuality ? How does it come to be ? The " Form " in any natural object is that which, when grasped by our thought, gives rise to the logical " universal,"— the *general nature* of the many different objects embodying it. The universal as the " Form " or essence of the particular object is called its *quidditas*, that is, its "what-ness" or nature; but beside possessing a general nature and answering to a general definition (*i.e.*, being a "what"), every man, for example, is this particular man, here and now. It is the question of the particularity or "this-ness" (*haecceitas*, as Duns Scotus afterwards named it) which was found embarrassing.

Albert and St Thomas agree in declaring that the "principle of individuation," by which the nature of any kind or class becomes embodied in different individuals, is to be found in "Matter" actualised in objects in time and space. The variety of individuals, they maintain, depends entirely on the division of "Matter," and, St Thomas adds, on the *quantitative* division of matter. The reference is evidently to the familiar fact that the natural objects of our experience are marked out from one another by relations of space and time. This explanation—if indeed it was intended to be an explanation—only carries the question a degree further back. What is the origin of the division of matter into spatial and temporal forms? The truth seems to be that St Thomas never intended to *explain how the individual comes to be;* he only intended to point out an invariable condition of the existence of individuals.[83] "Matter" itself contains nothing of individuality until it is actualised by "Form." Individuality is always unique. There is more in the individual than in the "species." The "Form" which actualises the "Matter" of an object may be produced under natural laws by another "Form," but the individuality of the object cannot be so explained. It can only be referred to the divine creative act. This consideration goes far to relieve a difficulty pointed out by critics of St Thomas both in his own time and afterwards. If individuality depends on " Matter," must we not conclude that individuality is extinguished at death, and that only the universal " Form " survives ? On this ground, Averroes had been led to deny the possibility of personal immortality. But if St Thomas means only that " Matter " is a condition of the appearance of individuality in the created world, no such consequence follows from his theory. The souls of men are immaterial " Forms," individualised by God in the act of creating them.

St Thomas explicitly affirms what modern biologists have called " ontogenetic " evolution, that is, the gradual growth of the individual animal from an embryo before birth to maturity : in the case of man, the gradual growth of the human embryo from mere " vegetative " life, through the life of the mere animal, on to the life of a rational being. " The higher a Form is in the scale of being," says St Thomas, " the more intermediate ' Forms ' and generations [stages of growth] must be passed through before that complete Form is reached. Therefore in the case of man there occur many intermediate ' Forms ' and generations." [84] But the doctrine of " Form " and " Matter," as he held it, requires a special interpretation of individual growth. He is aware, as we have seen, that it consists in a series of " stages," as we may call them. The earliest stage, the life of the embryo, he describes by a rather misleading metaphor as " vegetative " and compares it to the life of the plant. This is followed by the stage of animal life, which is both natural and sentient, and for a period the embryo lives the life of an animal; then ensues the life of the rational or distinctively human soul, which is infused from without. Now St Thomas repeatedly affirms that in the growth of a living being, the earlier and comparatively lower " Form " ceases to exist when it gives place to the higher. By this he means that it ceases to exist with a separate life of its own. It is merged in the higher " Form," which possesses all that the lower " Form " possessed, and much more. In this sense, and only in this sense, the " rational " contains the " sentient " and the " sentient " contains the " vegetative "; but we cannot discern the lower in the higher as a *separate kind of life*. Thus, there is an " evolution " in the life of the individual, but only in the sense that the lower " Form," in the natural order of things, must come first.

St Thomas never seems to have thought of what has been called " phylogenetic " evolution, or the *evolution of species from a common ancestor*. He sees a series of stages in the world of life at large. " A wonderful chain of beings is revealed to our study. The lowest member of the higher genus is found to border close upon the highest member of the lower genus: thus, some of the lowest members of the genus of animals attain to little beyond the life of plants; certain shell-fish, for example, have only the sense of touch, and are attached to the ground like plants." [85] He has in view the series, plant, animal, man; but to assume the derivation of all these forms of life from a common ancestor would, from St Thomas' point of view, be irreconcilable with the biblical account of creation, and thus would have presented very grave *theological* difficulties. On the other hand, it would probably not have presented any serious *philosophical or scientific* difficulties, provided that a clear and distinct meaning is placed upon it. He would never have been satisfied with such vague expressions as that later or higher forms of life have been " evolved from " or " out of " the lower. He would probably have insisted that, as in the life of the individual, so in that of the species, the " evolution " means scientifically nothing more and nothing less than the *order in time* in which the successive " Forms " of life have appeared. The lower " Form " must come first in order that the higher may emerge. If it had been possible for him to criticise the modern doctrine or doctrines of evolution, he would probably have taken a position very similar to that of James Martineau.[86] " Evolution consists in the perpetual emergence of *something new which is an increment of being* upon its prior term, and therefore more than its equivalent, and entitled to equal confidence and higher rank. This, however, though holding good throughout, has an exceptionally forcible validity at certain stages of the evolution. Though all the differences evolved are something new, and may fall upon an observer's mere perception as equally new, yet, when scrutinised by reason, some may retain their character of absolute surprise, for which there was and could be nothing to prepare us ; while others may prove to be, like an unsuspected property of a geometrical figure, only a new grouping of data and relations already in hand. . . . We may find examples without going back to any date anterior to the existence of *Life*. . . . We cannot doubt that from this point the next step in the ascent of being was to *Feeling*. . . . This next step is dependent, not on any modified conditions in the environment, so as to be calculable from them ; but on an increment quite heterogeneous turning up in the inward nature. It therefore constitutes a *new departure.*" In the language of St Thomas, " sentience " is a new and higher " Form " in which the earlier " Form " is merged. Thus, in the case of man, the total life of the soul includes not only the higher rational acti-vities distinctive of human nature, but also all the lower forms of life. The " soul-unit," so to speak, is a single unique substantial " Form," which con-stitutes " human nature " in endowing man with being, materiality, life, sentience, and rationality. These lower functions do indeed depend on bodily organs during our earthly sojourn. The dependence, however, is not necessary ; the soul, being immaterial, can and does maintain its own being when the body perishes.

The natural intimations of immortality, on which St Thomas lays most stress, are found in the rational capacities of the soul, which are not confined to the " here " and " now " but are able to pass ideally beyond every limitation. It is at this point that the Platonism in St Thomas makes itself felt. Every-thing which we desire is desired because it at least appears to be in some way a " good." Many " goods " thus desired are illusory. So far as they are really " good," it is because they share in the Absolute Good, which is God ; and it is this Absolute Good which our souls really seek through all and beyond all particular " goods." If we had, here below, the vision of that Absolute Good, our rational nature would at once recognise it as the true End of our being ; as we are, we can seek it only through the details of our experience. And our moral freedom lies in our power so to *think* about the things which we desire, that their real or apparent goodness, and their value for us as rational beings, may be made plain. The doctrine of degrees is essential to this conception of morality. The universal striving after God, since He is essentially intelligible, is revealed in its highest form in rational beings as a desire for that knowledge of Him which is at once knowledge and vision and supreme happiness. Such knowledge, however, is beyond all ordinary exercise of reason, and is only partially revealed to man here below ; and there is another kind of happiness to be realised here below in a normal human existence of virtue and friendship, with mind and body sound and whole and properly trained for the needs of life.

X.

St Thomas was deeply influenced by the study of Roman Law, which had attained a rapid and brilliant revival in Italy. The general idea of Law, regarded abstractly, is that of " an ordinance of Reason for the common good." It implies a community for whose good it is ordained, and an authority to ordain it. In our experience, in the widest sense of the word, four types of Law are found. In the *first* place, there is the Eternal Law or regulative Reason of God, revealed in the whole structure, order, and harmony of the created universe, up to the highest heaven. In the *second* place, there is Natural Law, being that part of the Eternal Law which refers to rational beings, and is discoverable by them. God has implanted in the human mind a certain knowledge of its unchanging principles, although the application of them may sometimes be obscured and perverted by bad education and custom. In the *third* place, there is Human Law, which, when it is *just*, is the adaptation of the principles of Natural Law to the circumstances of particular societies, deciding the details for which Natural Law gives no definite guidance, and supplying the force required to secure, among imperfect men, the observance of the most necessary rules of social conduct. In the *fourth* place, there is Revealed Law, consisting of the Decalogue and the Gospel combined, and going beyond Natural Law in directing the way to Eternal Life. As regards the Gospel, St Thomas followed St Augustine in distinguishing between absolute " commands " and " counsels." St Augustine found it necessary to judge between the extreme anti-worldly spirit animating some exponents of Christianity, on the one hand, and the necessities of secular civilisation on the other. He defended the life of marriage and temperate enjoyment of natural good against the attacks of the more extravagant advocates of celibacy and self-abnegation. So far as the Gospel inculcates these things, it is not as " commands " but as " counsels " recommended in order to avoid all contamination of sin. With St Thomas, nine centuries later, the emphasis is different. The evangelical " counsels " recommend, without positively ordering, the *monastic* life of poverty, celibacy, and obedience as the best method of effectively turning the will from earthly to heavenly things.

The doctrine of Natural Law implies a doctrine of what in modern times is called Conscience. Natural Law, though in its source it is one with the Eternal

Law, relates only to the free acts of rational beings. It is in the minds of men and angels. It obliges and binds, but does not constrain. The Eternal Law is like the sun bathing the heavens in a glow; the Natural Law is like the reflection of the glow in the sea; but it is one light. It is called " Natural Law " because it is found, more or less perfectly expressed, in all rational beings; and because a rational being, in order to attain its own maturity and perfection, must necessarily express that Law in and through itself. Now in order to state the manner in which the Natural Law operates in the mind, St Thomas makes use of the specially Christian idea of Conscience; but he makes an important distinction, using the word *synderesis* for that capacity of the soul by which the principles of the Natural Law are apprehended, and the word *conscientia* for the practical judgment by which they are applied to a particular case. Conscience, so understood, is no more infallible than any other human judgment. A man may fail to understand the motives and circumstances of his action; he may have " got hold " of the wrong general principle; he may be in error as to the application of his principle to the actual facts. In all these ways, Conscience may err.

The case is different, according to St Thomas, with respect to our grasp of the general principles. He believed that these principles, when clearly and distinctly understood and formulated, are *self-evident*. " The first principles of the Law of Nature," he says, " stand to the Practical Reason as the first principles of scientific demonstration stand to the Speculative Reason, for both sets of principles are self-evident." " From the very nature of his rational mind, it is proper to Man that as soon as he knows what a 'whole' is, and what a 'part' is, he knows that 'every whole is greater than its part'; and so of the other first principles. But whether *these particular things* are related as 'whole' and 'part,' can be known only by experience." Hence a proposition may be self-evident *in itself* and yet it is not self-evident to all of us: "In itself every proposition, the Predicate of which can be derived from consideration of the Subject, is self-evident. But to one who does not know the definition of the Subject, the proposition will not be self-evident. For example, the proposition, 'Man is a rational being' is self-evident in itself, because to name 'man' is to name something 'rational'; and yet, to one ignorant of what man is, the proposition is not self-evident." [87] This view of the first principles of Natural Law, if it is accepted, requires such an analysis of the principles claiming to be 'self-evident' as the late Henry Sidgwick gave in his once-famous book, *The Methods of Ethics*. St Thomas does not do this; but with skill and insight he works out a classification of the Virtues, and their contraries, based on Plato, on Aristotle, and—for its distinctively Christian elements —on St Augustine.[88] The most remarkable portion of his work, in the field of social theory, is to be found in the discussion of Law in the *Prima Secundæ* of the *Summa Theologiæ*. Its influence has been large and lasting—in the Catholic Church primarily, but indirectly among Protestants, especially in England. How much Hooker was indebted to St Thomas will be seen by anyone who compares the famous first book of the *Ecclesiastical Polity* with these sections of the *Summa*.

St Thomas looked for the foundations of Law in the nature of things; but we must distinguish his political doctrine of the nature and authority of the State from his Theory of Law. His political theory is embarrassed by an attempt to combine the free politics of which he read in his Greek authorities, especially in the *Politics* of Aristotle, with what he perceived of the actual tendencies of contemporary monarchical governments. He treated the problem with his usual systematic thoroughness; but for our present purpose, instead of concentrating on the doctrine of St Thomas, it will be more useful to give an interpretation of the type of political theory which generally prevailed among Christian thinkers during the thirteenth century. The serious study of the subject began with William of Moerbeke's translation of the *Politics* of Aristotle, which he completed in 1250.

What is called the "hierarchical theory of the Church" was uncompromisingly maintained.[89] It is necessary to have some *supreme authority* in matters of faith. This authority resides in the Pope, in whom is realised the unity of the Church and the presence of the Divine Government. To the Pope, therefore, is divinely entrusted the power to revise and control the ordinances of religion and to issue new confessions of faith when made necessary by the rise of erroneous beliefs or for other reasons. And since "error" is not limited to matters of theology in the strict sense, but may affect matters of political policy, the Pope has power to excommunicate a sovereign; and from the moment of the issue of a papal excommunication, the sovereign is deprived of all authority to rule, and his subjects are released from all allegiance to him. The limitations of monarchical power, thus defined,

were not universally accepted, even among churchmen ; but, in any case, the authority of the Pope
was not the only lawful check upon misgovernment
which was recognised. What we find is this : the
fundamental principle is always that the State exists
for the good of the citizens, and not the citizens for
the good of the State. This claim on behalf of the
citizens, individually and collectively, has a moral
and religious foundation. Personal " happiness," in
the sense of true welfare and blessedness (*beatitudo*),
is of infinite worth. " All souls are Mine " ; for this
Christ died.

Nevertheless, society, or social life, is necessary,
because the individual cannot attain the supreme
personal felicity of knowledge and love in a solitary
state. St Thomas knew Aristotle's statements to
the effect that man is by nature a " political animal."
He did not know Plato's statements, to which Aristotle
was almost certainly indebted. In the *Republic* Plato
represents Socrates as constructing the indispensable
minimum of a " city "—or, in our terminology, an
organised political State—from the necessities of
human life, food, clothing, shelter ; from the inability
of the individual to provide for these needs ; and
from the principle of the division of labour. Plato
was aware that the historic origin of the State is to
be looked for in the family and the clan ; but he
reserves the discussion of this aspect of the subject
for his last work, the *Laws*.[90] The mediæval thinkers
followed Aristotle, and through him followed Plato, in
regarding social life as essential to the fulfilment of
human nature ; but they were always prepared to
understand this in the light of the Christian doctrine
that man's soul is of infinite worth.

What kind of " social organism," then, did the mediæval thinkers regard as capable of being a political "unit"? What is the supreme social organism in the secular sense? We find that the answers to this question are not always and everywhere the same; they depend on the view taken of the " Empire," on the one hand as a contemporary political organisation and on the other as an ideal. It was obviously impossible to follow Aristotle in taking anything like the Greek " city-state " as the political unit. But however the answer to the question was formulated in detail, the fundamental principle was firmly grasped. The organised community exists for the service of the individual, and its good is the personal good of each and all of its members. Whether such a doctrine is to be described as one of " individualism " or not, depends on the meaning to be attached to this most ambiguous term; but it is a doctrine which implies belief in imprescriptible " natural rights " which the State can neither give nor take away. And the whole conception depends at bottom on the philosophical theory of the individual person as a " substance," by which is meant, a being created with an independent reality of its own. The State is not and cannot be in this sense a " substance."

This line of thought was worked out theoretically by the jurists and canonists, who brought the State and the Church under the principles of the Roman law of " Corporation," according to which a " Corporation " is neither more nor less than an association of individuals. This refusal to ascribe personality to a Corporation shows the sanity of the political thought of the Middle Ages. The unity which was ascribed to the social community is the unity of its members in co-operating for certain specific ends. The comparison of the State, or the Church, with a living body was only an analogical illustration.

The mediæval thinkers were acquainted with the communistic doctrine of Plato's *Republic* through Aristotle and other writers ; and they were practically familiar with social groups in which the principle of individual ownership did not hold—namely, the religious Orders. St Thomas, for example, had defended his own Dominican order against attacks on this ground, and had been driven to uphold the right to " all things in common," and to deny that private property was inalienable. The doctrine of St Thomas on this question, thoroughly and systematically wrought out after his manner, is typical of the mediæval attitude. He did not want to oppose communism (" all things in common ") on the basis of a principle which should be open to radical criticism, and in his constant memory of his own life as a Dominican friar he had to define precisely the sense in which private property is justifiable. He found that two questions are involved. In the *first* place, there is man's " right " to the use of material things. This is an inalienable right, springing from the roots of man's nature. If man exists, and is responsible for his existence, then he must necessarily have the " right " to the means without which his existence is impossible. This is a consequence of the Law of Nature ; but it is, so far, an abstract generalisation, and it leaves open a further and seriously practical question : Who is to hold the property or control its use ?

In the *second* place, therefore, there is the question

of the "right" to *private property*—that is, to the
division of material things among the individuals of
a social group, so that each one can say of certain
things, "These are mine, not yours." This arrangement is not dependent on the Law of Nature. It is
a matter of experienced necessity, and is to be defended
on the ground that without it worse things would
follow. It rests on positive human law under the
guidance of enlightened social prudence. It is not in
any sense contrary to Justice. Neither is communism
or community of goods contrary to Justice, but the
mediæval thinkers were convinced that communism is
an ideal too lofty to be ever here realised ; it implies so
much generosity, and such a vigour of public spirit,
as to be beyond the reach of fallen human nature.

In the beginning it was otherwise ; had human
nature remained as it was in Paradise, there need
have been no "mine" and "thine" in material
things. But afterwards, when selfishness and greed
grew out of the self-centred lives of men and led to
continual destructive strife and the supremacy of
might, experience gradually brought men to realise
that their only hope of peaceful intercourse lay in
the actual division of property and the establishment
of a system of private ownership ; and this can be
set aside only by men who are themselves perfect,
or had vowed themselves to pursue perfection. From
all this followed the conclusion that though the State
has theoretically the "right" to reverse the results
of history and re-establish common ownership, under
actual conditions this would be a violent and impracticable proceeding. It is evident that from a discussion conducted on these lines—as it was by St
Thomas—many propositions, isolated from their

context, could be quoted, and supported by the authority of his name, which did not represent his thought. His assertion of the impracticable nature of communistic organisation could be quoted by men looking for "authorities" in support of their individualistic theories; while others, like the friars of whom Wycliff and Langland spoke, quoted him only when he declared that "by Nature all things were in common," and that the communistic theory in itself is not contrary to the doctrine of the Church.[91]

The modern reader feels that the mediæval statements of these various social theories—and not least the elaborated systematic statements of them, as by St Thomas—are didactic, theoretical, and even *doctrinaire*, when considered in connection with the social history of the period. This fact increases their suggestiveness for modern times, since they are not intermingled with the discussion of events which have long passed away. None the less, they are enunciated *theories;* and they throw little light on the social standards involved in the contemporary actions of men. The tacit assumptions of men of action are as important as the statements of theorists. For example, the Church recognised the necessity of modifications in its general prohibition of "usury"; but the merchants of the time had evolved a working compromise between business and ethics in their dealings with each other. This is evident in their account-books and letters as well as in commercial law. This was not always in close connection with canonist theory; but it was not mere sharp practice. It belongs to the study of social ethics to inquire what was considered honest dealing by merchants as well as by bishops.

XI.

The Christian doctrines which St Thomas believed to be warranted by supernatural revelation and which are embodied in the creeds of the Church are expounded by him with the care and thoroughness which, in his view, their importance demanded. His purpose is not to prove the truth of these doctrines by reasoning, but by reasoning to repel objections which have been brought against them. To explain his treatment of these questions in any detail would lead us very far afield, and would involve continual references to the history of Christian doctrine ; but we may give illustrations of the way in which St Thomas treats these subjects.

The central problem of Christ's relationship to God and to man had been solved ; and the solution, formulated by the Church under divine guidance, could be explained or defended but never doubted. The Deity—in the absolute sense, the creative Source of all being—was one "Substance" in three "Persons" ; the Incarnate Christ had two natures, being perfect God and perfect man. St Thomas therefore had to face the problem, which lay behind the christological controversies of the fourth and fifth centuries, of doing justice to the complete humanity and to the complete Deity of Christ. He holds definitely that Christ was human in body, mind, and soul, capable of suffering in soul and perishing in body. On the other hand, as God, Christ had the full knowledge of the *comprehensores*, those who enjoy already the Beatific Vision. What we mean by "Faith" and "Hope" was foreign to His nature as God. Faith and Hope are possible only to the faithful on earth who are *viatores*, "wayfarers," "pilgrims." The prayers of Christ were uttered only to give us an example of prayer.

In fact, St Thomas elaborates into theory the dramatic presentation of the Incarnate Word in the Fourth Gospel, a Figure whose omniscience is full-orbed from the beginning, requiring neither to be sustained nor to be matured by experience ; whose Passion is no drift but an open-eyed choice, exhibiting marks of a royal advance ; who possesses an insight into His own career and fate which invests Him with a unique detachment and independence of spirit.

How then does the sacrifice and death of this transcendent Being become effective for the salvation of men ? What does His humanity mean spiritually and morally, for mankind ? The answer which St Thomas gives is crossed by the doctrine of the intercession of Mary and the Saints, and by the doctrine of the central authority of the Church as a means of imparting saving grace to men. The result, as regards the relation of Christ to those whom (St Thomas never doubts) He came to save is uncertainty and even obscurity. In a noteworthy passage St Thomas does not hesitate to suggest that the historic Incarnation was not necessarily final or exclusive : "after the Incarnation, the Father can still assume a distinct human nature from that which the Son has assumed ; for in nothing is the power of the Father or the Son lessened by the Incarnation of the Son : therefore it appears that after the Incarnation the Son can assume a human nature other than the one which he did assume." [92]

In his doctrine of the Fall and its consequences,

St Thomas builds on Augustinian foundations but reshapes many of the stones. One of the corner-stones is entirely new. The narrative of the first man, in the Book of Genesis, is interpreted in the light of the contrast between " nature " and " supernature," or the realm of reason and the realm of faith. We must distinguish between the purely natural qualities (*pura naturalia*) of the first man, which God, so to speak, was under the necessity of conferring upon him if He was going to make a " man " at all, and the supernatural endowments of " original perfection," with its perfect righteousness and transcendent mental powers : these are the result of purely gratui-tous munificence on the part of the Almighty. Even if man had remained endowed solely with the *pura naturalia*, and had never received the wondrous endowment of " original perfection," he could still have attained to a natural knowledge of God by observation and reasoning ; but with infinite gener-osity the Creator raised His creature, at the first moment of his creation, to the supernatural plane, and prepared for him as it were an ever-ascending pathway to the supernatural knowledge and possession of Himself in the Beatific Vision. St Thomas departs altogether from St Augustine in taking an essentially optimistic view of human nature in itself, even apart from the supernatural endowments enjoyed by the first man. Adam, failing under the test imposed upon him, " fell " not into a state of " corruption," but on to the natural plane on which he would have lived with-out the gratuitous exaltation involved in the bestowal of the supernatural gifts. This, however, introduced a disorder into the natural faculties of man ; their due harmony and proportion were disturbed and disarranged. This "disordered desire" is original sin. St Thomas does not hesitate to adopt the Augustinian paradox that this inherited sin is inherited *guilt*. Baptism, at the hands of the Church, abolishes the *guilt* of original sin, but leaves in human nature the *fomes peccati*, the "tinder of sin," the raw material of emotion, impulse, and instinct called "concupiscence," which in the baptised is not sin unless it is worked up and adopted by the will for evil ends. This admission that "concupiscence," in itself and apart from the consent of the will, is not sin in the baptised, must (on any other than a grossly mechanical theory of the efficacy of Baptism) ultimately involve the admission that it is not sin in the unbaptised ; in other words, that in itself it is not "sin" at all.[93]

XII.

In view of the commanding position afterwards attained by St Thomas, it is surprising to find that the impression made by his system on his contemporaries was one of bewilderment, hardening for various reasons into determined opposition. The vastness of the system, in its articulation and range, placed it beyond the comprehension of ordinary educated believers. Theologians who distrusted and misunderstood "Aristotelianism" saw in it a triumph of heathen speculation over Christian faith. The abler Franciscan critics saw in it serious philosophical errors, not merely in its technical development of the doctrine of Matter and Form, but above all in its clearly cut distinction of the realm of Reason and the realm of Faith, and its limitation of the function of the intellect to the extraction of "universals" from the facts of sense-perception. If St Thomas was right, it was no longer possible to maintain a difference of degree between the knowledge warranted by Reason and the knowledge warranted by Faith.

It is now almost universally agreed that the philosophy of St Thomas, like that of his master Albert the Great, so far as it claimed to be the work of unaided reason, was in its method and much of its material a Christianised Aristotelianism, and cannot possibly be identified with the Aristotelianism of Aristotle himself. What, however, was the view of the two thinkers themselves on this matter? The answer is that Albert and Thomas never regarded themselves as simply assimilating the doctrine of Aristotle; but they evidently believed that their version of Aristotelianism was truer to the teaching of "the Philosopher" than that of Averroes; and there was a superficial appearance of truth in the statement that "Thomism" represented a triumph of Aristotle over St Augustine. This impression was strengthened by the remarkable fact that among the lecturers in the Faculty of Arts at Paris, contemporaries of St Thomas, there were thoughtful men who claimed to be orthodox believers on all matters of Faith, and who nevertheless taught that Reason, unaided by revelation, led directly to the Averroist version of Aristotelianism. Now Averroism, as we have seen, contradicted the doctrine of the Church on several fundamental questions.

The only one of these teachers about whom any detailed information has come down to us is Siger of Brabant, who taught in Paris, and is believed to have been assassinated in Rome between 1280 and

1285. We are not concerned with his speculations in general, which were based entirely on those of Averroes, but with the extraordinary position which he adopted as regards Reason and Faith.

— There is a doctrine, the principle of which is sometimes defined as " the twofold nature of truth," and which is not found only in the Middle Ages. Expressed in general terms, it means that the realm of the " natural " is identical with that of the rational or the intelligible. Expressed more precisely, it means that there is one kind of truth attainable only by natural reasoning on the basis of experience, and another kind of truth known only by supernatural revelation and appropriated only by an act of faith. This revealed truth is beyond the power of natural reason to attack or defend. It may even be shown to be contrary to natural reason ; but this does not affect its claim on our acceptance. A remarkable presentation of this doctrine was given by H. L. Mansel, Dean of St Paul's, in his once famous Bampton Lectures, entitled *The Limits of Religious Thought*, delivered in Oxford in 1851. In these lectures his object is to demonstrate the inconceivability of every attribute, ascribed to Deity, which implies infinity. He ends by appearing to protect the orthodoxy of his time from attack by falling back on a moral and religious scepticism. He believes that he could cut the ground from under the feet of any objector to " the Christian revelation " by showing that in these matters human reason is incapable of offering an opinion. During the decline of mediæval thought we can find more than traces of an " apologetic " method similar in principle.

Such was not the method of Siger of Brabant.

On a certain number of questions two conclusions presented themselves to him ; and these conclusions were irreconcilable. On the one hand, there was the declaration of supernatural revelation, which was *true ;* on the other hand, there was the conclusion to which his unaided natural reason led. In such a case, since God cannot deceive, he adhered by an act of faith to the truth which God had revealed. Professor Étienne Gilson has called attention to the fact that Siger never described the results of philosophical speculation as " truth." He was satisfied when he had indicated the conclusions of unaided reason, and explicitly affirmed the higher claim of revealed truth. His position becomes more intelligible when we understand what he meant by " philosophy " or by the conclusions of unaided reason. Philosophical investigation, by the light of Nature, is the investigation of the arguments and conclusions of philosophers, and, above all, those of Aristotle ; but revealed truth is the highest and the supreme truth.

What is very probably the true explanation has been given by Professor Gilson. We know that in the age when Siger lived, and among all his contemporaries, it was natural and normal for all men to accept the Christian faith as a supernatural revelation of which the Church was the guardian. We also know, from experience, that even to-day there are believers capable of sincerely maintaining their belief in supernatural revelation and, at the same time, capable of accepting some doctrine entirely incompatible with it. If, then, in this twentieth century, some minds are able to overcome this minor conflict and hold fast by their orthodoxy, why should we assume to-day that Siger of Brabant was hypocritically con-

cealing his own convictions when he professed to
think as a philosopher and *believe* as a Christian?
We may carry Professor Gilson's suggestion further.
We know that as a matter of psychological fact the
mental furniture of some minds is divided, as it were,
into "compartments" between which there is no
communication, so that contradictory opinions and
beliefs may be held without any feeling of conflict.
Thus, there are some who, as a matter of religious
belief, accept without question the biblical narrative of the Creation, while they also accept without question, as a matter of secular knowledge,
the geological and biological facts which suggest an
entirely different view of the history of life on this
earth.

Nevertheless, although we may offer such psychological explanations of the position taken by Siger of
Brabant, there is no reasonable doubt that his influence, and the influence of some contemporaries of his
whose teaching was similar, promoted the doctrine
of the twofold nature of truth in a form which he
would never have sanctioned. Reason could claim
unlimited scope and freedom so long as the finality
of "faith" was formally granted. Any doctrine,
however sacred, might be intellectually analysed and
discussed; atheism, for example, might be shown
at length to be "reasonable," provided that the
opposite affirmation of "faith" was acknowledged.[94]
This, however, was not the position taken by Siger
of Brabant. In his mind convinced adherence to the
doctrine of the Church was primary and fundamental.
Perhaps this fact—together with human sympathy
with his fate—prompted Dante to place Siger in the
same celestial circle with the great Doctors of the

Church—Albert, Thomas, and others—and to say:
Esse e la luce eterna di Sigieri.

The "Averroism" of Siger, as his contemporaries
regarded it, was a very important factor in the opposition to Aristotelianism which prevailed in the thirteenth century; but, as we have pointed out, it was
not the only factor. On the whole, the Franciscan
thinkers distrusted the Aristotelian movement, and
their influence was adverse to the supremacy claimed
for Aristotle by the great Dominican masters. Political
and ecclesiastical as well as theological and philosophical influences were at work; and a temporary
triumph was secured when, in March 1277, Stephen
Tempier, Bishop of Paris, issued an official condemnation of two hundred and nineteen propositions,
and although most of these were "Averroist," the
bias of the whole demonstration was to implicate
the Aristotelianism of St Thomas with the errors of
Siger.[95] The Thomist doctrine of Individuation was
explicitly named and condemned. This, as we have
said, was only the temporary triumph of a league of
forces differing greatly in origin and worth. The fact
remains, however, that Aristotelianism never was
supreme in the age of St Thomas himself.

XIII.

The Dominican order produced two men of supreme
genius, Albert and Thomas; but the Franciscan
order produced a much larger number of original
thinkers. Apart from Albert and Thomas, the con-
servatism of the Dominican order stands in contrast
with the spirit of curiosity and inventiveness which

characterised the leading Franciscans. Indeed, it is
not too much to say that the Franciscans, through
their interest in the critical revision of current scientific
and philosophical theories, prepared the way for what
is called the " Renaissance." The home of the most
independent and influential Franciscan thought at
this time was in England and at Oxford,[96] and in
more than one direction it revealed tendencies characteristic of later British philosophy. We must not,
however, exaggerate this resemblance. It has been
suggested that the beginnings of British philosophy
are to be found within the " Scholastic " period ;
that the British intellect was at work in an age long
before Francis Bacon, and towards a result which he
and his followers are commonly thought to have been
the first to conceive.[97] Now, the distinctive characteristics of British thought, we may fairly say, are
exemplified in the spirit and method of John Locke's
Essay concerning Human Understanding. It is a
spirit and method which endeavours to keep close
to reality, and to verify all its conclusions by reference to the facts of experience ; which by a criticism
of knowledge, as it had been previously understood,
seeks a more adequate theory of its essential nature
and procedure ; which places action above thought,
and concludes that practice rather than speculation
is the real destiny of man, that for the practical guidance of life faith is a better guide than natural insight, and that probability serves where certainty is
not to be reached. To ascribe all these characteristics
to any mediæval thinker would, of course, be more
than misleading ; for instance, it would wholly mis-
represent the passion for symmetry and system which
ruled the work of St Thomas. None the less, when

we are thinking of the British Franciscans, and in particular of Robert Grosseteste, Roger Bacon, Duns Scotus, and William of Ockham, the characteristic tendencies of later British philosophy can be plainly traced. Grosseteste and Roger Bacon really saved mathematics, and the ideal of a science based on experience, at a time when the genius of St Thomas had led religious thinkers into an excessive pre-occupation with metaphysical divinity.

Robert Grosseteste was born in 1175, of humble parentage, at Stradbrook in Suffolk, and after studying in Oxford and (probably) also in Paris, he finally settled in Oxford, where he won considerable fame as a teacher, and was soon appointed to the Chancellor-ship of the University. Though not himself a member of the order, he became the first rector of the Fran-ciscan school there. The turning place in his life was his acceptance of the bishopric of Lincoln in 1235, when he at once undertook the reformation of morals and clerical discipline throughout his vast diocese. He was devoted to the hierarchical theories of his age ; and in English ecclesiastical politics he belonged to the school of Becket. The general tend-ency of modern writers has been to exaggerate his political and ecclesiastical services and to neglect his achievements as a scientist and scholar. His own contemporaries saw in him the pioneer of a literary and scientific movement : not merely a great ecclesi-astic who patronised learning in his leisure hours, but the first mathematician and physicist of his age, and the first Englishman to assimilate the new learning of Aristotle and the Arabians. In these fields of thought he anticipated some of the ideas to which Roger Bacon afterwards gave a wider currency.[98]

light. Light is the first divinely created " Form,"
inseparable from its " Matter "—its potentiality of
instantaneous self-diffusion in every direction. The
immediate result of this conception was the development of a positive and definite method of studying
Nature—namely, the mathematical method. Without
the study of geometry, he repeatedly affirms, it is
impossible to understand the phenomena of Nature ;
and the mathematical method he found to be immediately applicable to the laws of the propagation,
reflection, and refraction of light.

It was inevitable that Grosseteste should adapt
his theory of light to the Ptolemaic conception of the
universe, since no other conception was possible for
him. The immense sphere is the Ptolemaic universe.
Now light, the energy of which all things consist,
becomes more rarefied as the outermost limits of the
sphere are approached, and more condensed as its
centre is approached ; and when no further rarefaction
of the energy is possible, we have the " firmament,"
from which the rarefied energy turns back, as *visible*
light, towards the earth, the centre of the sphere.
The activity of this reflected light produces the series
of the celestial spheres and the spheres of the elements
—fire, air, water, and earth (*i.e.*, incandescent, gaseous,
liquid, and solid matter). How this comes about
Grosseteste is naturally unable to explain ; but, in
his mind, it leads to a remarkable view of the value
of this earth, as receiving and concentrating in itself
the activity of all the higher spheres.

Through all this speculation, half scientific, half
mythological, there runs an idea akin to one of the
fundamental conceptions of physical science to-day ;
and the same may be said of Grosseteste's general

theory of light as the energy of which all things consist and of which *visible* light is a special form. It is
easy to exaggerate these affinities, but they are real,
and they are remarkable. The varieties of wave-
motion, discovered and studied by modern mathematical physics, play a part in the universe akin to
that which Grosseteste assigned to the first-created
light-energy. " The tendency of modern physics is
to resolve the whole material universe into waves
and nothing but waves. These waves are of two
kinds : bottled-up waves, which we call matter ; and
unbottled waves, which we call radiation or light."
These conceptions reduce the universe to a world of
radiation *potential or active.* It has even been suggested
that the whole difference between " matter " and
" radiation " is that " matter " is nothing but a sort
of congealed " radiation " travelling at less than its
normal speed, and that radiation may be merely
matter moving with the speed of light, and matter
be radiation moving with a speed less than that of
light.[99]

XIV.

We have dwelt thus upon the work of Grosseteste
because the fame of his pupil Roger Bacon has obscured
the importance and originality of his work. The self-
centred claims which Roger Bacon makes for his own
achievement, his critical attitude to his contemporaries,
his monotonous dispraise of what he calls " authority,"
and his exaltation of " experimental science " (*scientia
experimentalis*) have endeared him to some modern
controversialists, who see in him " a martyr to science,

persecuted for his scientific studies," and indeed " the first prophet of modern science."

Roger Bacon was temperamentally an individualist and almost a rebel. When he joined a regular Order he took a step which had disastrous results for the whole of his life. He was born near Ilchester, in Dorsetshire, about 1214, and studied first at Oxford, where the teaching of Robert Grosseteste profoundly impressed him. He then spent a few years at the University of Paris, where he made the acquaintance of Alexander of Hales and Albert the Great, the leading thinkers respectively of the Franciscans and Dominicans, both of whom afterwards became the objects of violent tirades from his pen. Nevertheless his early lectures on the *Physics* of Aristotle, recently published by the University of Oxford—which are of slight scientific value—betray none of the characteristics of the later Roger. There is no suggestion that there are " errors in Aristotle " ; no complaints of the defects of the Latin versions ; no self-conscious censure of other expositors ; no hint of the need for a new scientific method, or even of interest in " experimental science," except in a long and curious account of the *clepsydra*, in which he runs entirely away from the *water-clock* meant by Aristotle to discuss the consequences of not making a vent (which he calls *clepsydra*) in a wine-cask ! It was probably during this period that he joined the Franciscan Order. About 1252 he returned to Oxford and began to lecture there ; and then the radical independence of his thinking began to appear. Owing to his temperamental aggressiveness and the resulting provocative character of his methods, he was obliged to abandon his work in Oxford, and was instructed to settle in

Paris, the headquarters of his Order. Here he was an object of constant suspicion, and intermittent persecution, until 1266. In that year Pope Clement IV., who when Cardinal-Legate in England had been acquainted with him, wrote ordering Brother Roger, notwithstanding any injunctions from his superiors, to write out and send to him a treatise on the sciences on which, he heard, Roger was working. The result was the composition of his best-known work, which he called *Opus Majus*, followed immediately by two supplementary works, *Opus Minus* and *Opus Tertium*. His literary activity continued until 1277, when a number of statements taken from his tracts on *Astrology* were included among the propositions officially condemned by Tempier in that year. The Head of his Order took this opportunity to secure his confinement to the Cloister. His last work (*Compendium Studii Theologiæ*) was composed in 1292, and after this date he disappears from history.[100]

Bacon is represented in an entirely false light unless we bear in mind his sincere belief in the entire subordination of philosophy to theology. This is made clear in the second part of the *Opus Majus*. There is one supremely perfect body of wisdom and knowledge which does and must dominate all other kinds of knowledge, and this is theology. Not that other kinds of knowledge are thereby depreciated. All knowledge of every kind is a divine revelation from one God and for one supreme purpose. Bacon is a true Franciscan in his loyalty to Augustinian Platonism. Indeed we may say that he is true to the main principles of Franciscan philosophy in his exposition of the doctrines of " Matter " and " Form " and the questions involved in it ; although, being

Brother Roger, he cannot avoid excessive discussion of small points of difference. Nevertheless his writings show that his interest was not in purely metaphysical questions; for the discussion of these he had not much aptitude. Nor was he specially interested in the study of philosophical theology, although, as we have seen, he was convinced of its supreme importance.

His real ruling interests were in the natural sciences —the science of language, the problems of mathematics, the beginnings of physics, chemistry, and astronomy. He was deeply dissatisfied with what passed for " knowledge " of these subjects, and was exasperated by what he supposed to be a complacent acquiescence in this state of things among the leading thinkers of his time. His attacks on " authority " were directed partly against veneration for mere tradition, partly against the commanding influence of great teachers like Albert and St Thomas, whose interests as thinkers were different from his own, and whose work he was incompetent to judge.

Roger Bacon believed very seriously that philosophy and science are the result of a divine illumination leading men to attain to wisdom. This, as we have seen, is the Franciscan view. But he transformed this conception into that of a special historical revelation. The whole contents of philosophy and science were divinely revealed to the first man, so far as a created rational being could comprehend them, and were known to the patriarchs; and, if we rightly interpret the pictorial and dramatic statements in the Bible, they can all be read there in figurative form. In reference to religious knowledge, these ideas were current among the Fathers of the Church, especially

the Alexandrians ; but Roger Bacon held this view
even in reference to natural sciences like mathematics
and astronomy. The result was an extraordinary
historical perspective. Through the working of the
evil wills of men, the primitive revelation was lost.
Solomon recovered it, but it was lost again, and
recovered once more by the Greek thinkers, among
whom Aristotle made philosophy and science as
perfect as they could be in his time. To those who see
in Roger Bacon a " prophet of modern science," we
reply that he saw in himself the prophetic restorer of
a revelation known to the patriarchs, to Solomon,
and to Aristotle.

This view of history is an example, among many
others which might be brought forward, showing
how entirely Brother Roger was a child of his time.
He was, as we know, a severe critic of " authority " ;
and yet he accepts without question a theory of
Medicine eminently based on authority—the system
of Galen, as further formulated and stereotyped by
Avicenna and the Arabs. The additions which he
makes look unpleasantly like the superstitions of
mere credulity. He believes that it has been proved
by certain " experiments " (*per experientias secretas*)
that human life can be greatly prolonged ; and a
certain man was thus enabled to live for over a
thousand years. Among the writings of Bacon,
previously unedited and recently published by the
University of Oxford, is one on the prolongation of
life ; it consists of curious recipes, many of them very
difficult to make out, conveying suggestions of wonderful secret knowledge, yet never leading to anything but the loosest generalities. One recipe, on
which he is prudent not to explain himself more fully,

is described as " medicine extracted from the mine of
the most noble animal."

It has been observed that all Bacon's discussions
of " experimental science " amount to little more
than a recognition of *experience* as a criterion of truth
and a promulgation of the phrase *scientia experimentalis ;* but there is more to be said. It is true
that Bacon sometimes confuses the issue by speaking
of " experimental science " when he means *observation.*
Thus, his explanation of the rainbow, which is his
longest illustration of the value of *scientia experimentalis,* is based on ordinary intelligent observation
and reasoning. Still, to insist on the importance of
wide and accurate observation was no small achievement at that time. Thus, at the close of his account
of the rainbow, he observes that tests with instruments are needed, and hence he will not assert that
he has reached the full truth of the matter.[101]

It is fair, however, to ask, What did he really
know or understand about *experiment* in science ?
We must first point out that experimental science as
we understand it—science which proceeds by hypothesis clearly and distinctly formulated and tested
by exact experiments—was unknown in the thirteenth
century. But Roger Bacon understood the general
possibility of purposive experiments in the sense of
" questions asked of Nature," although he gives no
directions concerning the proper field for experiment
or the proper conduct of experiment. On the other
hand, it must be remembered that the works on
which modern criticism of him are based are not
primarily treatises on Science at all. The *Opus Majus*
and the two supplementary treatises are propaganda
works, addressed to the Head of the Church when

Christendom was politically and socially in a dangerous condition. They were intended to put before him the resources of science and art, to urge him to take them into his own hands and gather round him a band of scientific workers, and to point out the power that science can put into the hands of men. And as regards his personal work, we may be sure that a pupil of Robert Grosseteste, and a man of the temperament and abilities of Roger Bacon, would " experiment," both secretly and openly, as much as he could, or as much as he dared.

When we get behind his superstitions, his contentiousness, his arrogance, we find a man moved by a passionate conviction that the natural sciences are of vast importance to humanity and to the Church, and that no further advance is possible but by an intellectual return to Nature. In this he was right ; and in this, rather than in any actual achievement, lies his title to fame. He had utterly abandoned the old belief that it is possible for man to know too much.* His official condemnation was not due to his scientific work. It was partly a matter of discipline within a regular Order and partly a matter of ecclesiastical statecraft. The Church, at that time, was in theory and in fact a political society based on first principles, claiming to be governed not by personal opinion or private judgment but by absolute *knowledge*, and pledged therefore to test every movement of thought by its probable effect on the faith which she was divinely charged to guard.

* See above, p. 34.

CHAPTER V.

THE TRANSFORMATION.

DURING the thirteenth century the constructive efforts of western Christian thought reached the highest level possible under the conditions of that time. In the early years of the century the two Orders of St Francis and St Dominic had brought the teachings of the Church into the homes of the people in a way unknown before. The School of Bologna had turned to account the stores of Roman Jurisprudence, and laid the foundations of the legal systems of the modern world. The great Universities had produced many men of originality and power, and a few men of supreme genius. Before the century ended they had all gone. Alexander of Hales—whose Augustinian Platonism prepared the way for St Bonaventura—had died in 1245, and Robert Grosseteste in 1253. St Thomas died in March and St Bonaventura in July in the same year, 1274. Albert the Great died in 1280, and Roger Bacon in 1294, or certainly before the end of the century. In 1300 Dante, aged thirty-five, after labouring to save Florence from tyranny or from anarchy, had been marked out in Rome for destruction :—

> So comes before mine eye
> The time prepared for thee. . . . So must thou
> Depart from Florence. This they wish, and this
> Contrive, and will ere long effectuate, there,
> Where gainful merchandise is made of Christ
> Throughout the live-long day.

We must not, however, isolate St Thomas, and assume that the constructive thought of the time culminated specially in his work. We might equally well say that it culminated specially in the work of St Bonaventura, whose conception of Faith in relation to Reason differed in principle from that of St Thomas.* These two thinkers were lifelong friends ; but they stand for two deep and divergent tendencies of religious thought. And Roger Bacon stands, away from St Thomas but not far from St Bonaventura, urging the claims of natural knowledge, because this also springs from a divine illumination intended for the good of man ; and because he had a vision of its possibilities going far beyond anything that his contemporaries conceived or imagined.

I.

It was a strange aberration of Bacon's mind if he assumed—as he seems to have done when writing to the Pope—that the natural sciences, properly studied and applied, could save Christendom from the social and political dangers which threatened it. What these dangers were is abundantly shown in the general histories of the time : in France, tyranny rampant under the rapacious ferocity of Philip IV. ; in Spain,

* See above, pages 152-153, and 173-174.

constant conflicts of Moor against Christian, and Moor against Moor ; in Germany, anarchy fostered by papal intrigue ; in Italy, a swarm of tyrants who had risen by destroying the republics. Dante was brooding over these things with a vision keener than that of Roger Bacon. He believed that the deepest need of all the world was for the souls of men to be purified from the poison of suspicion and fear from which their hatreds, their violence, and their injustice sprang. Hence his pictures of the hideousness of these sins, represented in the horror of their penalties, and his vision of the final blessedness of those who were permitted when purified to enter into the presence of God.

It is in the light of these convictions that we must regard Dante's dream of one united Christendom. It is a current doctrine in recent psychology that dreams are often the disguised expression of unfulfilled desires. Dante saw the condition of the world represented in his own beloved Italy. Weary of the endless strife of princes and of cities, and of the factions within every city against one another, seeing even municipal freedom—the only mitigation of turbulence —vanish with the rise of tyrants within the cities, he raises a passionate cry for some power to still the tempest, not to destroy liberty or supersede self-government, but to correct and moderate them, and restore unity and peace. To him it was no dream, but at once a strenuous argument, an uplifting vision, and a glorious prophecy.

Dante begins with first principles. Man was created in order that all his capacities, contemplative and active, may be realised ; and this can only be achieved under universal peace.[102] Now man's

nature is two-fold, mortal and immortal; the object
of his existence is therefore twofold, active virtue
on earth and the enjoyment of the vision of God
hereafter. Both these ends are divinely ordained.
God has made man subject to two orders, the temporal and the spiritual, and given him two guides,
reason and faith—philosophy and revelation—the
works of sages and poets, and the gospel. Each of
these two guides must be embodied and represented
in human life on this earth, one providing for man's
earthly blessedness, the other for his heavenly blessedness. To these ends man must come by diverse
means. For to the first we come through the teachings
of reason, provided we follow them by acting in
harmony with the moral and intellectual virtues; to
the second by spiritual teachings, provided we follow
them by acting in harmony with the theological
virtues, Faith, Hope, and Charity. But in spite of
reason and revelation, which make these ends and
means known to us, human self-will would reject
them, " were not men, like horses, held in the way."

At this point is made the transition which seemed
natural and indeed inevitable to the mediæval mind,
and which seems strange and impossible to us. Granting that every organisation, if it is to be effective,
requires a centre into which all is gathered and by
which all is controlled, granting that God has ordained
as it were two kinds of order in this world, the temporal
and the spiritual, each of these must be a kingdom
with a central source of order within it, which must
be embodied in a single Person—the Emperor in the
one case, the Pontiff in the other.

Historically this conclusion was of great importance.
Vital to it was the assumption that the temporal and

the spiritual authority are equally and directly God-given. The whole contention was a sustained protest against the assumption of any temporal power on the part of the papacy; and it is not surprising that Dante's book *De Monarchia* was at length placed on the Index of Prohibited Books. None the less, his doctrine of the twofold monarchy underlies much of the symbolism of the *Divina Commedia*. The journey through hell, purgatory, and paradise is man's journey after the double object of earthly and spiritual happiness. Virgil, his guide through hell and purgatory, represents reason and the temporal order; Beatrice, the supernatural aid without which, he believed, man cannot attain to his supreme end—to glorify God and enjoy Him for ever.

The question which is inevitably pressed by the modern mind still remains: why must the temporal or the spiritual order be embodied in a single Person here on earth? The arguments by which Dante defends his ideal of personal monarchy are amazing; but through the cumbrous and pedantic reasonings we seem to discern the unfolding of a prophetic vision. The picture ceases to be that of any historic person: it is that of a coming Messiah. We are vividly reminded of the ideal king portrayed by Isaiah and the Hebrew prophets of the eighth century before Christ: "A Man shall be as a hiding-place from the wind, and a covert from the tempest; as rivers of water in a dry place, as the shadow of a great rock in a weary land." At times the picture ceases altogether to be that of a person and comes to be that of a type or a principle. The ideal monarch or emperor is Justice, the foundation on which the order revealed in earth and heaven rests, now personified, throned and crowned, invested with majesty and honour ; and we seem to feel again the force of the ancient saying : "Human Ministers of Justice fail—but Justice, never." The just ruler is not only one who deals fairly, he is one whose rule proves his kingdom to be part of the eternal harmony on which the universe is built. When a tyrant reigns, it is as if a stroke of confusion disturbed the order of Nature or a shiver ran through the world, as once when the Veil of the Temple was rent in twain ; but when Justice reigns all is at peace.

The great jurists of the period worked out in theory what the position of such a monarch must involve. The result was a purely ideal theory, realisable only so far as human weakness permitted.[103] In Dante's mind the theory was inseparable from his ideal of the papacy. The occupant of the chair of Peter in Rome, when true to his divinely ordained mission, was the universal Bishop, the spiritual sovereign, charged to proclaim the law of Christ, and to guide the temporal sovereign and his subjects into the path that leads to eternal blessedness. But the Bishop had encroached on the province of his colleague and assumed the monarch's sword. Hence came confusion, no man knowing whom to obey ; hence disorder and tyranny in Italy, and wars all the world over. Dante's vision was of the whole Christian world living in concord as one community under its two divinely and legally appointed heads. The theory of a universal monarchy was not peculiar to Dante ; but none ever stated and argued it with such passionate conviction. The very intensity of his belief in the doctrine blinded him to the impossibility of giving effect to it. The sentiment of nationalism was already stirring ; and the problem of a united Christendom faces the world to-day in another form.

It has been said that in the world of thought the fourteenth century abandoned the great enterprise which was characteristic of the thirteenth. In what sense is this true ? The achievement of the thirteenth century, if we may use the language of diplomacy, had been to create an effective alliance between philosophy (including natural science) and theology— an alliance based on a treaty of peace and a definition of frontier-lines ; and it is true that the work of the thinkers of the following century went to destroy this treaty. If St Thomas had been granted a fore-knowledge of what was coming, he would have regarded it as a work of destruction ; he would have seen the nominally Christian " Averroists " increasing in number, and would have perceived that their formal recognition of " the Faith " scarcely concealed their radical unbelief ; he would have seen other thinkers giving up all attempts to reconcile faith with reason, and falling back on the inner experience of the soul as the foundation of beliefs which could never be warranted by logic ; and he would have seen men beginning to work in the conviction that there were more things to be discovered on earth than were dreamed of in his own philosophy, vast as its range had been.

II.

Of all chronological divisions, century-divisions are the most artificial ; and yet they sometimes correspond to deep periodic changes in the movements of men's minds. In passing from the thirteenth century to the fourteenth, we perceive such a change; but we see an outstanding figure, as it were in the midst of the transition, with an aspect of vigorous independence, and yet not quite sure of how he is moving. This is John Duns, better known as Duns Scotus.

Duns Scotus was born about 1270 and was a native of the South of Scotland. The Franciscans, perceiving his abilities, took him to Oxford, where he made extraordinary progress as a student. He entered the Franciscan Order, and lectured in the University until 1304, when he was summoned by the Franciscans to Paris. In 1308 he was obliged to leave France because of his open opposition to the anti-papal policy of Philip IV. He went to Cologne, where he was received with public honours; but he died there in November 1308. When Duns Scotus was at Oxford, the greater leaders of Franciscan thought in that city either had died or were on the Continent; but their influence remained and their writings were available. And in Paris Scotus studied under William of Ware, an English Franciscan who was lecturing there in the early years of the fourteenth century, and who had been a pupil of Bonaventura. We are not surprised to find that, although his personal interest in natural science is slight, he takes mathematics as the model of what a *strictly demonstrative science* must be.

Duns Scotus died in early middle life. If he had lived longer, he would, no doubt, have composed some kind of systematic exposition of his philosophy. As it is, he left only a mass of commentaries and special discussions of particular problems. His principles have to be disentangled from this body of voluminous exposition and criticism; and, unfortunately, the style and sometimes the temper of the criticism stand in the greatest conceivable contrast to that of St Thomas. In every problem which he takes up, Scotus tends to multiply divisions and distinctions to the utmost possible extent, until the essential factors of the question seem as it were to be reduced to impalpable particles, and the real issues are lost sight of. Hence it is often far from easy to trace the fundamental and essential portions of his argument. In Scotus, keen and powerful thinker as he was, the " scholastic " method overreached itself, and entered upon a subtlety which was one of the causes of its decline.* With good reason Duns Scotus was called *Doctor Subtilis*.

For our present purpose it will be sufficient to explain his leading principles, in contrast with those of St Thomas. His differences from St Bonaventura are not important ; but his writings are largely occupied by criticisms of St Thomas. We shall rely only on those works the authenticity of which is not open to dispute.

(i) According to St Thomas, while our unaided reason can discover and establish by argument a great body of truth, including natural religion and ethics, the truths distinctive of faith are revealed to, not discovered by, the human mind. On the other hand, it is possible for natural reason to refute arguments against these supra-rational truths ; and, so far, this is in effect to incline the mind towards their acceptance by reasoning. As we have seen, St Thomas never intended to assert an absolute separation, much less an opposition, between the two kinds of truth. But in the hands of Duns Scotus the distinction widens and deepens ; the range of philo-

* See above, page 88.

sophical and religious truth which can be demonstrated by our unaided reason is significantly restricted.

Duns Scotus is not satisfied with the simple distinction between truths discoverable by reason and truths made known only by revelation. Among the truths discoverable by reason, we must distinguish those which are matters of strict demonstration and those which, while they are not matters of strict demonstration, may be shown by argument to have a claim on our reasonable acceptance, and may be described as *credibilia*. In conclusions which can be made the subjects of strict demonstration—the kind of demonstration of which mathematical science is the standard and model—there are no " degrees " of *certainty ;* but there are " degrees " of *reasonable credibility* in all conclusions based on experience, as in natural science and natural life, and especially in those based on arguments *from effect to cause*. At the limit, as it were, we find conclusions for which, *from the point of view of natural reason*, there are no arguments at all. Now the arguments for the existence of God, hitherto brought forward by Catholic thinkers from the point of view of natural reason, are arguments from effect to cause. They are not therefore conclusive proofs, as St Thomas assumed that they were ; they are reasonable *credibilia*.

When Duns Scotus applies these distinctions to the accepted doctrine of the various " attributes of God," the results are serious. There are a number of attributes, ascribed to the Deity, which have been discussed by the philosophers : such are, among others, that God is a transcendent Being, the original Cause and final End of creation. These attributes, he admits, may be shown to be reasonably credible.

But Catholic thinkers ascribe to God omnipotence, omnipresence, perfect truth, righteousness, and love, and providential guidance of the whole of creation and especially of his rational creatures. For these attributes, our natural reason has so little to offer in the way of argument, that he points to supernatural revelation alone as the source of their credibility. With the warrant of revelation, they have the highest degree of credibility, but it is not a credibility based essentially on reason. The doctrine of the immortality of the soul is in the same position as the doctrine of divine Providence. The reasons offered for the doctrine, or the considerations brought forward in support of it, are *not proofs*. There is no demonstrative argument of which the doctrine in question is a necessary conclusion. Such was the position taken by Duns Scotus with regard to these fundamental questions. The effects of it were more far-reaching than he ever intended. He never said that a belief may be false for " reason " and true for " faith " ; but this conclusion was afterwards derived from his arguments. For him, theology is not—as it was with St Thomas—a rational science, capable of presentation as a speculative system. It is a practical science ; its object is to bring to our knowledge facts of supreme import, in order that we may govern our lives accordingly.

(ii) St Thomas teaches that intellect and will are never separated either in God or in man ; but in man their union is imperfect. Intellect is superior to will because it involves knowledge, contemplation, rational intuition, and is directly related to reality. An act of will is determined by the perception of good, and this perception is an intellectual act, so that an act of will is not possible without intellect. Moral freedom means that by an intellectual act of analysis and comparison, various possible lines of action are revealed, and the will decides for that one of them which is—rightly or wrongly—judged to be the best. In God the union of reason and will is perfect ; the divine will is the perfect expression in action of the divine nature, which is absolute goodness. An alternative choice would be less good and therefore comparatively evil. This conception is applied to explain the origin of the moral law as a divine command. God commands it because it is good. But the goodness which is commanded is not foreign to the divine nature ; it is an expression of the Perfection which is God.

According to Duns Scotus, this dependence of will on intellect destroys freedom of choice. If the will is free at all, its action must be wholly unrestricted. The intellect presents to the will the possibilities of its choice ; but the will is absolutely autonomous ; it is *motor in toto regno animæ, imperans intellectui*. And, as with the human will, so with the divine. Just as little can Duns Scotus admit an entire determination of the will of God even by His wisdom. The divine will is determined by nothing beyond itself ; it acts *ex mera libertate*, free from every kind of necessity. And this will of God is *summa lex*. Hence there is no necessity for the existence of the universe under its present constitution, forms, and relations.

Nevertheless these and kindred statements of Duns Scotus have sometimes been seriously misunderstood. It has been said that he places intellect at the mercy of arbitrary will, and that according to his teaching a thing is good only because God has willed and commanded it : which is understood to mean that God might have made good evil and evil good.

Duns Scotus does not teach that God " could " make a square round or make contradictories identical. He expressly rejects irrational assumptions of this kind. But God could have given to real beings other essences or natures than those which they actually have ; and then, the natures of things being different, the laws of Nature would be different from what they now are. It follows that, under the supposition stated, the laws of morality would be changed. Assuming that the content of duty depends on the constitution of human nature, it follows that if human beings were constituted differently in certain fundamental ways, then the content of morality would be fundamentally altered. There is, however, no evidence that Duns Scotus intended to teach that morality could be determined differently by the will of God, human nature being constituted as it is. But the anti-moral conclusion was afterwards derived from his statements. It was argued that nothing is *in itself* either righteous or sinful, but only because God has commanded or forbidden it, and that the divine commands are made known to men only by the Church.

(iii) Duns Scotus agreed with Albert and St Thomas in maintaining the threefold existence of the " universals " ; * but he rejected the Thomist doctrine of individuation. What was the question at isue ?

Any being having a nature of its own, which no other being can possess for it, is an individual. Such a being of rational grade is a person. Hence the

* See above, pages 105 and 159.

question is this : Can we explain or conceive the means
by which a being acquires individuality involving a
nature which no other being can possess for it ?
St Thomas, as we have seen, assumed that individuality originates when a universal " Form " becomes
embodied in " Matter " *signata quantitate*—in other
words, determined in reference to time and space ;
and then we have " this " or " that " individual,
man, or tree, or whatever it be. Duns Scotus maintained that the distinction of the universal essence
and the individualising limitations does not coincide
with the distinction between " Form " and " Matter."
The individualising qualities are as truly " Form "
as the universal essence. The latter may be called
quidditas (the " what-ness ") and the former *hæcceitas*
(" this-ness "). Just as the genus becomes the species
by the addition of further qualities, so the species
becomes the individual by the addition of fresh forms
of difference. As " animal " becomes " man " by
the addition of *humanitas*, so " man " becomes
" Socrates " by the addition of the qualities signified
by *Socratitas ;* and then we have the actual individual
Socrates, and no other—his *hæcceitas*. Thus, in
criticising St Thomas, Scotus introduces a third
principle which is neither " Matter " nor " Form,"
and which is spoken of as if it produced or created
the concrete individuality, for example, the personality
of the man as a particular individual.

At first sight, such statements appear to be open to
two criticisms. They are merely an example of the
illusory " explanation " which consists in naming
over again the fact to be explained : " Socrates is an
individual because he has individuality." Or, if not,
then such statements are an example of a more

serious fallacy—of treating the concrete existence involved in individuality as a logical quality like the " differentia " of a genus which makes it a species. On examination we find that neither of these criticisms is relevant to the writer's real intention. The individual form is for Duns Scotus an original fact ; no further question as to its ground is permissible. He describes individuality (whether individual being, or individual occurrence or event) as " the contingent " (*contingens*), in other words, as that which cannot be deduced from anything more general but can only be verified as actual fact.

For Duns Scotus, " the individual is the real." He seems to have seen more clearly than St Thomas that the problem of individuality is of central importance in any philosophy. It may be argued that from the nature of the case the problem is insoluble, since we cannot " dig up the roots of our own being " ; but the real nature and tendency of a philosophy depend on its grasp of the nature of this problem. We may say that he saw further than St Thomas also in reference to the closely related problem of " Matter." He is convinced that all created things —angels and men and all things—consist of " Matter " and " Form " ; but he is not satisfied with the definition of " Matter " as *mere* potentiality or *mere* possibility. It has a positive character and actuality of its own, with a natural " inclination " towards some particular type of " Form." It is a *real* possibility, and, so far, it is *subjectum omnis receptionis*, the *radix et seminarium* of the world. Rational souls are its " flower," and pure intelligences (angels) are its " fruit." The result is a conception of Nature as consisting of beings ever striving towards more complete and perfect individuality. The highest type of embodied existence is the human body, because it is the organ of the rational soul.

" When we read St Thomas, we are in touch with a man whose first concern is to say what is true ; and when we read Duns Scotus we are in touch with a man whose first concern is to prove his originality by disagreeing with someone else." There is some truth as well as point in the epigram. But the opposition between Duns Scotus and St Thomas is one of principle, and went deep enough to perpetuate itself in two antagonistic schools. And when it is remembered that matters of acute theological controversy were involved, and that the respective Doctors were impressive representatives of two different religious Orders, it is not difficult to account for the feuds of " Thomists " and " Scotists " during the fifty years following the death of Duns Scotus.[104]

III.

In the meantime another stream of influence was growing in strength—independently of the " Thomist " and " Scotist " parties and, in principle, hostile to both. It originated in the work of William of Ockham, a man whose ability, originality, and acumen are not inferior to any of the thinkers whom we have already named. He was born in Ockham, Surrey, towards the end of the thirteenth century. He entered the Franciscan Order when a young man, studied and lectured in Oxford, and was a pupil of Duns Scotus in Paris. He shared in the revolt of the Franciscans against Pope John XXII., and afterwards he supported Ludwig of Bavaria in the latter's famous contest with the same Pope. For these reasons he was obliged to take refuge with Ludwig, and lived in Munich from 1330 until his death in 1349 or 1350. During his life-time he was best known for the position which he took up against the Vatican : but his work as a philosopher and theologian was influential enough to earn for him the titles of *Doctor Invincibilis* and *Venerabilis Inceptor*.[105]

From Munich he issued a series of elaborate works circumscribing and limiting the authority of the Pope. The issue with the Franciscan Order concerned the duty of " evangelical poverty." John XXII. had issued formal declarations condemning this practice ; and the Franciscans maintained against him the ideal of strict imitation of Jesus in His poverty and obedience. The immediately practical question involved in all this was the right of the clergy to hold property. The issue with Ludwig of Bavaria raised the whole question of the Pope's authority as against that of the Emperor. Ockham's arguments in effect cut at the root of the spiritual as well as the temporal supremacy of the Pope. The temporal supremacy is openly and deliberately attacked. Independent civil power is declared to be as much an ordinance of God as spiritual power ; and in the created world the authority of the State is supreme.[106]

Ockham's philosophical and theological works consist mainly of commentaries on the *Liber Sententiarum* of Peter the Lombard and on the logical treatises of Aristotle. It is a mistake to underestimate the importance of these as compared with his political writings. It is usually said that he was instrumental in bringing about " a revival of nominalism." This expression is admissible only if we remember that it is not the nominalism of Roscellinus, whether understood as "extreme" or as "moderate," but a new nominalism wrought out with originality and thoroughness. Some historians—to distinguish it from the earlier versions of the doctrine—have described it as "Terminism."

Ockham is convinced that sound thinking in philosophy must always be guided by a supreme principle or rule of method. We are not entitled to assume the existence of anything more than is necessary to account for our actual experience : *entia non sunt multiplicanda præter necessitatem.* This expression, usually attributed to Ockham, is not to be found in his published writings, but is an accurate statement of his intention. The first and fundamental application of this principle appears in the doctrine that *the individual is the real.* I see "a man"; but "manhood," apart from the qualities of this, that, or the other man, I do not see ; I see "a table," but "tablehood"—so to put it—I do not see apart from the table ; I see "a stone," but I have no experience of its distinctive qualities apart from the particular thing itself. Ockham's philosophical work is a sustained protest against the tendency to treat an idea, derived by abstraction from perceptual experience, as if it could have a substantial existence of itself, or as if it could correspond to (or be a copy of) anything having such existence. He finds this fallacy in all forms of logical realism.

If, then, the individual is the real, it follows that the foundation and natural form of our knowledge is *intuition,*—that is, immediate perception or apprehension. By intuition, so understood, we come into direct contact with reality, with what is "given," and know whether something exists or does not exist ; and then the intellect can "judge" or make statements about what is thus apprehended. Such immediate or intuitive knowledge is of two kinds. In sense-perception we have direct apprehension of the facts of the outer world (*sensibilia*) by means of the various bodily senses ; and we have equally direct apprehension of the inner activities of the mind— activities of thinking, feeling, and willing. We experience these in ourselves, although for them there is no sense-organ (*nec sub aliquo sensu cadunt*). Ockham is a strong "realist" in the modern meaning of the word. He expressly repudiates anything resembling the later doctrine of "representative perception" (that we know things only by the intervention of mental copies). The mental act of apprehension and the objective fact are directly related to each other ; and truth consists in the completeness of this relation.

We have then innumerable acts of sense-perception directly related to external objects. Every such act leaves behind it a mental trace or mental disposition (*habitus*) resembling itself ; and when several such acts, or their mental traces, occur together, their common elements (*consimilia*) are assimilated. This is why *perception* always tends to pass into *classification* : I see a moving figure, and say that is "a man." The intellect is nothing but a derivative continuation of this primary sense-elaboration of given material. That it should be so, is a fundamental law of the mind which we have simply to accept. The procedure of the intellect is always the same. Abstracting from the variable particulars of sense-

experience, it retains the common or permanent
elements; and with the indispensable help of language forms what Logic calls " class-concepts." The
only existence which the concepts have consists in
these ever-recurring acts of mental abstraction,
which, again with the indispensable help of language,
are combined into propositions and arguments.
" Universals " are therefore artificial products of our
mental activity, although indispensable to mental
discourse. A " universal " has no existence or meaning but what it derives from the particular concrete thing or group of things whose place it takes.
These are its *suppositio*—a term which Ockham
employs largely in this technical sense. And when
we use a class-name (" animal," " man," &c.) we
mean, or logically " intend," the many individuals
regarded from the point of view of certain important
common qualities. He often calls the " universals "
fictions, but he does not mean that they are necessarily
a falsification of reality; he means that there is
nothing in reality corresponding to them which is
separate from or independent of the particular individuals named. Hence " universals " are *ficta quibus
in esse reali correspondent vel correspondere possunt
consimilia ;* a class-name *non est universale nisi per
significationem quia est signum plurium.*

The question which Ockham appears to leave
unanswered is a fundamental one. All forms of
Nominalism have to meet it sooner or later.* What is
the real basis of the *consimilia* whose objectivity
Ockham admits? Natural objects are found to fall
into classes of individuals resembling one another,
not merely in non-essential or comparatively un-

* See above, page 189.

important qualities like colour but in essential qualities. The essential qualities are those on which many other qualities are seen to depend, as when we class together various human beings—for example, negroes, Europeans, Indians, Chinese—as having in common the attributes of " man." Again, natural events are found to resemble one another when under similar circumstances similar results occur, as when an unsupported object falls more or less quickly to the earth. Is there any real connection between the similar objects and similar events in such cases? If not, every such resemblance is nothing but a chance coincidence, and science is impossible.

Ockham comes nearest to facing this question when he considers the causes of *motion*, with special reference to the case when an object continues to move after the impelling force has ceased to act, as in the case of a stone thrown from the hand or an arrow shot from a bow. He rejects the supposition that the motion continues because something is transmitted from the source of motion to the object which it moves ; because when he brought his hand slowly and gently into contact with an object, the latter did not move. He therefore adopts the conclusion which seems simplest because it involves the fewest assumptions. The source of motion must be within the moving body itself ; movement, once initiated, is everlasting. This was a remarkable anticipation of the first Law of Motion—that every body in motion continues to move in a straight line with uniform velocity until acted on by an extraneous force— friction, resistance of the atmosphere, interposition of other objects, and the like. Ockham, however,

fails to do justice to the doctrine of " Form " and
" Matter " in its application to material motion ;
for in this reference (at any rate as the Franciscans
formulated it) it had certain affinities with the
modern doctrine of Energy, "potential" and "kinetic,"
and its " transformations." He seems to have been
on the way to affirm a real connection between
natural causes and their natural effects ; and if there
is such a connection, then every universal which has
any scientific value is more than a *suppositio* for the
fact that natural events happen to resemble one
another in some ways. We may say of him that
while his manner of expression and method of
expression are distinctively mediæval, his thinking
reveals a new mental energy and a " modern " spirit.
His appeal is constantly to experience. His central
doctrine that the individual is the real, meant in its
application that investigation is directed to the
actual concrete facts.

When we turn from Logic and natural science and
ask after the bearing of Ockham's principles on theology, we find a very different state of affairs. If
reason consists only in the elaboration of facts given
to us by sense-perception and by introspection, then
no article of faith, whether of natural or of revealed
religion, can be rationally demonstrated. In the case
of some dogmas, his conclusion is that they are not
only indemonstrable but irrational. The idea of God,
though not irrational, is one whose truth cannot be
demonstrated. It is a composite idea, whose parts
have been abstracted from various aspects of normal
experience. The mind can form the idea of God only
by the artifice of abstraction, assuming the qualities

thus abstracted—wisdom, goodness, and the like—to be magnified indefinitely, and then making them into " attributes of God." We can therefore have no *knowledge* of the Supreme Being in Himself ; we can only acquire a relative notion, whose truth-value remains an open question.

There is not the slightest reason to believe that such arguments on Ockham's part imply " an ironical scepticism concealed under the mask of orthodoxy." He holds that the soul has a faculty of its own for apprehending super-sensuous truth. This is the significance of his distinction between man as " pilgrim " or " wayfarer " (*viator mortalis*), limited to the world of sense, and man as " blessed " (*beatus*), endowed with the privilege of Faith. There is no doubt that the distinction between truth acquired according to the laws of logical thinking, and truth acquired under the rules of Faith, was used by others as a means of attacking Faith while appearing to acknowledge its authority, and that Ockham's influence actually contributed to the spread of theological scepticism. Nevertheless, the characteristic effect of his teaching was not scepticism but mysticism. More than one of the influential exponents of Christian mysticism in the fourteenth and fifteenth centuries had deeply studied Ockham's writings. We find, for example, that an adherence to terminism and empiricism on Ockham's lines, a rejection of metaphysics, and a mystical doctrine of the basis of religious belief, are combined in the doctrines of Cardinal Pierre d'Ailly (Petrus de Alliaco, d. 1420), and of Johannes Gerson (d. 1429), his successor as Chancellor of the University of Paris. Cardinal d'Ailly wrote on meteorology, astronomy, and geography, as well as on theology. It is probable that his geographical and meteorological writings influenced Christopher Columbus and Amerigo Vespucci.

IV.

Mysticism is a feature of western Christian thought in the fourteenth century which had various sources. The influence of the " Ockhamists," in dissolving what we have called the " treaty of peace between reason and faith," was only one of these sources. The abuses of the papal government ; the scandalous lives of many of the clergy ; the disastrous political circumstances of Germany in the first half of the century ; the Black Death which swept over Europe in 1848 : all these events, working on the lives of men whose religious instincts had not been wholly destroyed, threw them back on the inner sources of spiritual strength. Thus, for example, arose the societies of " Friends of God " (*Gottes Freunde*), spreading from Switzerland, over the south and west of Germany, to the Netherlands. They formed no exclusive sect. They often took opposite sides in politics, and they differed in the type of their religious life ; but they always desired to strengthen one another in living intercourse with God.[107] The kind of priest whom they admired and desired is portrayed in Chaucer's *Prologue* :—

> *A good man was ther of religioun,*
> *And was a poor Persoun [parson] of a toun;*
> *But riche he was of holy thought and werk.*
> *He was also a lerned man, a clerk*
> *That Cristes gospel gladly wolde preche;*
> *His parishens devoutly wolde he teche.*

R

This noble ensample unto his sheep he gaf,
That ferst he wroughte, and after that he taughte:
Out of the gospel he the wordes caughte,
And this figure he addid yit thereto,
That if gold ruste, what schude yren doo?

A bettre preest I trowe ther nowher is.
He wayteed after no pompe ne reverence,
Ne maked him a spiced conscience,
But Christes lore, and his apostles twelve,
He taught, and ferst he folwed it himselve.

The revival of definite mystical teaching is associated with the great personality of Heinrich Eckhart. Born about 1260 at Hochheim, near Gotha, he studied first in Paris, rose to a high position in the Dominican Order, and became famous, both as teacher and as preacher, at Cologne and in many other parts of Germany. During his later years at Cologne, opposition to his teaching became strong enough to promote a prosecution for heresy, and Eckhart appealed to Rome. The papal " bull," condemning a number of propositions selected from his writings, was not issued until 1329, two years after his death. It made little difference to his influence; and tradition has fittingly entitled him " Meister Eckhart."

Eckhart was a distinguished son of the Church; but in reading his works we feel at once that we have passed into a realm of thought different from that of the churchly mystics of whom St Bernard is the greatest representative. We seem to leave the cloister behind and to breathe a freer atmosphere. In Eckhart the attitude of the churchman and traditionalist is abandoned. Instead of systematising dogmas, he appears to evolve a philosophy by the free exercise of reason. His system enables him to give a profound significance to the doctrines of the Church ; but, instead of the system being accommodated to the doctrines, the doctrines—and even the historical facts—acquire a new meaning in the system, and often become only a symbolic representation of philosophical truth. Indeed, the philosophical doctrines of the masters are treated by Eckhart in a similar way. As a convinced Dominican of Paris and Cologne, he was a great student of Aristotle, Albert, and St Thomas ; but in his mind their doctrines are systematised in a new way and are infused with another spirit. It is the spirit of mediæval Platonism set free.

Nevertheless, to say that Eckhart's interest in religion is purely intellectual, would be far from the truth. If that were true, he could never be classed with the mystics. In his nature intellect and feeling are largely fused ; his apparently abstract statements are the expression or formulation of religious feeling. Hence it is not surprising that many of his followers were to be found among the " Friends of God." Such were John Tauler, of Strasburg, who died in 1361 ; Heinrich Suso, of Constance, who died in 1366 ; and John Ruysbroek, of Brussels, who died in 1381. In Tauler's sermons, while the standpoint is the same as Eckhart's, the philosophical groundwork is less insisted upon ; the appeal is directly religious and practical. The case of Suso is different. He has been described as " a remarkable combination of self-torturing asceticism with an inexhaustible play of poetic fancy "—the " poet-prophet of the love of God." Ruysbroek's mysticism, like that of Tauler, is of a practical cast. He is chiefly occupied with the means by which the *unio mystica* is to be attained ;

and Suso's way of self-torture is not, for Ruysbroek, the true way.

Eckhart's religious point of view is indicated very simply in his tract on the Lord's Prayer. He points out first of all that we are not bidden to pray for anything " temporal " ; because " temporal " things, as compared with eternal things or as seen in the light of eternity, are " nothing " (*nihil sunt*) ; and to pray for things that are " nothing " (*pro nihil*) is not to pray at all. Now this statement might be used to justify the most extreme depreciation of bodily life and of all material things, and the most extreme practices of self-torture. On the other hand, it might be used to justify the most extreme indulgence of every bodily instinct and desire, since these all are " nothing." Neither of these extremes can for a moment be attributed to Eckhart. Coming to the petition " Give us this day our daily bread " (*panem nostrum cotidianum da nobis hodie*), he explains it as meaning in the first place spiritual food, and in the second place bodily food. " This day " means during this life, or while we are wayfarers in this world ; for we need material bread so long as we are mortals and capable of suffering. But we are bidden to pray, not for wealth or luxury, but for " bread," that is, for the necessaries of life : " lest we, who seek to attain to the Kingdom of God, should cling too closely to the things of this world " (*ne quæremus in hoc seculo diu manere*). If we may use the language of the Anglican liturgy, we may say that in this petition Eckhart recognises a reference to " those things which are requisite and necessary, as well for the body as the soul."

Eckhart was a strong thinker of an intensely

speculative temperament. We are not surprised, therefore, to find that he begins his mystical doctrine with a theory of the divine Nature. His primary distinction is between the divine Person and the divine Nature—between God and the Godhead. The divine Nature is incomprehensible, because it is beyond every possible predicate that our thought can frame. The Godhead is not God as known to us. God as known to us proceeds from the Godhead. How is this process to be thought of ? It is a process of self-expression. The Absolute in expressing itself realises that supreme personality which we know as God. This realisation must take a trinitarian form. Why that form, necessarily ? Because in thus realising itself the Absolute becomes personal and self-conscious : and this involves a duality and a relation between two aspects or terms. God as knowing himself is the Father ; that which he knows of himself is the Son ; and the unity of the two in one life is the Spirit. It is evident that this differs widely from the traditional doctrine of the tri-personality of the Godhead.

What, then, of the world ? The realisation of the divine Son involves the creation of the world ; for the Son is God's mind in expression, and that expression involves creation. Creation is therefore an eternal process. On this basis Eckhart uses the traditional theological phrases in reference to God's relation to the world. But he is in contact with the fundamental difficulty—the origin of the *material* world. That which is created in the Son is the *ideal* world. Whence comes the material world, with its imperfections and evils, and its apparent independence of everything ideal ? Eckhart has no answer. He does not reduce the actual world to a mere illusion. Neither is it absolutely independent of God. The material world is in some mysterious way involved in the divine process called creation. It follows, then, that the Son of God, who is God in expression, is actually immanent in the material world. This is the downward movement from the divine to the earthly.

With the downward movement there arises also an upward movement. All beings have arisen from God and all desire to return. All beings have ultimately arisen from the Absolute or the Godhead, so that what all desire is not only God but Godhead ; and Godhead is beyond God. The soul, says Eckhart, receives from the Trinity (from God) all that can be measured by the faculties of the soul ; but from the absolute Godhead, a light shines into the very being of the soul, which the soul's faculties cannot receive. This is the ineffable state, the mystical ideal beyond any faculty or condition of the soul that speech can name.

In man the upward movement is realised and its nature seen. Man has the power of returning to the Absolute ; this is his chief end. The return is possible because there is a point of identity between even the natural man and the Absolute, because from the Absolute all things have come. The point of identity is found in the divine *scintilla* or " spark " in the human soul. As the intensity of that spark grows, it consumes our finiteness and the evil that springs from it, and only the divine is left.

How is the *scintilla* to be set free so that its intensity may grow ? Eckhart's sayings suggest that he failed to see how deep is the difference between the negative and the positive way of answering this question.* The negative way of seeking salvation assumes a sheer identification of man with man and of man with God. Spiritual progress consists in destroying the illusion of separateness. We are accustomed to say " I am not you," " You are not I." That is false ; we reach the truth by leaving out the " not." We are all one, and that one is the Son of God. There are not many sons, but one Son. The practical issue of this doctrine, when it is taken seriously—as similar doctrines, when held to-day, are not usually taken—is to destroy the value of all the instincts and desires which link us on to the actual world and the actual individuals around us.

Beside this negative ideal of the disappearance of all human endeavour, Eckhart has in view a positive ideal. Two of his most concrete statements of it are thus rendered by the late Baron von Hügel : " That is beautiful which is well ordered. The soul ought, with its lower powers, to be ordered under the higher, and with the higher, under God. . . . The right and perfect state of the soul would be, not simply that it should practise virtue, but that all the virtues should constitute its state (should have become the soul's second nature), without being practised with de-liberation." This is the way not of the suppression of desire, but of its right regulation and control. He condemns those who say : " If we have God and God's love, we can do whatever we like ! " The man who can do anything against God's command, is without God's love.

Eckhart, like many other mystics, teaches that evil is nothing positive. It consists in being without good ; it is a privation and a defect. This doctrine

* See above, page 73.

is sometimes supposed to spring from a tendency to explain away the real character of moral evil. But nothing of the kind can be attributed to Eckhart. " The question has been asked "—he said in one of his sermons—" what it is that burns in hell. The masters generally say it is self-will. But I say, in truth, it is *privation* which makes the burning of hell. Learn this from a parable. If you take a coal, glowing with heat, and place it on my hand, and I were asked what it is that burns me, I would say it is *privation*, because the coal has something which my hand has not. If my hand, by its very nature, had all the heat that the coal has, I should feel no pain. In like manner, I say, if God, and those who stand before His face, enjoy that perfect happiness which those who are separated from him possess not, it is the privation, the *not having*, which torments them."

John Ruysbroek, the great representative of mysticism in the Netherlands, and an earnest student of Eckhart, saw equally with his master the mischief of that morbid spirituality which, straining after an absorption of self in the Infinite, is in danger of passing over into its opposite and making self into God. But he saw more clearly where the root of the mischief lay. Even in its uttermost attainment the creature remains a creature. We must be conscious of ourselves in God, and conscious of ourselves in ourselves. Though we may rise above Reason, still we are not without Reason. Hence we perceive that we touch and are touched, love and are beloved. We are continually renewed and return back to ourselves. We come and go. Although love absorbs the soul, consumes it, and even demands of it what is impossible ; and although the soul longs to resolve itself into love as into nothing; yet it can never perish but will always endure. It belongs to our nature to look up to God and to strive towards him; and this endeavour will abide eternally with us.

While Ruysbroek thus earnestly contends that we can never lose our nature as created beings, and can never, through all eternity, cease to be different from God, he teaches with as firm a conviction that our being is rooted in and vitally united with an eternal ground, which is God. It is part of our nature to be thus, in the innermost, joined by a vital bond to God. In this sense, we combine a created and an uncreated life; a life subject to time, and a life beyond the power of time. Our created life, though we share it with the angels, and though like their life it is immortal, is not in its own nature blessed (*beatus*). It can become a blessed life, by God's Grace, if we attain to Faith, Hope, Knowledge, and Love. In attaining to these, we practise the virtues which are well-pleasing to God. We rise above ourselves and are united to God. Yet the creature never becomes God. What Ruysbroek said, speaking as an exponent of practical religion, is in entire harmony with the constant endeavour of St Thomas to avoid every possibility of confusing the creature and the Creator. The distinctions on which St Thomas insisted, in order to avoid this danger, disappear in the teaching of Meister Eckhart.[108]

V.

Protestant historians have sometimes represented the mystics of the fourteenth century as " precursors of the Reformation." In a sense this is true; Luther was an earnest student of Ockham, and was directly and greatly influenced by Tauler. But such statements convey a false impression if they are understood to mean that these men protested against the doctrines of the Church in the way in which the Reformers felt themselves called upon to do. " There is no sign that Tauler, for example, or Ruysbroek, or Thomas à Kempis, had felt the dogmatic teaching of the Church jar in any single point upon their religious consciousness. Nevertheless, mysticism did prepare men in a very real way for a break with the traditional system. Mysticism instinctively recedes from formulas which have become stereotyped or mechanical into the perennially fresh experience of the individual. In the *first* place, therefore, it brings into prominence only those broad and universal doctrines which it finds to be of vital and present moment for the inward life, while others, though they may have an important place in the churchly system, are unconsciously allowed to slip into temporary forgetfulness. It is thus we must explain the almost total absence of Roman Catholic doctrine in Thomas à Kempis, which makes his *Imitation of Christ* as acceptable to Protestants as to Catholics. In the *second* place, mysticism accustoms men to deal with their experience for themselves at first hand, and to test the doctrines presented to them by that standard. This growth of spiritual freedom is especially to be marked in the German mystics. It is to be noted, however, that mysticism affords in itself *no foundation for a religious community*. Its principle is pure inwardness, but it possesses no rule by which the extravagances of the individual may be controlled. Thus, when the Reformers appeared to do their work, the mystics

were found opposing the new authority of Scripture
to the full as bitterly as they had opposed the old
authority of the Church." [109]

If we are to find, in the fourteenth century, any
stream of influence which went to swell the force of
the Reformation, we must look for it in the political
doctrines of men influenced by Ockham and who
thought as he did. And if we are to name an outstanding leader whose influence worked powerfully
in this direction we shall name not Ockham himself
—whose political writings attracted little attention
outside the official papacy—but another writer and
thinker, whose principles entered so completely into
the doctrine of his successors in the work of national
development and Church reform that it has been over-
shadowed by their greater fame.

When speaking of Ockham's political work we
referred to the events in connection with which they
were produced. The Emperor Henry VII. died in
August 1313, when the complete failure of his adventure in Italy—from which Dante had hoped impossible
things—was evident to all. There were two candi-
dates for the imperial throne, Ludwig of Bavaria and
Frederick of Austria ; and the electoral votes were
equally divided. Neither of them would give way ;
and several years of war ended in the defeat of
Frederick in 1322. The Pope John XXII., resident in
Avignon, supported the Austrian candidate by every
means in his power. His supporters contended that
the authority of the Emperor was valid only when
it was confirmed by papal sanction. In itself this
was, of course, only a renewal of the old conflict ; but
it produced a new and drastic treatment of the question
at issue—the relation of the Church and the State.

The Emperor Ludwig eagerly availed himself of the assistance of Ockham's pen in contesting the claims of the papacy, and gave him his protection. When Ludwig was in Nuremberg in 1326 there came to him from Paris a man who had been a distinguished teacher there, and who had just published a book defending political principles akin to those held by Ockham. This was Marsiglio of Padua, whose book *Defensor Pacis* shows that he was one of the most independent and far-seeing political thinkers of the age. When a young man he had left his native city and migrated to Paris—the University which was then the natural goal of all intellectually ambitious men. When he joined the Emperor he became one of the latter's most trusted advisers—interested as he was in defending the rights of the civil authority against encroachments by a power claiming to be beyond civil control.

In explaining the political doctrine of Marsiglio, much depends on where we begin. If we begin by stating his view of the rightful authority of the State over the Church, we may easily represent him as anticipating Hobbes, who made the Church little more than a Department of the State. As a matter of fact, Marsiglio advocates for the Church an organisation which anticipates the principles of the Presbyterian order, and for the secular State a limited monarchy and majority government. In order to reach to the root of his doctrine, we must ask, what, in his view, is the foundation of political authority? The fundamental and effective source of Law, in other words, of organised political authority, is the the whole body of the citizens, *or a majority of them*, acting of their own free choice openly declared in a

general assembly, and prescribing something to be
done, or not to be done, in civil affairs—that is, enact-
ing a law to be exercised over them. The body of
citizens may directly act of itself, or it may appoint
one or more persons to act for it ; but the authority
of such person or persons is derived from the body
of citizens, to whom the making of laws is committed. To the object that " the multitude " are not
competent for this purpose, he replies that the greater
part of the citizens are not evil-minded and not
unintelligent as regards the greater part of the questions which concern them and for the greater part of
the time. If the making of laws were entrusted to
a few, there would be a danger of the common good
being overridden by selfish interests.

Marsiglio is convinced that the best form for the
authority delegated by the general body of citizens
is that of a limited monarchy where the sovereign is
chosen by election. For reasons which are not clear
he entirely rejects the hereditary principle. That
such a monarchy is limited is obvious from the nature
of the case. The sovereign is responsible *for* the execu-
tive government, but he is responsible *to* the real
law-giver, the community of the citizens (*civium
universitas*), who may restrain or even depose him if
he goes beyond the bounds prescribed for him.

What then is the place of the Church in this
organisation ? Marsiglio carefully distinguishes different meanings of the word : the Church as a building ;
the Church as the body of the officiating clergy—and
in mentioning these he refuses to distinguish between
" presbyters " and " bishops " ; the Church as the
clergy of the chief cathedral, which " in recent times "
has come to be the Cathedral Church of the city of

Rome. But in the original and true meaning of the word, the Church is the whole body of believers who call upon the name of Christ, whoever and wherever they may be.

In defining the authority of the priesthood, Marsiglio insists repeatedly on the difference between the character of the priest as a religious " expert "—as a theologian and religious teacher—and the claim made by the Roman priesthood to *coercive jurisdiction* of the kind exercised by a judge in a civil court. He argues elaborately, appealing to Scripture and to the Fathers of the Church, to show that neither the Bishop of Rome, called the Pope, nor any other bishops, presbyter, or deacon, has a right to coercive jurisdiction over any priest or layman of whatever kind. The civil ruler alone has a right to exercise such jurisdiction. To the civil ruler all clergy are subject ; and his authority is created by the free choice of the community of the citizens. The effect of these conclusions on the doctrine of " clerical exemption " is evident ; the whole doctrine appears as a baseless invention of priestcraft, most dangerous to the common weal. Marsiglio points out how, in pursuance of their doctrine of clerical exemption, the Roman bishops were trying to include as many kinds of persons as possible under the term " clergy." He protests against the successors of the Apostles accumulating wealth and exercising the power of territorial magnates. And as regards the supremacy of St Peter, his argument is strictly historical, and resembles what might be expected from any well-informed and fair-minded Protestant controversialist in modern times. That Peter was ever designated as the divinely appointed head of Christendom, or that any such authority was passed on to his successors, is uncompromisingly denied. But the probability of Peter's presence in Rome, and of his leadership of the Christians there, is freely admitted ; and Marsiglio admits also that the bishopric of Rome represents an ancient and honourable tradition of sound doctrine and practice, and that it is entitled to the reverence and within limits, to the obedience of Christendom.

His opinion of many of the clergy of his time is shown in the following passage : " Now, however, on account of the corruption of the Church administration, the greater part of the priests and bishops are but little versed in sacred Scripture ; and the temporalities of benefices are gained by greedy and litigious office-seekers, through servility or importunity or bribery or physical violence. And I declare before God and the company of the faithful, that I have known numbers of priests, abbots, and other Church dignitaries of such low quality that they could not even speak grammatically. And I have seen a man less than twenty years of age, and almost completely ignorant of the divine law, entrusted with the office of bishop in a large and important city, when he not only lacked priestly ordination, but had not passed through the diaconate or subdiaconate."

The most important part of the second book of the *Defensor Pacis* is occupied with Marsiglio's programme for a working General Council of the Church. It is of great historical importance owing to its connection with what is known as the " Conciliar Movement," which was championed by the great Parisian teachers, Cardinal d'Ailly and Johannes Gerson, grew in strength during the last quarter of the fourteenth

century, and was not defeated until the middle of
the following century. Its purpose was to substitute
the authority of General Councils, each representing
the whole Church, in place of the papal supremacy
as previously understood. This subject belongs to
the general history of the Church. For our present
purpose we need only give a brief statement of the
position taken by Marsiglio. The foundation of the
authority belonging to the General Council, as of
that belonging to the civil government, is the community of the citizens, now regarded—from the point
of view of the Church—as " the faithful." In cases
of doubt as to the meaning of the divine law in reference to any important question of faith or of life,
it is the duty of the civil ruler to call a General Council
of all the faithful, or of their elected delegates, to
decide the question. The laity as well as the clergy
are to be represented ; and, in cases of final difference
of opinion, the question is to be settled by a majority
of the whole Council.

" If the Pope of Rome," says Marsiglio, " or any
other one bishop had authority of this kind, or if
the decrees or encyclicals of the Roman Pontiff were
of greater authority than the decisions of a General
Council, then all nations, governments, and individuals of whatever rank or condition would be subject
to the coercive jurisdiction of the Roman bishops.
For this is what Boniface the Eighth declared in his
edict beginning *Unam sanctam catholicam ecclesiam*,
and ending, ' We proclaim, declare, and establish,
that henceforth it is a necessary article of faith that
every human creature is subject to the Roman
Pontiff.' " Marsiglio's argument is that this is fundamentally false, and most injurious to the welfare of

civilised peoples ; and he scornfully points out that
Pope Clement V., who removed the papal court to
Avignon, and was entirely subservient to French
interests, had been obliged to modify or explain away
those portions of the bull *Unam Sanctam* which were
particularly offensive to the King of France. Nevertheless, it is doubtful whether he perceived the
significance of the rise of independent " sovereign
States," as we see them to-day, although this had quite
evidently taken place, in his own time, in the case
of England and of France ; and there is no evidence
that he even imagined the possibility of a Christendom
divided into many different Churches and sects, each
claiming to be " the true Church." And yet his work
was unconsciously prophetic. The principles which he
defended were expanded and developed, at portentous
length and in the worst " scholastic " style, by John
Wycliffe in the next generation ; and they entered
into the spirit of the Reformation.[110]

VI.

Our interpretation of the leading tendencies of
Christian thought during the fourteenth century has
already taken us into the transition to a new outlook
—or rather, into the period of new and rapid growth,
growth in breadth and depth, of an outlook on the
world which in the fulness of its variety and confusion characterises what we call modern thought.
What was the essential nature of the " new outlook " ?
In its essential nature it was an ever-increasing realisation of this present world in the manifold vastness of
its appeal to the mind of man. The contrast between

" this world " and " the next world " remained ; but the centre of gravity was shifted to this world.

The so-called " Renaissance " was only one factor—it would be nearer the truth to say, only one result—of this movement. When we look at it as it appeared in Italy, the " Renaissance " shows itself in an enthusiastic search for manuscripts, for the sake of their dissemination and wider distribution ; in an intense devotion to literary form ; in a revival of classic taste in architecture ; in a growth of painting and sculpture away from the symbolism of spiritual qualities towards realism or romanticism ; in a contempt, often unreasoned and lacking understanding, for the trivialities into which the exercise of " scholastic " methods of argument were degenerating. The invention of printing gave the movement a stronger and wider influence than it would otherwise have attained. And in its search after knowledge it was in full harmony with the spirit of adventure which characterised the age and led to the discovery of " the New World."

In England the movement naturally took a form different from that which it had taken in Italy—a form less akin to literature and art, but more religious and more practical in its bearing on religion and politics. An ideal representation of the spirit of the English " Renaissance " is seen in the work and influence of John Colet, from the time when he returned to Oxford in 1496, fresh from contact with Italian learning in the Florence of Savonarola's time. The Italian " Renaissance "—beginning with a rediscovery of the Hellenic ideal of free creation, free life, free enjoyment, free access to reality or what seemed to be such—had worked itself out into a practical paganism, which substituted the attractions of art for the claims of religion and morality, and tolerated the outward observances of religion without faith in the truths which they symbolised. Men like Colet reacted against the paganism of the Italian scholars, and they adopted opinions about the classical authors less liberal and more " mediæval " (in the conventional, and historically false, meaning of the word) than those of John of Salisbury and the School of Chartres in the twelfth century. The effect of his Florentine studies was to throw Colet back on the New Testament read in the original language. In his free criticism of the earlier Scriptures, his tendency to simple forms of doctrine and confessions of faith, and the stress which he laid on practical Christianity, Colet struck the keynote of a mode of religious thought as strongly in contrast with that of the later Reformation as with that of Catholicism itself.

In Germany the failure of the Conciliar Movement for the reform of the Church from within gave rise to the Reformation from without. On its negative side it was a revolt against the system of ecclesiastical dogma which made " reform from within " impossible. Intellectual and moral cravings, which had been blindly gathering force for generations, found expression, and in Martin Luther a man appeared who was fitted to take the lead.

Yet the Reformation had its own " dogmatism," its own " obscurantism," and its own " scholasticism." It made the Bible into a true idol, and made the worship of the Bible, as an oracular idol, necessary for every Christian. In fifty years it produced creeds which in the voluminousness and minuteness of their dogmatism far exceeded all that the ancient

Church had done in three hundred years. In Germany the reformers fulminated against the Universities as the homes of the hated " scholastic " philosophy and theology ; and the denunciations of " carnal knowledge," and the proposal of the Barebones Parliament in London to abolish the Universities, sound like echoes from " the Dark Ages." But Melanchthon came to the conclusion not only that a developed theological system and a regulated order of instruction were vitally necessary even for a Protestant Church, but also that these ends could not be attained without the help of philosophical principles. Whence then were these principles to be derived ? A new philosophy could not be created— this he took for granted as beyond question ; and since philosophy was indispensable, it was necessary to choose from the philosophies of antiquity. He found the Epicureans too atheistic, the Stoics too fatalistic in their theology and too extravagant in their ethics, Plato and the Platonists either too indefinite or too heretical. Aristotle alone, as the teacher of form and method, could meet the wants of the new as he had met those of the old Church. Accordingly, Melanchthon published expository commentaries on the logical, psychological, and ethical works of Aristotle ; but, like the other leading reformers, he was as indifferent to the rising interest in what we understand by " natural science " as Gregory the Great or St Bernard of Clairvaux had been.

We said that the ecclesiastical Reformation was only one factor in the transformation of the mediæval outlook on Nature and Man. The movement went much further than the aims which Luther himself had at heart. He advocated the abolition of institutions for the cultivation of formal asceticism because to him they stood for indolence rather than true self-sacrifice. He approved the restriction of ecclesiastical exercises because to him they were mere external compromises with heaven. The true reconciliation was through faith, an inner condition of the emotions and the will. These were Luther's conscious aims ; but the thoughts of men were instinctively turning earthwards, and the spirit of the age took the ultimate issues out of Luther's hands. The reaction against institutions for the cultivation of formal asceticism became the expression of the desire for secular civilisation and comfortable living ; and the restriction of ecclesiastical exercises was valued because it left time for more important worldly affairs.

It has been said that the place given to natural science is the surest indication of the character of a civilisation. In this matter Francis Bacon proved a true prophet. Bacon dated the beginning of the modern era from the period of the invention of the nagnetic needle, of gunpowder, and of printing. His whole philosophy of science is based on the ideal of natural knowledge as a source of power. Its possibilities, as he conceived them, are set forth in imaginative form in one of his latest works, the *New Atlantis*, a picture of the ideal civilisation of the future. Its central and supreme institution is a vast organisation of workers engaged in investigation and research in every department of science. Their common aim is " the knowledge of causes," for the sake of increasing the *regnum hominis*, the " kingdom of man," and for " the effecting of all things possible." Under the auspices of this organisation innumerable things of interest and utility are done, among which the following achievements are specially noteworthy : the prolongation of human life ; the production, by artificial selection and breeding, and also by vivisectional surgery, of new species of animal and vegetable life ; the wholesale vivisection of animals, in order to throw light on what may be done with the bodies of men ; the perfecting of all kinds of optical instruments ; the manufacture of cannon of enormous power, of flying machines, and of submarine boats.

With less power of imaginative intellectual prophecy, but with far greater grasp of principles, Bacon's younger contemporary, Descartes, formulated a programme of reforms in " philosophy "—by which, in this connection, he meant chiefly natural science. He urged the pursuit of a *practical* philosophy, " by means of which, knowing the force and action of fire, water, air, the stars, the heavens, and all the other bodies that surround us, we might apply them to all the uses to which they are adapted, and thus render ourselves masters of Nature."

If such thinkers as Bacon and Descartes could rise to-day and survey what the intervening generations have accomplished, on the lines which they thus laid down in advance, they would not deny that the labour has been both earnest and successful. They would also admit that the extension of the " kingdom of man " by these means has brought about some results which, in the enthusiasm of the sixteenth century, they had not anticipated.

The place of science in the transformation of mediæval thought was foreseen with an insight deserving to be called prophetic. But another series of connected changes, not so dramatically predicted, has worked itself out through these centuries. Visitors to parts of Europe where the old mediæval cities still preserve most of their original appearance, have remarked that these places take their character from their churches round which they were gathered as the original centres of their life. In the modern cities the State buildings predominate : the palaces, the courts of justice, the Government offices, the barracks, the railway stations, the prisons. The Church, the characteristic and dominant institution of mediæval times, has been supplanted by the State, the characteristic and dominant institution of modern times. The State has become a comprehensive institution for the advance of civilisation.

This is no place for an attempt to judge concerning the gains and losses involved in all these changes. One thing, however, may with confidence be said. With the disappearance of " mysticism " as a force in modern religion, we have lost the sense of *wholeness*, the sense of the totality of being in which we and all things exist. For all the greater religious teachers of the " Middle Ages," this was a primary and direct experience—the central experience of the religious life. In this mood Saint Francis hailed " Brother Sun " and " Sister Moon," " Brother Fire " and " Sister Water " and " Mother Earth," because they had their being in the same universal life of which he was a part. In the modern world we find division. Nations, classes, persons—ideals, tasks, duties—are divided from one another. They seem to be as separate from one another as sun and moon or earth and fire and water. Our loyalty is called for in many different ways at once, and we fail to satisfy them all. Knowledge and Compassion and Justice and Love fall apart ; and yet we know that not one of these can find its perfect work without the others. We have seen how the men of a distant age tried to unite them. Our place in the long ascending spiral of history seems now just over the place where the men of that time stood. In the light of a clearer day than theirs, with a wider field and a clearer vision, it is for us to-day to take up the old task with dauntless hearts.

BIBLIOGRAPHY AND NOTES.

How vast is the literature of the History of the Middle
Ages, in all its branches, will be evident to a reader who
even merely turns the pages of the Bibliographies attached
to the successive volumes of the *Cambridge Mediæval
History;* and the revised edition (1931) of Paetow's
Guide to the Study of Mediæval History shows that the
stream is not diminishing. It must be distinctly understood that the references given in the following Notes
are for the most part limited to books which are written
in English, and in which readers who are interested in
particular topics may find guidance for further study.

On the general subject there is no comprehensive work
in English ; on the other hand, many important contributions have been made by English and American scholars
to the understanding of special problems arising out of
the history of mediæval thought, and references to a
number of these are given below. In this connection we
must point out an important result of the discoveries and
studies which have been carried out in the department of
western Christian thought (not to mention other branches
of mediæval history). The extent of the field is now so
great, that the historian who is not concentrating on some
special monograph but desires to deal with some considerable period in the history of mediæval thought, finds
himself faced with only two possible alternatives. He
must either make large and deliberate omissions and give
an interpretative account of tendencies, concentrating
on the work of a limited number of thinkers of outstanding
importance ; or he must make what is really an encyclopædic dictionary of the subject, with the topics and
heads arranged in chronological instead of in alphabetical
order. To a great extent this is illustrated in the fifth
edition (Louvain, 1925) of M. de Wulf's *Histoire de la*

Philosophie Médiévale, of which there is an English translation by Mr E. C. Messenger. Much more is it the case with that monument of industry, accuracy, insight, and scholarship, *Die Patristische und Scholastische Philosophie*, by Professor Bernhard Geyer, published in 1928 as part of the eleventh edition of Ueberweg's *Grundriss der Geschichte der Philosophie*. An English translation of the work would be a formidable undertaking, but is much to to be desired. The *Beitrage zur Geschichte der Philosophie des Mittelalters*, edited by C. Bäumker and G. von Hertling, of which the first volume was issued in 1891, is a series of special studies as valuable for the original Texts as for the scholarly expositions by the Editors. The brilliant and illuminating contributions of Professor C. H. Haskins, of Harvard, and Professor É. Gilson, of the Sorbonne, are of the greatest value to students, and most of them are referred to below. We may also mention here a rather older but valuable French work, *Esquisse d'une Histoire générale et comparée des philosophies médiévales*, by M. F. Picavet (second edition, 1907).

An interesting and instructive first introduction to the subject will be found in *The Legacy of the Middle Ages*, by various authors, edited by Messrs C. G. Crump and E. F. Jacob (Oxford, 1916). With this may be read chapters from the companion volumes, *The Legacy of Israel* (1927) and *The Legacy of Islam* (1931). In the fifth volume of *The Cambridge Mediæval History*, Mr W. H. V. Reade has contributed an excellent summary under the title " The Philosophy of the Middle Ages " (Chap. xxiii.) ; and in the sixth volume we must mention in particular Chap. xvii., " The Mediæval Universities," by the late Hastings Rashdall ; Chap. xviii., " Political Theory to 1300," by Mr Reade ; Chap. xix., " Ecclesiastical Doctrine to 1215," by Professor A. H. Thompson ; and Chap. xx., " Heresies and the Inquisition," by Professor A. S. Turberville.

Vivid accounts of the popular life and beliefs of the period are given in *The Waning of the Middle Ages*, by Professor J. Huizinga, of Leiden (London, 1927), and in *Medieval Faith and Fable*, by Canon J. A. MacCulloch (London, 1931).

NOTES.

[1] (p. 4). The first paragraph in this chapter is taken from *The Message of the Middle Ages to the Modern World*, by S. H. Mellone (Essex Hall Lecture, London, 1928). The points of view from which the Middle Ages are now regarded by impartial historians are summarily stated in the brief but suggestive surveys by Professor J. H. Shotwell, article " Middle Ages," in the eleventh edition of *The Encyclopædia Britannica*, and by Professor F. M. Powicke under the same title in the recent fourteenth edition.

[2] (p. 6). See *Chivalry: its historic Significance*, by Members of King's College, London (1928).

[3] (p. 8). See *Virgil and his Meaning to the World of today* (New York, 1930), by J. W. Mackail. The references to the *Æneid* are : Bks. i. 278-79 and vi. 851-53.

[4] (p. 10). The most trustworthy accounts of the moral and spiritual condition of imperial Rome appear to be derived, directly or indirectly, from Friedländer's classical work, *Darstellungen aus der Sittengeschichte Roms*, of which the eighth edition appeared in 1910.

[5] (p. 12). The quotation is from Harnack's striking article " Montanism " in the eleventh edition of *The Encyclopædia Britannica* (abridged in the recent fourteenth edition). " Leaving to it everything except its gods " : it would be a serious historical mistake to assume that the Church became nothing more than " a slightly modified *world*." She grappled with some of the destructive forces in the world and brought them under control. Here it is sufficient to say that the Church enforced an ideal of *self-mastery*, understood at first with special reference to bodily purity, but capable of a deeper and wider application ; she severely condemned and finally succeeded in suppressing the practice of *exposing and abandoning infants ;* she brought about an effective abhorrence of

the barbarism of *gladiatorial combats;* she produced an immediate moral mitigation of *slavery* and a strong encouragement to emancipation; and she greatly extended the charitable provision made for *the sick and the poor.* In general, she made beneficence a form of divine service, and identified *piety* with *pity*—except where " heresy " was concerned !

[6] (p. 15). See *The Invasion of Europe by the Barbarians* (posthumously published Lectures, 1928, by J. B. Bury). These Lectures are an important contribution to the understanding of one of the great " watersheds " of human history, the period between Constantine and Charlemagne, where we see Western Europe in the making. An earlier but valuable work, *La fin du monde antique et le début du moyen age* (1897), by F. Lot, deals with the whole period apart from the thought-world of the time. But of this we have now a much-needed history in English, *Thought and Letters in Western Europe,* A.D. 500 *to* 900, by Professor M. L. W. Laistner (London, 1931).

[7] (p. 18). The breach between East and West, culminating on the political side in the coronation of Charlemagne by the Pope, had been prepared also by diversities of temper and outlook on the ecclesiastical side. It was in the East, where men were more given to speculation of every kind, that the great Christological controversies arose and spread ; and after the first Council of Nicæa (A.D. 325) the same controversies went on in other forms. The Western Church accepted the Nicene Creed (as expanded at the Council of Constantinople, 381) as final, with the addition of the word *filioque* in reference to the " procession " of the Holy Spirit. The Eastern insistence that the Holy Spirit " proceeds " from the Father *only* was a remnant of the doctrine of the Alexandrian theologians that the Son is in some sense subordinate to the Father, and for that reason it was resisted in the West. Then there emerged the " iconoclastic " controversy, when in 726 a strong emperor in the East, Leo III., forbade the use of images in worship. This practice, though made a reproach against Christianity by Jews and Mohammedans, was too widespread to be easily sup-

pressed. From the beginning the attempt to abolish the images had been resisted by Rome ; and after many years of intrigue and violence it was abandoned in the East. The renewal of persecutions by the iconoclast parties when the Empress Irene was deposed in 797 (thus almost coinciding with the coronation of Charles) completed the ecclesiastical breach between East and West.

[8] (p. 21). The quotation is from Cicero, *De Republica*, III., xxii., 33.

[9] (p. 25). John of Salisbury, writing in the middle of the twelfth century, feels most deeply the importance of the international unity of Christian civilisation under the universal Roman Law and the universal spiritual dominion of Rome, as against the separatist tendencies of the national States, whose authority in the last resort is one of force alone (see the references given by Poole, *Illustrations of the History of Mediæval Thought*, second edition, 1920, pp. 205-09). John frankly and unsparingly denounces the stupidities, hypocrisies, and vices of many churchmen of his time, while he whole-heartedly defends the supremacy of the Church over the world. Poole seems to put the emphasis in the wrong place when he speaks of the universal dominion as " a mere theory " and " purely ideal." The contrast in John's mind is not merely between the " ideal " and the " actual," but between an office of supremely sacred import and the many unworthy men who have held that office. Nearly two centuries later Dante, keenly and bitterly conscious of the prevailing corruption, boldly expresses his conviction that the Popes were the principal authors of it (*Inferno*, xix., 104 ; *Purgatorio*, xvi., 97-105 ; *Paradiso*, xviii., 120 ; xxvii., 20-25, 40-45).

[10] (p. 26). See *The Moral Basis of the League of Nations*, by Lord Robert Cecil (now the Rt. Hon. Viscount Cecil) : the Essex Hall Lecture, London, 1923.

[11] (p. 31). See " The Mediæval Universities," by Hastings Rashdall, in the *Cambridge Mediæval History*, Vol. VI., p. 601.

[12] (p. 33). For the metaphor of " Light," see Plato,

Republic, VI., 508-10 ; and for the journey of the soul, see the " Speech of Diotima," *Symposium*, 201-12.

[13] (p. 34). Seneca, *Epistle*, lxxxviii., 36.

[14] (p. 35). Saint Bernard, *Sermones in Cantica Canticorum*, xxxvi.

[15] (p. 37). See Gilson's Essays on " Le sens du rationalisme chrétien " and " La signification historique du Thomisme," in *Études de Philosophie Médiévale* (Paris, 1921).

[16] (p. 39). Recent research has shown that natural science has in the main had a continuous development of its own, in which the conventional periodising of " Middle Ages " and " Renaissance " is not only irrelevant but thoroughly misleading. Professor Lynn Thorndike's *History of Magic and Experimental Science* (1923-34, in four volumes) is an instructive account of hundreds of writers, famous and obscure, and with its excellent index can be used as a dictionary of the subject. Dr Charles Singer's remarkably interesting work *From Magic to Science* (1928) gives a reliable version of the history of science from the Roman Republic to the " Renaissance," with special studies of particular documents. The second volume (1931) of Dr G. Sarton's monumental work *Introduction to the History of Science* covers the whole field of scientific thought in connection with its cultural background during the period. Professor C. H. Haskins, in his *Studies in the History of Mediæval Science* (1927), has made a very important contribution to the history of the renaissance of the twelfth century and the influence of Eastern culture on the West (see also his *Renaissance of the Twelfth Century*).

[17] (p. 40). For this quotation I am indebted to Dr C. Singer, *History*, Vol. XII., p. 64 (April 1927).

[18] (p. 48). Augustine, " Confessions," X., xxxv., 55.

[19] (p. 50). " City of God," X., 9.

[20] (p. 50). " City of God," V., 7 ; " Confessions," VII., vi. 8.

[21] (p. 50). " Christian Doctrine," II., xxix., 45.

[22] (p. 50). "Confessions," V., iv., 7 ; " On the Trinity,"
IV., i. ; and " Sermons," lxviii.

[23] (p. 52). " On the Trinity," X., xiv. ; " Confessions,"
VI., v., 7.

[24] (p. 52). On the Cartesian version of this argument,
see Mellone, *The Dawn of Modern Thought*, Chap. ii., pp.
27-28.

[25] (p. 55). See the standard edition by A. Souter,
Commentary of Pelagius on Thirteen Epistles of Paul,
Part i., 1922 ; Part ii., 1926 ; Part iii., 1930 (in the
Cambridge series, *Texts and Studies*).

[26] (p. 56). On this view of the State, see, for example,
Seneca, *Ep.*, XIV., and Irenæus, *Adversus Haereses*,
V., 24.

[27] (p. 58). The logical doctrines of Aristotle are contained in six small but masterly treatises which afterwards,
on account of their affinity, were collectively referred to
as the *Organon*. They are usually quoted by the English
or Latin titles here given : (1) *The Categories*, a philosophical introduction to Logic ; (2) *De Interpretatione*
(on expression in words), dealing with Terms and Propositions ; (3) *Analytica Priora*, dealing with formal
deductive reasoning ; (4) *Analytica Posteriora*, an account
of the methods of demonstrative science (as in Mathematics) ; (5) *Topics*, an account of reasoning in matters
where complete demonstration is unattainable ; (6)
Sophistici Elenchi or " Sophistical Refutations," an
account of various kinds of fallacious argument. Boethius
translated the *Categories* and the *De Interpretatione* into
Latin and wrote explanatory commentaries on both ; he
did the same with Porphyry's *Isagoge* (" Introduction "
to the Aristotelian Logic) ; and he also composed an
account of deductive reasoning, in his own words, but
based on Aristotelian principles.

[28] (p. 58). The most convenient edition of the theological tracts and the *Consolatio* is by Stewart and Rand

in the *Loeb Classical Library*. The reference is to *De Trinitate*, S. and R., pp. 5, 31.

[29] (p. 60). See *Consolatio Philosophiæ*, VI., 6. The quotation is almost in the words of Wicksteed's translation (Note " H " to the first Essay in *Studies in Theology*, by Carpenter and Wicksteed, 1903, p. 45).

[30] (p. 64). On Isidore's sources, consult Mr W. M. Lindsay's edition, *Isidori Etymologiarum Libri XX.*, two vols., Oxford, 1910.

[31] (p. 64). In connection with the " encyclopædists " we must mention an earlier writer (not an adherent of Christianity) whose work became influential in the Carolingian period and afterwards. This is Martianus Capella, who flourished in the middle of the fifth century. He wrote a treatise on the liberal arts in a fantastic allegorical form, *De nuptiis Philologiæ et Mercurii* (see " Martianus Capella and his ninth century commentators," by Professor M. L. W. Laistner, *Bulletin of John Rylands Library*, XI. (1925), pp. 130-38).

We must further observe that the unique position of Beda (" The Venerable Bede ") in the English Church must not be taken to imply that he was in any distinctive sense an English churchman. As theologian and student of traditional science, he was a European Catholic Christian ; and the influence of his writings on the Continent was akin to that of the " encyclopædists."

[32] (p. 67). The story of the " Carolingian Renaissance," on its cultural side, is well told by Professor Laistner, *Thought and Letters in Western Europe to Charlemagne*, especially Chaps. vii.-xiv.

[33] (p. 68). This capitulary is quoted in English by Laistner, *op. cit.*, pp. 153-54.

[34] (p. 69). On the Library and School of York, see Poole, *Illustrations of Mediæval Thought and Learning*, second edition, pp. 18-19.

[35] (p. 77). A careful account of the philosophy of the *De Divisione Naturæ* is given by H. Bett, *Johannes Scotus*

Erigena (Cambridge, 1925) ; and for an estimate of John's work, see Poole, *op. cit.*, Chap. ii. The fullest accounts of the man and his work are those given by German scholars. See, for example, Manitius, *Geschichte der lateinischen Literatur des Mittelalters*, I., 323-39 ; II., 803 ; Traube, *Monumenta Germaniæ Historica* (Poetæ), III., 518 (for the poems) ; Grabmann, *Geschichte der Scholastischen Methode*, I., 202-10.

[36] (p. 81). G. M. Trevelyan, *History of England*, Part I., Bk. ii., Chap. 4 (ed. of 1926).

[37] (p. 84). Professor F. M. Powicke has called attention to the importance of the *Chronicon* of Otto of Freising, in an instructive review of the American translation by Mr C. C. Mierow ; see *History*, XV. (1930-31), pp. 145-46.

[38] (p. 85). Apart from its use as a historic label, the adjective " scholastic " has acquired a special meaning, as descriptive of a kind of reasoning or discussion characterised by excessive intellectual subtlety or formal rigidity of method, or pedantically systematic development of minute details devoid of real significance. These defects, however, are not peculiar to historic " scholasticism," and they are characteristic of it only in its decadence during the fifteenth and sixteenth centuries. Here we find unlimited analyses corresponding to no real differences in the nature of things ; elaborate discussions of questions having no relation to reality ; and a terminology which went far beyond what was required for defining genuinely philosophical ideas or discriminating really scientific distinctions. " The philosophers and divines," says " Folly " in Erasmus' famous satire, " are deeply in my debt, as it is I who bestow upon them that self-love in which they look down upon the rest of mankind, while they are themselves protected by so vast an array of magisterial definitions, conclusions, corollaries, propositions explicit and implicit, and have so many loopholes of escape that no chain can hold them so fast but they will contrive to extricate themselves ; for which purpose they are provided with a multitude of fine distinctions with which they can cut all knots more easily

T

than the sharpest axe, and with a vast supply of newly invented terms and words of prodigious length." Erasmus, whose " Praise of Folly " was published in 1676, thought that the " scholasticism " of his own time was an attempt " to discover in thick darkness what in reality has no existence whatever." But to assume that all this is true of the whole " scholastic " period is to take a grossly biassed and perverted view.

39 (p. 99). Anselm's version of the argument from what I have called " Degrees of Goodness " is in principle the argument worked out by Descartes and expounded with great force in his third " Meditation." In the fifth " Meditation," and also in his " Principia " (Part i., section 14), Descartes states a version of the " ontological argument," which he claims is free from the objections to which earlier versions of the argument are liable ; but the justice of the claim is very doubtful. The principle of Gaunilo's criticism of Anselm is the same as that of Kant's criticism of the ontological proof in his *Critique of Pure Reason* (see the English translation by Professor Norman Kemp Smith, 1929, pp. 500-507).

40 (p. 101). For some observations in this account of the *Cur Deus Homo*, I am indebted to the late Dr P. H. Wicksteed. Not much work on Anselm has been done in English in recent years. The best short account is by Dr C. C. J. Webb in his *Studies in the History of Natural Theology* (Oxford, 1915).

41 (p. 102). The reference is to the *Metalogicon*, in which John of Salisbury discusses the position, utility, and prospects of logical study (see note 53 below).

42 (p. 103). See Bain, *Mental and Moral Science*, 1884, p. 179. This " empiricist " view of universals had its origin in the work of Locke and Hume ; and, as a logical doctrine, it was earnestly but confusedly defended by John Stuart Mill in his *System of Logic*.

43 (p. 106). See J. G. Sikes, *Peter Abailard*, 1932, Chaps. i. and ix. So far as I know, this is the first book in English to give a reliable and comprehensive account of Abailard's work and influence.

[44] (p. 107). See Justin's *Apology*, I., 46; II., 13; and elsewhere.

[45] (p. 108). An interesting discussion of the " errors " of Abailard, in the form in which they were condemned at Soissons, is given in the article " Abélard " in Vacant et Mangenot, *Dictionnaire de Theologie Catholique*, Vol. I., col. 43 ff.

[46] (p. 109). The important passages are in his *Introductio in Theologiam*, and may be found in Migne, *Patrologia Latina*, Vol. 178, col. 1050 ff.

[47] (p. 109). See Sikes, *op. cit.*, Chap. ii. ; and Geyer's excellent summary, *op. cit.*, pp. 214 ff.

[48] (p. 114). See Professor A. Boudinhon's article " Canon Law (general) " in the eleventh edition of the *Encyclopædia Britannica;* Professor H. A. Hazeltine's Essay " Roman and Canon Law in the Middle Ages," *Cambridge Mediæval History*, Vol. V., Chap. xxi. ; and Professor F. M. Powicke's Essay on " The early History of Canon Law," *History*, Vol. XVIII., p. 11 (April 1933). The vigorous growth of the study of Civil and Canon Law at this time is evidence of an effective desire for national and international order and peace.

[49] (p. 115). See Gilson, *Introduction a l'Étude de St Augustine*, Part iii., Chap. 3 (pp. 275 ff).

[50] (p. 116). See the quotation in Geyer, *op. cit.*, p. 233.

[51] (p. 118). An instructive account of Gilbert's doctrine will be found in R. L. Poole, *Illustrations of the History of Mediæval Thought*, second edition, pp. 112-15, 156-70.

[52] (p. 120). On the importance of Adelard's work, see Geyer, pp. 231-32 ; and Haskins, *Studies in the History of Mediæval Science*, Chap. ii.

[53] (p. 122). The standard editions of the *Metalogicon* and the *Policraticus* are those edited by Dr C. C. J. Webb,

both published by the Oxford University Press. The same author has published a convenient and reliable account of John and his work, *John of Salisbury*, in Methuen's " Great Churchmen " series. The account given by Poole, *op. cit.*, Chap. vii., is also based on special study, and is valuable.

[54] (p. 123).   Gilson, *La Philosophie au Moyen Age*, pp. 94-95, and *Études de Philosophie Médiévale*, Essay I.

[55] (p. 130).   Bernard, *De Diligendo Deo*, Chaps. x., xi.

[56] (p. 131).   The quotations are from the *Sermones in Cantica Canticorum*, xli. 3 and lxxiv. 5.

In recent years some valuable work has been done on Saint Bernard in English. Bernard's most important interpretations of his own religious experience (apart from the Sermons on " The Song of Solomon ") are the *De Diligendo Deo* and the *De Consideratione*. We now have an English translation of the former by E. G. Gardner, 1916, and a critical edition of the text by W. W. Williams, Cambridge, 1926 ; also an English translation of the *De Consideratione* by G. Lewis, Oxford, 1908. In 1927 Mr Williams published a suggestive volume, *Studies in Saint Bernard of Clairvaux*. An excellent short sketch by Lavisse is translated in Munro and Sellery's *Mediæval Civilisation* (New York, second edition, 1907). This book gives a series of short historical selections, dealing with various important topics, most of them translated or adapted from standard French and German works.

[57] (p. 132).   Walter of St Victor, who died about 1185, is an exception to this statement. He heaped abuse upon the " summists " and the " dialecticians " alike, declaring that the " summists " have as much to say against the existence of God as for it, and that the " dialecticians," having gone to school to the heathens, have forgotten over Aristotle the way of salvation. Walter of St Victor was a reactionary, whose influence appears to have been slight.

Richard of St Victor, great exponent of mysticism as he was, had almost a passion for the philosophical statement of the contents of Christian faith. He deserves more attention from students of the subject than he has yet received. Illustrative extracts are given by Geyer, pp. 267-70.

[58] (p. 132). A clear and concise account of the "heretical" movements of the twelfth and thirteenth centuries is given by Professor A. S. Turberville, *Cambridge Mediæval History*, Vol. VI., Chap. xx., on "Heresies and the Inquisition in the Middle Ages" (1929). Two chapters in *Studies in Mediæval Culture*, by Professor C. H. Haskins, on "The Inquisition in Northern France" (Chap. x.) and "The Heresy of Echard the Baker of Rheims" (Chap. xi.) will be found to throw light on the general subject as well as on the particular topics named. On the work of Henry Charles Lea, see Haskins, pp. 256 ff. On the very living subject of "sect-life" as contrasted with "church-life," see Troeltsch, *Social Teaching of the Christian Church*, Eng. tr., Vol. I., pp. 328-78.

[59] (p. 141). For several observations in this account of Joachim and his work, I am indebted to the late Dr P. H. Wicksteed.

[60] (p. 143). On the character of the mediæval translations of Aristotle, with special reference to the strictures of Roger Bacon, see Mr W. H. V. Reade's concise and effective statement, *Cambridge Mediæval History*, Vol. V., pp. 811-14. On the importance of Toledo as a centre, see Sarton, *Introduction to the History of Science*, Vol. II., Part i., p. 114; and on the work of Gerard of Cremona, *ibid.*, pp. 338-39.

[61] (p. 145). On the general subject of Saracen civilisation and thought, see *The Legacy of Islam* (Essays edited by the late Sir T. Arnold and Mr A. Guillaume, Oxford, 1931). The Essay by Dr and Mrs C. Singer in *The Legacy of Israel* (Oxford, 1927) on "The Influence of the Jewish Factor in Mediæval Thought" appears to the present writer to exaggerate this influence so far as the Christian thinkers are concerned.

[62] (p. 148). There is no adequate account, in English, of Averroes apart from scattered articles not very accessible ; but we must refer the article " Averroes," by Baron Carra de Vaux in Hastings' *Encyclopædia of Religion and Ethics*, and to Dr G. Sarton's concise statement, *op. cit.*, Vol. I., Part i., pp. 355-61. A comprehensive summary of the system is given by M. Horten in Geyer, *op. cit.*, § 28 (pp. 287-355), with many references.

Professor Étienne Gilson has observed : " Si l'on veut savoir si quelque commentateur médiévale est averroiste ou non, il suffit de consulter son *Physicorum* à la question, *utrum mundus sit aeternus*, et son *De Anima* à la question *utrum intellectus sit unus numero in omnibus hominibus*. La response fourni est un symptome concluante " (*Philosophie au Moyen Age*, p. 108).

[63] (p. 150). On the Mendicant Orders, see Dr A. G. Little's chapter under this title in the *Cambridge Mediæval History* (Vol. VI., Chap. xxi.), with references to a portion of the vast literature on the subject. Two useful studies of St Dominic and his work are *The Life of St Dominic*, by Bede Jarrett, new edition, 1934 ; and *Saint Dominique*, by P. Mandonnet, 1921. The standard life of St Francis is by P. Sabatier, *Life of St Francis of Assisi*, English translation by Louise Houghton (1894). See also Saint Francis, *Essays in Commemoration* (edited by W. W. Seton, 1926, the seventh centennial of his death) ; and A. G. Little, *Studies in English Franciscan History* (1917).

[64] (p. 151). See Rashdall, *Universities of Europe in the Middle Ages*, Vol. I., pp. 345 ff.

[65] (p. 153). See page 32 above, and note 12.

[66] (p. 153). As far as I am aware, this has for the first time been adequately stated by Professor Gilson in his *Philosophie de Saint Bonaventure* (1924) ; see especially Chap. xii.

[67] (p. 164). The quotation is from Professor A. E. Taylor's brilliant sketch of Aristotle's work : *Aristotle* (in the series entitled " The People's Books ").

68 (p. 170). On Albert the Great there is little of importance written in English. The article by P. Mondonnet in the *Dictionnaire de Théologie Catholique* (Vacant et Mangenot) is a trustworthy and instructive review; see also his *Siger de Brabant*, Vol. I., Chaps. i. and ii. (2nd ed., 1911).

69 (p. 171). A reproduction of the picture is given in *The Legacy of Israel*, facing p. 266.

70 (p. 175). See *Of God and His Creatures*, pp. 38 and 122 (Fr. J. Rickaby's abridged translation of the *Contra Gentiles*, London, 1905).

71 (p. 175). See *Contra Gentiles*, II., Chap. lxxv.

72 (p. 176). See *Western Mysticism: neglected Chapters in the History of Religion*, by Dom Cuthbert Butler (London, 1922). In this book the author concentrates attention on mysticism as " the endeavour of the human mind to enjoy the blessedness of actual communion with the Highest." This definition is from the article " Mysticism " in the *Encyclopædia Britannica* (9th ed., abridged in the recent 14th ed.); and the historical examples are those of St Augustine, Gregory the Great, and St Bernard.

73 (p. 176). I adopt this paraphrase (" and all the stars") in preference to the literal " and the other stars " (*l'altre stelle*).

74 (p. 178). See Plato, *Laws*, 895*a* (from Professor A. E. Taylor's translation, p. 286).

75 (p. 178). Taylor, *op. cit.*, Introduction, p. liv.

76 (p. 180). The quotation is almost a translation from the *Compendium Theologiæ ad fratrem Reginaldum socium suum carissimum* (Part i., section iii.). This work is a wonderful achievement of concise and lucid exposition, written probably immediately before or during the composition of the *Summa Theologiæ*.

77 (p. 181). From the *Compendium*, I., xxi.

[78] (p. 182). From the *Compendium*, II., ci. See also *Summa Theologiæ*, I., qu. vi., art. 1, and *Contra Gentiles*, III., xvii., xviii.

[79] (p. 185). From the *Compendium*, I., xxvii. St Thomas defends the principle in many passages ; see, for example, *Contra Gentiles*, I., xxxii.

[80] (p. 186). See, for example, *Summa Theologiæ*, I., xvi., 7 ; I., xxxv. ; *Contra Gentiles*, I., xxvi.

[81] (p. 187). See the *Epistle to the Hebrews*, Chap. xiii.

[82] (p. 192). Some of the most important references are given by Gilson, *La Philosophie de Saint Bonaventure*, Chap. x.

[83] (p. 198). See Gilson, *Le Thomisme*, p. 183 (3rd ed., 1927).

[84] (p. 199). See *Contra Gentiles*, II., 89.

[85] (p. 200). See *Contra Gentiles*, II., 68.

[86] (p. 201). From Martineau's suggestive discussion of "hitches in the evolutionary deduction" : *Types of Ethical Theory*, 3rd ed., Oxford, 1889, Vol. II., pp. 393 ff.

[87] (p. 206). From the *Summa Theologiæ*, Part II., division i. (usually referred to as *Prima Secundæ*), qu. li., art. 1, and qu. xciv., art. 2. The section on Law (qu. xc.-cviii.) may still be regarded as a valuable introduction to the study of the subject.

[88] (p. 206). The most important passages for understanding the ethical doctrine of St Thomas are given (in a French translation) with explanatory notes, by Professor Étienne Gilson, *Saint Thomas d'Aquin* (Paris, 1925, in the series " Les moralistes Chrétiens ").

[89] (p. 207). St Thomas expounds the hierarchical doctrine of the Church in the *Summa Theologiæ*, Part II., division ii. (usually referred to as *Secunda Secundæ*), qu. i., art. 10 ; in *Contra Gentiles*, iv., 76 ; and other passages.

⁹⁰ (p. 208). See Plato, *Republic*, 369-72, and *Laws*, 672-80.

⁹¹ (p. 212). The best guide to this whole subject, for English readers, is Fr. Bede Jarrett's *Social Theories of the Middle Ages* (London, 1926). The writer gives a competent discussion of the social and political theories of St Thomas ; but specially noteworthy are his references to men, comparatively little known, such as Humbert de Romano and St Antonino of Florence. The former was a practical preacher, whose business it was to relate the Church's teaching to the lives of his hearers. St Antonino, born and bred in a city of banking-houses, was conversant with international commerce and finance, a man of the world as well as a saint.

⁹² (p. 214). Passages illustrative of what is here said will be found in the *Summa Theologiæ*, Part III., qu. vii, art. 3 and 4 ; ix., 2 ; xxi., 1 ; xxxiv., 4 ; xlviii., 2. For reference to the extension of the Incarnation, see III., iii., 7.

⁹³ (p. 216). English readers who desire to understand the philosophy of St Thomas, but who are perplexed by the difficulties of an elaborate and unfamiliar terminology, have now an admirable introduction in the late Dr P. H. Wicksteed's Hibbert Lectures on *The Reactions between Dogma and Philosophy illustrated from the works of St Thomas Aquinas* (London, 1920). If anyone still doubts whether St Thomas is a great thinker and a great interpreter of religious truth whose work is one of the permanent treasures of our intellectual inheritance, he may be recommended to give careful consideration to this estimate. Wicksteed's earlier work, *Dante and Aquinas* (1913), is helpful. Professor Étienne Gilson has given a penetrating exposition in his *Le Thomisme : introduction au système de saint Thomas d'Aquin* (third edition, 1927 ; the existing English translation is from an earlier edition). And from an equally competent student in Germany we have *Thomas von Aquin: eine Einführung in seine Persönlichkeit und Gedankenwelt*, by Professor M. Grabmann (5th ed., Munich, 1926) ; English translation by

V. Michel (London, 1928). Guidance for further study is
given in the books already named. The extent of the field
will be seen in consulting Geyer, *op. cit.*, pp. 421-44 and 743-
57. To the labours of the English Dominican Fathers we
owe the following English translations: *The Summa Theologica*, in 22 volumes, London, 1911-25; *The Summa
Contra Gentiles*, in 5 volumes, 1925-30; and *On the Power
of God (De Potentia)*, in 3 volumes. The great revival and
extension of Thomist studies in the nineteenth century
was due to the progressive policy of Pope Leo XIII.,
whose encyclical *Aeterni Patris* (1879) is a defence of
Thomism. Under his auspices and with his financial
support the " *Leonine* " edition of the works of St Thomas
was completed.

[94] (p. 220). All recent investigation of Sigor de Brabant
starts from the work of P. Mandonnet, *Siger de Brabant
et l'averroisme latin* (2nd ed., Louvain, 1911). Important
explanations of Siger's position have been made by
Professor Gilson in *La Philosophie au Moyen Age*, Chap.
viii., and in *Études de Philosophie Médiévale* (pp. 51 ff. :
" La doctrine de la double verité ").

[95] (p. 221). See Mandonnet, *op. cit.*, Vol. II., pp. 175 ff.

[96] (p. 222). We now have a valuable series of studies
of leading English Franciscans by Miss D. E. Sharp,
Franciscan Philosophy at Oxford in the thirteenth century
(Oxford, 1930), with many quotations from the original
sources. Professor Gilson considers that the English
Franciscans inherited and developed the spirit of the
School of Chartres—" platonic, humanist, and mathe-
matical " (*La Philosophie au Moyen Age*, pp. 57 ff. and 204).

[97] (p. 222). See G. Croom Robertson, *Philosophical
Remains* (London, 1894), pp. 32-38.

[98] (p. 223). The best account (in English) of the
life and ecclesiastical activities of Grosseteste is by F.
Stevenson, *Robert Grosseteste, Bishop of Lincoln* (London,
1899). The best accounts (in English) of his philosophy
are those of D. E. Sharp, *op. cit.*, Chap. i., and L. Thorn-

dike, *History of Magic and Experimental Science*, Vol. II., ch. lv. In Germany attention has been given to Grosseteste by L. Baur, who in 1912 published a critical edition, *Die philosophische Werke des Robert Grosseteste*, followed in 1917 by the best existing account of the Bishop's scientific and philosophical work, *Die Philosophie des R. Grosseteste*. See also Baur's essay on " The influence of Robert Grosseteste on the scientific work of Roger Bacon " (in *Roger Bacon Essays*, ed. by A. G. Little, Oxford, 1914).

[99] (p. 227). See Sir J. Jeans, *The Mysterious Universe* (2nd ed., 1932), p. 69.

[100] (p. 229). In 1914 considerable interest in Roger Bacon and his work was aroused by the celebration in Oxford of the seventh centenary of his birth ; and in connection with this, the volume *Roger Bacon Essays*, named above (note 98), was published. As a corrective to the tendency to over-estimate Bacon and treat him as an isolated phenomenon, we may refer to Professor L. Thorndike's articles, " The true Roger Bacon," *American Historical Review*, Vol. XXI. (1916), pp. 237 ff., 468 ff. ; and " Roger Bacon and the Experimental Method," *Philosophical Review*, May 1914. A valuable critical survey will be found in the same writer's *History of Magic and Experimental Science*, Vol. II., pp. 616-720. Miss D. E. Sharp's exposition of Bacon's philosophy (*op. cit.*, pp. 115 ff.) is specially useful through its quotations from the original sources. Among other important recent works we must mention R. Carton, *L'expérience physique chez R. Bacon* (Paris, 1924), and C. Bäumker, *Roger Bacon's Naturphilosophie* (1916) ; and the comprehensive summary and references given by Geyer, *op cit.*, pp. 463-73 and 760-61. Of Bacon's principal surviving work the best edition is that of J. H. Bridges, *The Opus Majus of Roger Bacon*, with introduction and analytical table, Vols. I. and II., London, 1897 ; Vol. III., with emendations and additional notes, 1900.

[101] (p. 232). The account of the rainbow will be found in the *Opus Majus*, Bridges, Vol. II., pp. 172 ff.

[102] (p. 236). "Pax universalis est optimum eorum quae ad nostram beatitudinem ordinantur" (Dante, *De Monarchia*, I., 5).

[103] (p. 239). On the theoretical ideal of the mediæval Empire, see Bryce, *The Holy Roman Empire*, Chap. xv. (in the revised and enlarged edition of 1922) ; and his contribution to the volume *Dante : Essays in Commemoration* (London, 1921, the sixth centenary of the poet's death).

[104] (p. 249). The fullest account, in English, of Duns Scotus and his work is by C. R. S. Harris, *Duns Scotus* (2 vols., Oxford, 1927 : Vol. I., "The place of Duns Scotus in mediæval thought" ; Vol. II., "The philosophical doctrines of Duns Scotus"). The exposition suffers slightly from a propagandist tendency to exalt Scotus, as a thinker, above St Thomas ; and suffers seriously from the writer's acceptance as genuine the work *De rerum principio*, the genuineness of which is very doubtful (see the references given by Miss D. E. Sharp, *op. cit.*, pp. 284-86). The best recent accounts of Scotus are by Fr. E. Longpré, *La philosophie de B. Duns Scot* (Paris, 1924) ; by Miss Sharp, pp. 279 ff. ; and the summary and references by Geyer, pp. 504-17, 765-68. The edition of the works of Scotus, published in 1639, has been republished by the Franciscan Fathers in 11 vols. (Paris, 1891-95), but includes several works which are not genuine.

[105] (p. 250). For a list of the surviving writings of Ockham, see A. G. Little, *The Grey Friars in Oxford* (Oxford, 1892), pp. 224-34. Some of his works have never been published ; and, apart from the article by R. L. Poole in the *Dictionary of National Biography* (Vol. XLI.), no good monograph on his work has appeared in English. A very instructive account is given by Professor Gilson, *La philosophie au Moyen Age*, Chap. XI. ("Guillaume d'Occam et ses prédécesseurs" ; "L'Occamisme philosophique" ; "L'Occamisme scientifique") : a masterpiece of lucid exposition. For further references, see Geyer, pp. 571-83 and 781.

[106] (p. 250). It is not easy to form a coherent system

out of Ockham's various and sometimes diffuse and complicated discussions of this subject; but their general meaning was plain enough for the Pope and for the Emperor. The best exposition which I have seen is by J. Sullivan, *American Historical Review*, Vol. II. (1896-97), pp. 409 ff. and 593 ff. Mr Sullivan makes an instructive comparison between William of Ockham and Marsiglio of Padua, whose political doctrine was akin to that of Ockham, but not identical with it.

[107] (p. 257). See The Rev. F. J. Powicke's article, " Friends of God," in Hastings' *Encyclopædia of Religion and Ethics*, Vol. VI., p. 138 ff.

[108] (p. 265). The best edition of Eckhart's German works is still that of F. Pfeiffer, first published in 1859. These are for the most part in the " high German " dialect of south-west Germany. The Latin works were neglected for more than four hundred years, and have only recently been adequately examined. An edition of the Latin works, edited by Dr R. Klibansky of King's College, London, and Fr. Théry of Rome, is in course of publication; and the quotations given are from the tract *De Oratione Dominica* in that edition. English readers may be referred to R. M. Jones, *Studies in Mystical Religion*, 1909; von Hügel, *The Mystical Element in Religion*, 2nd ed., 1909; W. R. Inge, *Christian Mysticism*, Bampton Lectures, 2nd ed., 1912. Most of the special work on Eckhart is in German: see Geyer, pp. 553 and 579-80. The careful summary given in Geyer, pp. 561-71, is by J. Quint, and is partly based on recent work by the late Professor A. Lasson of Berlin, whose book *Meister Eckhart*, published in 1868, is still valuable. An instructive French book is Hornstein's *Les Grands mystiques allemands des* 14me *siècle* (1922). The value of Tauler's teaching may be discerned in Susanna Winkworth's translation of a selection from his sermons: *John Tauler*, with Preface by Charles Kingsley. On Ruysbroek, see Evelyn Underhill, *Ruysbroek*, 1912. See also the references given in Mr Powicke's article referred to above.

[109] (p. 267). The quotation is from the late Professor

A. S. Pringle-Pattison's article " Mysticism," *Encyclopædia Britannica*, 9th ed., Vol. XVII., p. 134 (abridged in the recent 14th ed.).

[110] (p. 273). Very little that is at all satisfactory on Marsiglio of Padua has appeared in English. The best exposition of the *Defensor Pacis* which I know of is by Professor E. Emerton, " The Defensor Pacis of Marsiglio of Padua," in the *Harvard Theological Studies*, Cambridge, U.S.A., 1920. There is a very careful summary in R. L. Poole's *Illustrations of Mediæval Thought*, 2nd ed., Chap. ix., which should be compared with the account of Wycliffe in the following chapter. We have now an adequate modern edition, *The Defensor Pacis of Marsilius of Padua*, edited, with introduction and notes, by C. W. Previté-Orton, and published by the Cambridge University Press.

INDEX OF NAMES.

Printed in Great Britain by
WILLIAM BLACKWOOD & SONS LTD.